A COMPREHENSIVE GUIDE TO RAILWAY REQUEST STOPS

A PERSONAL ODYSSEY TO VISIT EVERY ONE IN BRITAIN

For my daughter Anna, as without her constant love, affection, support and enthusiasm for the things I do, this book may never have been written. She selected the butterfly photographed at Tonfanau, so it is for her, not only because she does love her butterflies, but that is how I often think of her, beautiful and yet fragile.

Also to my son-in-law Lance for having the idea that I could turn my journey into a book, something that would never have occurred to me. For his contacts and guidance, without which I would not have known where to start, and his kind words about my writing as it progressed.

To the memory of my parents, firstly my mother whose fortitude and determination got us through the dark and difficult days. Secondly my father for instilling in me my love of railways and getting me up onto the footplate that first time at Reading, and standing with me at Shippea Hill.

A COMPREHENSIVE GUIDE TO RAILWAY REQUEST STOPS

A PERSONAL ODYSSEY TO VISIT EVERY ONE IN BRITAIN

Anthony Hart

PEN & SWORD
TRANSPORT

AN IMPRINT OF PEN & SWORD BOOKS LTD.
YORKSHIRE - PHILADELPHIA

First published in Great Britain in 2021 by
Pen and Sword Transport
An imprint of
Pen & Sword Books Ltd.
Yorkshire - Philadelphia

Copyright © Anthony Hart, 2021

ISBN 978 1 52678 112 3

The right of Anthony Hart to be identified as author of this work has been asserted by him in accordance with the Copyright, Designs and Patents Act 1988.

A CIP catalogue record for this book is available from the British Library.

All rights reserved. No part of this book may be reproduced or transmitted in any form or by any means, electronic or mechanical including photocopying, recording or by any information storage and retrieval system, without permission from the Publisher in writing.

Typeset by SJmagic DESIGN SERVICES, India.

Printed and bound by Printworks Global Ltd, London/Hong Kong.

Pen & Sword Books Ltd incorporates the imprints of Pen & Sword Books Archaeology, Atlas, Aviation, Battleground, Discovery, Family History, History, Maritime, Military, Naval, Politics, Railways, Select, Transport, True Crime, Fiction, Frontline Books, Leo Cooper, Praetorian Press, Seaforth Publishing, Wharncliffe and White Owl.

For a complete list of Pen & Sword titles please contact

PEN & SWORD BOOKS LIMITED
47 Church Street, Barnsley, South Yorkshire, S70 2AS, England
E-mail: enquiries@pen-and-sword.co.uk
Website: www.pen-and-sword.co.uk

or

PEN AND SWORD BOOKS
1950 Lawrence Rd, Havertown, PA 19083, USA
E-mail: Uspen-and-sword@casematepublishers.com
Website: www.penandswordbooks.com

CONTENTS

	Acknowledgements	6
	Introduction	7
CHAPTER 1	Why Berney Arms?	9
CHAPTER 2	What Do You Mean Cancelled?	15
CHAPTER 3	The Joy of Lists	29
CHAPTER 4	The End of the Line	33
CHAPTER 5	Through the Tunnel	52
CHAPTER 6	Repeat After Me, Cynghordy	67
CHAPTER 7	Railway Mindfulness	77
CHAPTER 8	Returning to the Scene of the 'Crime'	89
CHAPTER 9	The Soggy Walkers	104
CHAPTER 10	What, No Chips?	122
CHAPTER 11	The Home of the Hump	138
CHAPTER 12	The Wilderness	153
CHAPTER 13	Get on Yer Bike	172
CHAPTER 14	Oh Bullocks, What Do I Do Now?	185
Appendix I	Abbreviations	200
Appendix II	Alphabetical List of Request Stops	201
	Bibliography & Sources	203
	Notes	204
	Index	206

ACKNOWLEDGEMENTS

When it was first suggested that I could record my round Great Britain journey in book form, I must confess to having major doubts. Accordingly I must thank family and friends who convinced me that I could and should actually do this.

Many thanks to Anna for her sketch of fireman Hart at work.

I have used many books as a reference point in varying degrees and a selected bibliography is included on page 203. Three books that deserve particular mention are:

Butt, R.V.J., *The Directory of Railway Stations*; Jowett, Alan, *Jowett's Railway Atlas of Great Britain & Ireland*; and Quick, Michael, *Railway Passenger Stations in Great Britain: A Chronology*.

Many websites were consulted, and the ones I found most useful are listed in the bibliography/sources section. Wikipedia was perhaps the most used, albeit with caution as the information comes from many and sometimes unverified sources. Nonetheless it did provide the list of request stops, and much other invaluable information.

A big thank you must go to Shannon Turner for her consent to use the plans/maps I made using her website, metromapmaker.com.

Finally a thank you to all the railway men and women I encountered on my journey who, despite working unsocial hours and coping with inevitable delays and cancellations, still managed, without exception, to be cheerful, helpful, friendly and often genuinely interested in my endeavours.

All photographs are by the author.

INTRODUCTION

The Beeching Report, *The Reshaping of British Railways*, published in 1963, called for the closure of 2,363 stations and many miles of track.[1] Thankfully some stations and lines did manage to survive, but most of the closures went ahead according to plan, leaving many small communities to rely on much vaunted local bus routes, many of which are now themselves under threat. Not only were numerous small stations swept away, but with them went a way of life; no more do people have a parcel to collect at the local station, from staff who probably knew them by name.

The railway of today is busier than it has ever been and passengers are often whisked along at great speed in air-conditioned comfort with the all-important at-seat trolley service, and nearby power points, essential for keeping one's devices fully charged. Heritage railways are increasingly popular, and there people can experience travelling as it once was, with the window open on a warm day, allowing the occasional waft of steam to come in, perhaps even coughing in a compartment full of smoke when they go through a tunnel. Little boys can get too near an open window and then go to a parent to get a smut removed from an eye. Anyone who can remember pre-Beeching times will be able to recall that these things were once an everyday occurrence; taken for granted, a part of our normal lives. At that time, you could go from almost anywhere to almost anywhere by rail. Passing through big stations with the ubiquitous train spotters, small and sometimes bigger 'boys' who never tired of watching the passing cavalcade, each with their notebook and a bag containing sandwiches and a bottle of drink. Glimpsing smaller stations along the route, some a junction for a branch line, with a gently simmering tank loco waiting to transport a handful of lucky passengers to a rural haven. Noting a life that seemed to be moving at an enviable and altogether different pace.

My plan to journey around the National Rail system, documenting request stops, began simply enough. I would visit all the request stops on mainland Great Britain. A journey that not only involved travelling in excess of 20,000 rail miles, but it also became a real voyage of discovery, on several levels. Then, at somewhere around the halfway stage, my son-in-law suggested I might write a book about my experiences. Hesitation gave way to, well, perhaps ... and the rest is, as they say, history.

My rail odyssey taught me that from a green valley in Cornwall that holds the delightful Looe branch line, to the magnificent isolation at Altnabreac in the far north of Scotland, some of that world which has always occupied my memories does still remain. It is true very much has been lost, but locations reflecting that world do still exist for anyone who cares to find them. As my journey unfolded I quickly realised that I was no longer simply documenting the request stops of Great Britain, but seeking the spirit of the lost places of my youth. Sadly much has changed; request stops are now nearly always a single platform, and mostly with just a bus stop-style shelter. The goods yard and parcels office are gone, the station buildings either demolished or converted to private use. The arrival of a train, instead of being heralded by the clunk of a semaphore signal, is now to be seen on an electronic information screen, and the only human contact is a remote voice coming through the speaker of a 'help point', but at least the stop is still there and we must be thankful for that.

Beeching the axeman didn't get them all. In fact some lines and stations have re-opened in recent years, surely evidencing that he got it wrong. There is even the promise that more may follow – let's hope it is many more, although the profit motive and expediency are still alive and well. Therefore we should not be complacent, and take note of the fact that Kildonan on the 'Far North Line' survived a recent closure attempt in 2018, reportedly to save four minutes on the Inverness to Thurso journey time of around three hours and forty-five minutes.

Some request stops exist in areas that are quite urban, but the vast majority are in rural, even isolated, locations. Arriving at one of these stops, then standing alone on the platform and watching the train depart, is to be free, if only briefly, from the prisons without bars or guards that we call towns and cities.

As this around Great Britain odyssey took about a year and a half to complete, and cost the equivalent of several good overseas holidays, a good question would be, was it worth it? Perhaps the fact that currently I am looking at the possibility of visiting all the request stops on heritage lines answers that, and if not I would emphatically say yes: worth every penny, twice over.

I discovered much about the almost hidden parts of our rail system, and much also about myself. Realising just how deep my love of all things railway are, and where this love first formed, did in some ways surprise me, although I suppose I always really knew.

To anyone else who is tempted to try this, or something similar, I would say: do it. If you don't have my obsessive desire for completeness or the sheer bloody mindedness to complete all the stops no matter what, just visit some. What is important, and vital, is not to hurry. Take time, and lots of it. Allow yourself to become part of the place and of the moment, and hopefully you will experience the railway magic that I felt the first time I stood on the platform at Berney Arms.

CHAPTER 1

WHY BERNEY ARMS?

I have a lifelong love of all things railway – partly inherited, but also partly the little boy who refuses to grow up. It is a sort of refuge from our ever increasingly hectic, angry, selfish and alienating world. A world where material things have such importance that happiness becomes confused with and takes second place to possessions, leaving the simple joy of just being alive to become lost in a world where many people seem to be in such a hurry to go nowhere – so many people with such little purpose.

My interest was never limited to locomotives and the trains themselves, exciting though they were, especially to a young boy witnessing the final days of steam. The railway station has always fascinated me, and to this day standing at the end of the platform looking down the line is a sight I never tire of, particularly if it is somewhere new to me and the line curves away into the distance; just what is around that corner? The grandeur of the large stations is something to admire certainly, but also to pass through without lingering. A country station however, now that is something else. Growing up in the Oxfordshire village of Goring-on-Thames, my local station was the former Great Western Railway (GWR) Goring and Streatley, a true country station despite its location on the London to Bristol main line. For me it was the starting point of many adventures.

This is not to say that being on the main line did not have its advantages. Platforms 3 and 4, the fast lines, were rarely used for stopping trains, in fact I cannot recall ever seeing a train stop on Platform 4. The fast trains that passed were an awesome sight, and my favourite would have to be the 'Bristolian' which I often watched thundering through the station as it headed back to London – something it did without even a sideways glance towards the inconsequential local stopping service from Didcot on Platform 1 that I was there to meet, usually hauled by a lowly and grimy Prairie tank locomotive. Perhaps with its headboard and polished brass, the express believed itself to be altogether superior. My father, who had just got off the local service, would meet me and say something like, "Did you see it? Must have been doing over ninety," and once, "it came through that fast last week that the lamps on the front had blown themselves out." I never did find out if that was true, but I doubt it – just something grown-ups tell kids, although I did naturally believe it at the time.

Station staff, I remember, included a stationmaster who lived in the nearby stationmaster's house, and although he never wore the top hat of days gone by, he did always dress immaculately and remained very aloof, unlike his staff who knew everybody and everything about them. Tickets were sold by a friendly lady booking office clerk who worked until the early afternoon, after which time one of the three station porters would appear to sell any other tickets required. When I say a porter would appear, what I mean is that he would leave the sanctuary of the parcels office, where porters were mostly to be found with their constantly boiling kettle. The parcels office at this time still handled a lot of packages: boxes of fresh fish destined for local shops, a crate of day-old chicks chirping, even a cat in a travel basket. Packages of every size and shape imaginable, wrapped in brown paper and all guarded and sorted by the three porters whose other duties would be to collect used tickets and keep the station immaculate, something they certainly achieved. The small garden and fish pond complete with goldfish on Platform 1 were always tended with great care – all this, needless to say, pre-dates our world of graffiti, empty plastic bottles, soft drink cans and discarded crisp packets blowing in the breeze.

My father was a sensitive but deeply troubled man, and when young he undoubtedly had, as they say today, 'issues'. His first thought on leaving school was to join the railways and become, eventually, an engine driver, something his father, for his own reasons, obstructed. So he became an apprentice carpenter instead. The Second World War denied him even that when he was called up and found himself in the Royal Artillery. Away for four-plus years from his new wife and daughter, fighting the Japanese in the jungles of the Far East, and what is sometimes described as a 'bad war', left him on his eventual return with issues that were spiralling out of control. Today it is called combat post-traumatic stress disorder but in 1946 it had no name and victims were told to be a 'man' and pull themselves together. But he still loved his railways and no matter how much difficulty he had getting through the day he never let it show to me, not at first anyway.

My dad and I spent most of our spare time together visiting all the places that a young boy would most want to go to, and we naturally always travelled by train. Our days out often involved going to London and, travelling from Goring, many trains were direct. The problem with these was they were slow, calling at numerous stops. The answer was simply to change at Reading and get a fast train, although he would always ask me, "Shall we get a fast?" – a silly question really, and changing at Reading became the norm for us. We would wait at the end of the platform to check the loco, usually an ex-GWR Castle Class: the heat, the steam, the smell and the polished brass as alive now in the fog of my mind as they were then.

"Can the boy come up?" my father would ask the fireman, who would then look across to his driver who would nearly always shake his head, since they were waiting for the 'right away', the whistle and green flag from the guard, the signal to move off. Then on two occasions we got a "Yes – have to be quick." That first time, standing dumbstruck in front of that fire, feeling the heat on my face and seeing all those pipes and levers, created a sensation that went so deep it has never left me. The guard's whistle blew, the fireman called "Right away driver" and we scrambled down and in through the first carriage door as the train pulled away. Little did I realise then that one day it would be me up there saying "Right away driver." It became our practice once the train had picked up speed to use dad's watch to time the quarter mile-posts and work out our speed; sometimes as much as 90mph. I never worked out who was the more excited, him or me.

My father did manage briefly to work on the railway for the signalling department, but then all his jobs tended to be brief. One day during this time, 1955 I think, we were on the end of the platform and a train pulled in, but unlike any train I had ever seen before. No Castle Class here but an experimental gas turbine locomotive '18000', although it easily could have been a spaceship straight off the cover of *Eagle* comic, piloted by no less than Dan Dare himself. Dad lifted me up to look into the cab – all those switches and dials, I had never seen anything like this before except in the aforementioned *Eagle*, but this was real and right here.

"Probably come up all the way from Penzance," my dad said.

"Where's Penzance?" I asked.

"At the end of the line," he replied.

The end of the line? I knew about Paddington, the beginning of the line, but it had never occurred to me that there was an 'end of the line'. Penzance, spelt with a Z – even the name was strange. But now, realising that there was an 'end of the line', I wanted to go there. It would be quite a few years before I finally made it, on a cold and very wet winter day, but make it I did. Arriving at or leaving Penzance, 'the end of the line', even after all these years, still feels special. As a railway employee my father had the right to wander wherever he wanted, or at least that's what he seemed to think. After seeing '18000' he decided to walk me over to the yard to look at the locos awaiting their next duties. He walked over live running tracks with an 8-year-old in tow, and no yellow vests. It would be a good many years before these would become essential everyday wear; we just had our gabardine macs. My mother had always insisted gabardine provided good protection but I think she was thinking more about a light shower and much less about a train at speed.

We headed for a loco that had a crew on board.

"Can we come up?" my father asked, and the reply being positive we climbed aboard. "I think the boy would like to do this when he's older," my father said. He usually referred to me as 'the boy' when talking to other people.

The particularly friendly fireman asked, "Would you?" I nodded, dumbstruck yet again. "Would you like to ask anything?" I shook my head, still dumbstruck. As we left the driver handed me the copy of *British Transport Commission News* that he had been reading. Locomotive 18000, Penzance, the 'end of the line', a locomotive cab visit and *British Transport Commission News* – just how much magic can an 8-year-old boy take in a day?

On Monday, 30 April 1962, at the age of 15 years and 4 weeks, I started work in the locomotive sheds at Reading as an engine cleaner. Arriving on my first day, the booking clerk handed me my brass pay check number 426, which enabled me to book on and off at the start and end of each working day. Then I was taken to Eddie Fullbrook, the cleaners' charge hand. Eddie gave me the tools of the trade: a bucket of cotton waste balls soaked in oil and a pot of brick dust with a leather pad. The oily waste to be used for the paintwork and the brick dust for the brass. He then walked me to a locomotive that already had a team of cleaners at work.

"This is Harty," he said, and to me, "Just follow the others."

Half an hour from walking through the gates and I was already at work, with a new name. I would always be known as 'Harty' during my time as a cleaner.

The various trades in the shed had their own rest rooms known in railway parlance as 'cabins'. The cleaners' cabin was like nothing I have ever experienced, before or since. Not a single pane of glass in the windows, no handle or catch on the door and a long table and bench that had more grease on them than on most of the locomotives outside. The people responsible for shed maintenance had given up trying to keep the cabin in any sort of good order. Cleaners apparently could and did break windows faster than anyone could replace them. The lack of windows was definitely an issue during the winter months, but had a simple solution: old hessian sacks wedged in place by wooden boards, to keep the wind out. For warmth we had an enormous 'Tortoise' stove, and we always kept it glowing red hot, made easy by the endless coal supply just outside the door. It would be reasonable to say my fellow cleaners were a fairly rough lot and some were certainly 'characters'. One of these was a lad from Tutts Clump, a village just outside Reading, who nobody liked. I recall the day he found himself shut in the smokebox of a Castle Class, with the door shut tight. He emerged moments later covered in soot, through the chimney, looking like a chimney sweep from a Charles Dickens novel.

One of the crew, named Titch, loved engines to the point where he would sometimes go without his meal break and carry on cleaning, oily cotton waste in one hand, cheese roll in the other. Then there was Snagglepuss, or sometimes Snaggle for short, so-called because he reminded us of the popular TV cartoon character of the time. Snaggle had a thing about lamps and never missed a chance to retrieve dirty ones from a locomotive and give them a polish. Then there was Gutteridge, kicking the cabin door open and throwing a bucketful of light, thin, cleaning oil onto the red-hot stove, engulfing the entire cabin in a fireball of the sort usually seen only in Hollywood movies. A good laugh?

Well it definitely amused *him*, judging by the maniacal grin on his face, illuminated momentarily by the glow of the fireball. There was no harm done, just a few singed eyebrows.

Eddie, the charge hand, was a lovely man and to this day I do feel somewhat guilty about the way we treated him. We were never what you might call nasty, but we did run him ragged. He would often lose track of us, while we on the other hand always knew where he was from our vantage points: under a locomotive, on the tender, I could go on, but suffice it to say an engine shed has many places to hide. Eddie, now nearing retirement, had been a driver until he failed his regular eye test, when he got lumbered with the cleaners' charge hand job. His cabin was a real home from home, with breakfast a revelation: frying pan, lard, eggs, bacon, the Full English. The cabin was always warm and smelled of a recent fry-up. He loved to talk about his life on the railway. He probably began work on the GWR just before the start of the First World War, because he remembered seeing engine 111, *The Great Bear*, the only 4-6-2 Pacific locomotive the GWR ever had. He always treated us fairly, even after being smoked out of his cabin when someone climbed onto the roof and blocked his chimney with cotton waste (and the less said about the frog in the teapot incident the better). I do hope you are doing well in the great engine shed in the sky Eddie.

In April 1963, I attended Southall shed for my firing training, a two-week course with a lot of emphasis on the rule book. The rule book had many safety implications and even as a 16-year-old it was essential to understand your role in the event of an emergency. The workings of a locomotive were also covered, but much had been learned during my time as a cleaner, particularly hanging round with and helping firemen in the shed, who were often not much older than myself.

Back in Reading and I went straight out firing, mostly on short freight trips to begin with, but with some passenger work. Then it became my turn to say "Right away driver" at last. My father never knew that I had begun to do what he had wanted for himself, at least I don't think so, because I'd lost all contact with him four years previously. The memories of my firing days, short-lived though they were, are very special, a time when going to work was more like an adventure, a day out. Very early on, possibly from day one, I learned the fireman's pose when going through stations. That is, head out of

the window, arms on the window ledge, in the hope that any local girls on the platform might be impressed. A forlorn hope no doubt, but I could always dream.

One passenger turn I really enjoyed involved going through Devizes, which included my first experience of single-line working, and I managed to disgrace myself twice in the same day. On arrival at Devizes I went to the signal box to make the tea, whereupon I managed to drop my container of tea and sugar, which went all over the polished floor.

"Have you got a brush?" I asked the signalman.

"I'll do it," he replied through teeth that were most definitely gritted.

I beat a very hasty retreat. Those signalmen were very proud of their boxes. A little later we were pulling into Seend, with me hanging out of the cab clutching the single-line token in my hand ready to hook it on the post as we passed. What could go wrong? I could, and did, miss the post.

"What do I do?" I called out.

"Throw it down," the driver shouted.

I complied, and the token landed halfway down the platform. I can still remember the signalman shaking his fist at me while running to retrieve his token. Looking on the bright side, he seemed to be puffing somewhat, so perhaps the exercise was beneficial.

My time firing proved to be short-lived, partly due to uncertainty surrounding the Beeching cuts, and also due to being very young and unsure of what I hoped for in life. After a little short of a year I left the job and my life took a different direction. I lived overseas, which proved to be great fun. I have no real regrets about leaving; that would be very negative, but seeing on my return to England in 1979 a high speed train (HST) for the first time I did think to myself, and have done occasionally since, 'What if?' Perhaps if I had stayed in the job I might not have gone overseas, I might not have even met my wife, or more correctly put, my ex-wife – now there's a thought. Sometimes I do now allow myself the luxury of standing on the end of a platform when a steam special has arrived. I watch the admiring crowd jostling for their photographs and peering into the cab, and I silently harbour the smug thought that I was up there once doing that for real, when it was real.

I read in the April 1984 edition of *Railway Magazine* an article about a request stop in East Anglia called Berney Arms, an isolated rural idyll that looked as authentic a country station as any could possibly be, and thought to myself, 'I must go there.'[1] Life however, as it so often does, always got in the way and it was many more years before I finally got round to it.

Berney Arms
Annual passenger usage: 996
Least used station rank: 51
Postcode: NR30 1SB
Ordnance Survey national grid reference: TG460053

In August 2017, and now retired, I found myself in East Anglia for a few days touring the local bookshops. Remembering the article about Berney Arms, I seized the opportunity to finally go there. On 17 August, I boarded a train at Great Yarmouth and felt very special, and a little excited, as I said to the guard, "Berney Arms please." Little did I realise that I had at that moment actually started on an odyssey that would take me quite literally to the four corners of the British mainland railway map. Seven minutes later I alighted from the train. Watching it depart into the distance and being left alone on the platform fully lived up to my 33-year-old expectations. Although it has to be said that the thought of a two and a half hour wait in the middle of the Fens for the train that would take me back to Norwich left me with a feeling of slight trepidation. Two and a half hours with nothing to do, just me and my camera. Just what would I do?

The platform at Berney Arms is delightfully tiny, with the guard only able to open one door, although signs exist in the undergrowth that suggest it was once much longer. Station facilities consisted of a small bicycle rack and a help point; no seat or bench, although that has improved since my first visit. The small waiting shelter of previous years that I had seen in photographs had gone. But who needs station facilities? They're for the towns and cities. This is a request stop, and less is most definitely more. Berney Arms has no vehicular access which makes it the most remote station in England, but with an annual passenger usage of 996 it is definitely not the least used. The only access, apart from by train, is by the River Yare, a third of a mile to the east, or on foot. The Weaver's Way long-distance footpath crosses the railway line close to the end of the platform, while the Wherryman's Way follows the banks of the River Yare at this point. A walk of 3 miles is the least anyone who misses the last train can expect though.

In perfect weather, with the only sound being the breeze blowing in the reeds, supplemented by occasional birdsong and the mooing of cattle grazing nearby plus the huge Norfolk sky overhead, a three-mile walk to the nearest road became a revelation. I almost instantly became absorbed in my surroundings, untroubled by the madness and hurry of the world outside the oasis of calm that is Berney Arms. I took my photographs, lots of them, pictures of the platform, the nameboard and all the obvious things, then found myself focusing on small details. Pictures of insects, the rusty bolt of a gate, flowers, and the swans on the nearby water. I began remembering how much I used to enjoy birdwatching with my daughter when she was younger. People in a hurry never notice the details, they miss far more than they ever see. Time passed amazingly quickly, so fast in fact that standing on the platform with my arm out to stop the homeward train, I felt somewhat cheated that my time had come to an end, but it was only over for the present. I didn't realise it then, but in almost exactly two years' time I would return, and what a return that would be!

The only reason Berney Arms exists is because the local landowner, Thomas Berney, made it a condition of the land sale to the Yarmouth and Norwich Railway. The station opened in 1844 and then closed in 1850 due to lack of patronage. When Thomas Berney protested, the Eastern Counties Railway (ECR), which had acquired the line, told him that the agreement to build a station did not extend to actually having trains stop. Only after a lengthy dispute did services resume in 1855, with the courts finally ruling, in 1860, in Thomas Berney's favour, that trains would stop in perpetuity.[2]

Perhaps it could be said that Berney Arms should never have been built in the first place. After all, it serves no real purpose does it? My view would be that the fact it serves no real purpose in being there is its reason for being there. The magic of the place (and it does have a magic) if you have time to see it, is that it exists, it does not *need* to, it just *does,* standing quietly, awaiting the next visitors and hoping to share a little of its tranquillity and magic with them. Oh please spare us from a world in which everything has a purpose, or a monetary value.

Eventually arriving into Norwich station and the other world that so many of us are forced to spend our time in, I was immediately engulfed by hordes of hurrying people, home from the shops, home from work, all looking hot, tired, anxious and stressed. How many of them had had a good day? Hopefully some of them at least might find occasionally their version of Berney Arms, whatever that is, wherever it is.

Shortly after my Berney Arms experience my thoughts turned to wondering just how many request stops there might be. I looked at Wikipedia which, at that time, December 2017, listed 152. Realising that because many would be difficult to reach this would be a real challenge, my feeling was: *I'll visit them all.* I formulated a plan to visit, spend time at and photograph each and every rail request stop in mainland Britain (I do not believe that Northern Ireland Railways have any request stops). But why would anyone want to do such a thing? Why spend so much time, effort and money (on train fares but also on several weeks of hotel bills)? Simple – because such stops are in the main remote and difficult to get to, the services are at the best infrequent and I like a challenge. Rail operators would like to abandon some of these services, leaving only the occasional 'parliament' required train (the minimum service to avoid the trouble of actually closing a stop): "You've just missed it sir but not to worry there is another one, same time next week." Stops that have one train a day, even one train a week, really do exist.

It became much more than a simple challenge. Total determination on my part has taken me to places where they don't want people to go, but my attitude has always been that I will find a way. This time life did not get in the way. "I am retired and have a railcard, so I'm off." This then is my record of that odyssey, a journey through a world where time moves more gently and people stop to say hello instead of pushing you out of the way in their headlong dash to nowhere. A world where it feels good to 'just be'. I downloaded the timetables and began planning. I set my own strict definition of 'visiting' – boarding or alighting from a train at each stop, usually both. Not always though: I arrived at some by bus or taxi, on foot or by bike. Plans, no matter how meticulous, and people tell me mine are meticulous-plus, can go wrong. I was rescued twice by taxi when trains were cancelled, one of these trips involving a journey of 50 miles. I'm glad GWR, and not myself, had the £130 bill for that. I was trapped in a waiting shelter by a less than friendly dog, and I also had a highland bull, the type with horns not a sporran, take a worrying interest in me.

Berney Arms was a revelation. The list was prepared, timetables downloaded. How many other stations like this exist in the corners of our rail system? Only one way to find out. Let's do it I thought – one down, only 151 to go.

CHAPTER 2

WHAT DO YOU MEAN CANCELLED?

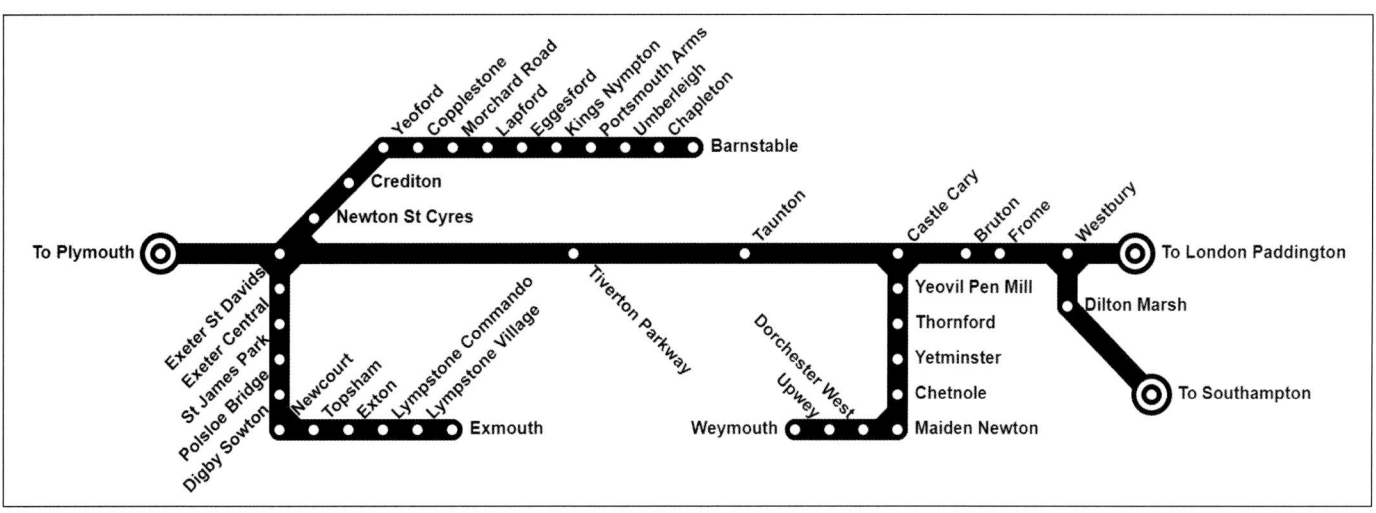

Dilton Marsh
Annual passenger usage: 20,302
Least used station rank: 340
Postcode: BA13 4DF
Ordnance Survey national grid reference: ST855500

On a very cold and bright morning in February 2018, I stood on Platform 2 at Swindon station with a return ticket to Dilton Marsh. Dilton is only 33 miles distant, making it my local request stop; I was starting with an easy one you might say.

Shortly after moving off, the guard walked through the train. "All tickets please," he said.

I offered mine up for inspection.

"Dilton Marsh? What are you going to do in Dilton?"

"Just hit the shops and check out the nightlife," I replied.

He smiled and said, "I can see the platform from my house, change at Westbury."

The first thing I saw on arrival were men in orange workwear. This was definitely not what I had hoped to find, since I had photographs to take. Fortunately, work had only just got underway so I did manage to get most of the photos I wanted. If I had arrived a week or two later, it might have been a different story. A major station refurbishment had just begun. The existing shelters and platforms were all constructed of a type of plywood and definitely showing their age. I did revisit about eighteen months later to see the completed works, which had transformed the station into a clean, modern, functional and, to me, soulless place.

There has been a stop here since 1937 when the GWR opened Dilton Marsh Halt. BR dropped the suffix in 1969 and it became just Dilton Marsh. BR did attempt to close the station in the late 1960s, however a vigorous campaign by local people and a poem by John Betjeman averted closure and it still remains in use today. A slightly unusual feature is that the two platforms are staggered and separated by the high street. Anyone wishing to change platforms here would have to go down the access ramp onto the road, under the rail bridge and up the other ramp, a distance of approximately 100 metres.

Having taken my photographs it was time for tea. I always carried a flask for what became, from day one, my traditional platform tea drinking ceremony; especially useful if it is a frosty February morning. I then headed back to Westbury and on home to the warm, with the knowledge that I had just visited not only Wiltshire's lone request stop but also its least used station.

Four weeks later and in possession of a 'Heart of Wessex Ranger' ticket I boarded a train at Bath Spa, and shortly after leaving I asked the guard to stop at Thornford, the first of three stops in Dorset, the other two being Yetminster and Chetnole. My intention was to visit them all in a single day. I had checked them out on the internet as part of my planning, and they looked very rural, isolated even, and just what I was looking for. What could possibly go wrong?

Thornford
Annual passenger usage: 3,448
Least used station rank: 133
Postcode: DT9 6PT
Ordnance Survey national grid reference: ST593125

Thornford was opened by the GWR in 1936, with the name Thornford Bridge Halt. It was renamed Thornford Bridge in 1969 and then Thornford in 1974. Built with wooden, staggered platforms separated by a road, it also had wooden shelters and a lamp hut.[1]

I arrived at Thornford on time, and found myself to be the only person who alighted, standing on the single platform in a wonderful rural location with not a house in sight. Facilities were quite basic: a noticeboard, help point and a shelter with a bench seat complete with a working payphone, something of a luxury. I found a few more of these on my travels, though rarely in working order. This one however did actually have a dialling tone. The station is constructed entirely of concrete, not the most attractive of materials, but this is offset by its location in the 'Heart of Wessex', with a perfect view from the end of the platform of a single line curving into the distance. Exiting the station is no mean feat because the only way to the road is a climb up a long flight of steps, then go through a gate, which would be a real problem for those with mobility issues. (Throughout this book I often comment on the ease of access for people whose mobility is challenged, as conditions can vary considerably from station to station.) The gate had an ice warning sign on it, possibly left over from a recent Everest expedition I thought. Not until I reached the road bridge did I catch sight of human habitation – the tiny village of Thornford a mile distant, a community that this station has served since its opening.

Yetminster
Annual passenger usage: 7,618
Least used station rank: 207
Postcode: DT9 6LH
Ordnance Survey national grid reference: ST597108

My next call was Yetminster, just a little over a mile away by rail. Adjacent to the village, it appeared almost busy when I arrived with two fellow passengers alighting with me and three people getting on. Something borne out by the Office of Rail and Road (ORR) statistics, which show passenger numbers here as double those of the preceding stop, Thornford. The facilities are what you would expect at a request stop: noticeboard, help point and a waiting shelter of the typical bus-stop variety, plus a small car park. I did not get the feeling of isolation here, because I found Yetminster to be busy by small village standards, but nonetheless it was a very pleasant place to pass a couple of hours in the spring sunshine.

Built by the GWR in 1857, signs of its past are very evident. A platform that is more than ample in length for the two- or three-car diesel multiple units (DMUs) that comprise today's services. The original station building still exists although sadly no longer in railway use, though it has been put to good purpose by local businesses. Clearly visible is an abandoned and overgrown second platform indicating that there had been double track here in the past. Also apparent is the former stationmaster's house, which has become a rather imposing and cared-for private dwelling.

Chetnole
Annual passenger usage: 2,998
Least used station rank: 119
Postcode: DT9 6EP
Ordnance Survey national grid reference: ST597075

The GWR opened Chetnole Halt in 1933. It then became Chetnole in 1969. Constructed with wooden platforms and shelters, the platforms were again staggered, with a roadway in between.[2]

I was heading south again, to what would be my last stop of the day at Chetnole, only 2 miles distant. I approached the guard and requested my stop.

"Sorry we can't stop there," he said.

"But you have to stop. I want to get off," I replied.

He then explained that we were travelling in one of the three-car Class 166 Thames Turbo DMUs and while not new, they were new to this line, having recently been released from the Thames Valley routes. It transpired that he could only release all the doors together, and had no way to open them selectively, which presented no problems with the longer platforms, where they originally worked, but at Chetnole with its short platform it would not be safe. I had a momentary vision of massed passengers throwing themselves out of open doors and plunging into the abyss like lemmings in a mass suicide. I would probably be interviewed by the press: 'Swindon man saw it all'. Even though I pointed out that because no one else had requested Chetnole, could he please let me off, health and safety ruled the day and we were not stopping. The best I could hope for at that moment would be to wave 'hello' and 'goodbye' to Chetnole when we whipped through.

As a GWR guard, this man was both reasonable and resourceful and had a solution to my problem. Stay on the train (I did not think I had a choice) and get off at the next stop, Maiden Newton. There, waiting in the passing loop, should be the next train going north. I could then sprint over the line, jump aboard and ask the guard for Chetnole, always assuming it was not a Thames Turbo, in which case I might spend the rest of the day going up and down, passing, then re-passing, Chetnole but never actually arriving, a sort of railway version of the *Flying Dutchman*.

Hurrying over the footbridge at Maiden Newton, I could see the other train at the platform waiting for me. My guard had called over to let them know I was on my way. I felt particularly relieved to see a Class 150 DMU with only two coaches. The day was saved, I thought, Chetnole here I come, a little late, but on my way.

I stepped down from the train and checked the station nameboard just to make sure I had actually arrived, and yes it said Chetnole. This station is almost a duplicate of Thornford, two stops up the line, hence it has that same rural feel to it. With an annual passenger footfall of a little less than 3,000, it is the least used station in Dorset. This is hardly surprising – the nearby village, which can only be seen when you climb up to the road bridge, has a population of around 350.

Checking the shelter out, I found a nice touch: someone had left some copies of the local *Wriggle Valley Magazine*, named after the local river; what a charming name. An excellent photograph of a nuthatch graced the front cover, and this was particularly apt, seeing as a short while later I would be able to photograph one of these delightful little birds from the platform myself. This was the first time I had really noticed the flora and fauna surrounding a stop, and this became an increasing feature of my visits, to the point where I carried a small pair of binoculars in my bag.

Taking a stroll down the platform and passing the information point, the thought came to me to try it out. Two buttons were evident, the first for information and the second connecting to a call centre if you needed assistance. I decided to give the former a try, even though I didn't need information, because I knew exactly when my train would arrive; or at least that's what I thought. Screeching into life the box announced: "This station is Chetnole," and then, "Your attention please, we are sorry that the 15.42 to Gloucester has been cancelled."

I knew that the next train would be the 18.03, which would have meant another two plus hours to wait. My flask by this time was unsurprisingly empty, and the sun that earlier had felt good had become both weaker and lower in the sky, and the thought of a few hours in that concrete shelter, in the middle of March, really did not appeal.

Only one thing for it. Press the help button. The box screeched into life again, but this time a woman answered. I explained my problem in that I wanted a train to Bath Spa.

"I'm sorry sir, the 15.42 has been cancelled."

Of course I already knew this but sought clarification. "What do you mean, cancelled?"

This lady could be described as both pleasant and helpful, but she did not seem to understand the concept of a rhetorical question and repeated what she had just told me.

"I can't wait here for four hours can I?" was my response, desperately hoping she would not say yes.

After a brief silence she replied, "Please wait sir and I'll call you back." She did call me back, with the welcome news that a taxi had been called. A delay would be inevitable, thanks to its coming from Weymouth over 20 miles distant, but she assured me it would arrive.

In a little over an hour my car arrived and I was away. I asked the driver where he planned dropping me and expected him to say Yeovil, from where it would have been easy to catch a homeward rail service.

He replied, "Bath." Perhaps he thought I looked a little concerned and told me, "Don't worry it's all paid for. I've told them the bill for this will be £130."

What else could I do but sit back and relax, safe in the knowledge that Bath Spa would be the next stop.

Dockyard
Annual passenger usage: 4,432
Least used station rank: 148
Postcode: PL2 1RX
Ordnance Survey national grid reference: SX453558

A week later found me heading for Dockyard in Devon for a single-stop outing. Opened by the GWR in 1905, like many others it originally had the suffix 'halt', but this was dropped in 1969.

Travelling west from Plymouth, Dockyard is the second stop and less than 2 miles along the main line to Cornwall. The track here is double, dictating the need for two platforms, with only the westbound platform having a shelter, which does not have a single piece of plexiglass left in it, giving the whole place a rather unloved feel. Facilities are minimal, just a help point and the usual noticeboards. Situated near a naval base and with rows of houses stretching into the distance, it is a wonder Dockyard isn't busier than it is. Exploring, I noticed a couple of nice details. Firstly I found an original mile-post marker on the up platform, and then some bricks which were embossed 'Cakemore'. The Cakemore brickworks, based in the Dudley area, has been known by various names over the years including the 'South Staffordshire Blue Brick Company Ltd'.

Waiting for a train back to Plymouth, I had time for tea and a nibble while watching a blackcap happily singing the joys of spring from the top of a sycamore tree on the other platform – food for the body and the soul perhaps? A satisfying end to this visit I thought to myself, trying to remember the last time I had seen a blackcap.

A couple of days later I continued my trek westwards into Devon, this time visiting two request stops on the 'Avocet Line' south of Exeter. These being Exton and Lympstone Commando. I also intended to stop at Topsham. While not a request stop, there is a rather good bookshop and a coffee shop that sells top of the range carrot cake. After all, man cannot live by request stops alone.

Exton
Annual passenger usage: 24,886
Least used station rank: 380
Postcode: EX3 0PR
Ordnance Survey national grid reference: SX980863

Exton opened for traffic in 1861 as 'Woodbury Road', and its name was changed to Exton in 1958. The suffix 'halt' was added in 1965 and removed in 1969, when it became plain Exton once again.

The station facilities are the usual shelter, help point and noticeboard, but what it lacks in amenities it makes up for with its beautiful location right on the banks of the Exe. During my visit it was low tide and a profusion of waders were scouring the mud flats. Avocets are sometimes seen here, but unfortunately not on this day.

The platform seemed to be much longer than required for the Class 143 DMUs that were passing, a sure indication of the longer trains of yesteryear, when people went on their holidays by train, with the excitement of the journey being part of the experience, instead of piling the kids and bags into a people mover and hurtling down the motorway, with tunnel vision engaged, stress levels high and getting higher. I must stop here before I begin to see lemmings again.

Lympstone Commando
Annual passenger usage: 61,456
Least used station rank: 642
Postcode: EX8 5AA
Ordnance Survey national grid reference: SX982857

On arriving at Lympstone Commando my thoughts were, just what will I find? Built in 1976 by BR for the exclusive use of the army camp, stories abound regarding the attitude of the Ministry of Defence (MOD) to this stop. The MOD has in the past claimed that the station is private and the public are not allowed to get off here. Some people have described being told they cannot alight and others told not to take photographs. Following a freedom of information request the MOD conceded that the station is the property of Network Rail (NR) and therefore they cannot prevent the public from stepping onto the platform. Before arriving I did take the precaution of letting the guardhouse know of my intended arrival, and was advised this would attract attention and not to point my camera in the direction of the base. While on the platform it became clear that my presence had indeed attracted the attention of security staff, but at no point was I spoken to or approached.

Lympstone Commando is a very basic station with a platform made of second-hand concrete sections recovered from another site. One interesting feature is that under each station nameboard is a red sign with the legend in white, 'Persons who alight here must only have business with the camp'. A statistic to note is that with an annual passenger figure of 61,456, it is the busiest request stop in Great Britain.

I can a claim a link to Lympstone Commando, albeit extremely tenuous. My son-in-law's father is an ex-marine and trained there, and he tells stories of swimming across the Exe. While looking out across the river I saw what may have been a cormorant on the water, more likely a shag, but I did allow myself to fancy that it could have been the head of marine 'Cole' having a last swim across to Starcross for a quick pint and then back to barracks.

Still moving westwards from Swindon, I planned to tackle the 'Tarka Line' in Devon, which runs from Exeter to Barnstaple, a distance of just under 39 miles with nine request stops. Consulting the timetables I soon realised this would take careful planning, because some of these stops had a service limited to morning, late afternoon and evening services. Eventually I hatched a plan: four could be done on single days out, and the others merged into a two-week Cornwall adventure which was next in the pipeline.

Umberleigh
Annual passenger usage: 34,784
Least used station rank: 467
Postcode: EX37 9AB
Ordnance Survey national grid reference: SS609238

I reached Umberleigh incident free, despite a tight time allowance to change trains at Exeter, arriving late one Monday morning on board a Class 143 Pacer DMU, which did not give the smoothest of rides. I stepped onto the platform and made a quick check to ensure the journey hadn't shaken any of my tooth fillings or dentures loose and then I was off on a walkabout, camera at the ready.

The North Devon Railway (NDevonR) built this line, with Umberleigh opening in 1854. When I visited it was a very clean and nicely presented station, with spring daffodils in flowerpots. There is a wooden station sign suggesting Southern Railway (SR) heritage, and although probably not authentic, it is still a nice touch nonetheless. The original station house, which has now become a private dwelling, is a sign of busier, more important days, also indicated by the second platform, overgrown but still visible. Today's facilities are basic but adequate, with a help point that displays the train details in real time.

Morchard Road
Annual passenger usage: 12,134
Least used station rank: 268
Postcode: EX17 5LR
Ordnance Survey national grid reference: SS750051

After about an hour I headed back in the direction of Exeter on the same Pacer. This time my destination was Morchard Road. Passing me, the guard did not ask for my ticket, he just said "Where to this time?"; he knew what I was up to, something that was to become familiar to me as my journeys continued.

The NDevonR opened Morchard Road in 1854. It became Morchard Road Halt in 1965, but lost the halt suffix in 1969. I found the old station house to be a private home. On the platform is a bus stop-style waiting shelter and the whole station had a generally cared-for look. At the end of the platform is a mile-post informing anyone interested that it is a little over 187 miles to London, a good distance to have between myself and the capital, I thought.

As the village of Morchard Bishop is more than 2 miles away, I decided to content myself with photographs and a local exploration only. This allowed me time to sit quietly until my train arrived. The realisation of how important this quiet time was began here, but at this stage I didn't understand quite what was happening – that would come later.

When the train had left I stood alone on the platform and with the exception of the breeze rustling in the trees, quiet ruled. However, after sitting for a while things began to come to life. The birds who were not evident a short while before started to sing and flit from one tree to another. Small creatures rustled through the undergrowth; it seemed they had accepted my presence and were honouring me by allowing me to share their world.

Copplestone
Annual passenger usage: 15,262
Least used station rank: 299
Postcode: EX17 5NE
Ordnance Survey national grid reference: SS767031

My southward train came into view, and I was standing with my arm out to give, as the sign puts it, 'a clear indication' that I wished to board. I was in luck – it was a Class 153 Sprinter DMU, a touch of luxury with proper seats. It was a shame that Copplestone, my destination, was under 2 miles away.

Copplestone is fairly typical of many other stops described in this book. An old gradient sign still exists. The platform has other signs of grander days gone by; it is a lot longer than necessary, and there is also a disused second platform, clearly visible opposite. The main platform's central section has been raised with the use of plywood, and while this is totally justified to eliminate the not insignificant step down from a train, personally I feel it nevertheless detracts from the overall charm of the place. Such is the price of progress. Copplestone is nevertheless a very pleasant spot to linger.

The station house still exists, now unsurprisingly a private dwelling. Passengers have a typical plexiglass and aluminium shelter to keep the wind and rain off, adequate and definitely better than nothing. Our insect friends are very much better catered for though, because at the Exeter end of the platform some kind person has made them a home of their own, in the form of a miniature signal box filled with fir cones, bits of wood and all sorts of other things that provide the nooks and crannies they need. Here the local bugs can spend the winter days and long dark nights snug. It even has a Copplestone signboard on the front: delightful.

The village of Copplestone is a pretty and seemingly busy place, marred only by the fact it has, like so many villages, an A road racing through the centre of it. In the middle of the village, Copplestone Cross is worthy of note. Some stories claim it marks the geographical centre of Devon, others that it marks the site of a murder. Personally I cannot attest to the veracity of either claim. Both are good stories though.

Yeoford
Annual passenger usage: 18,156
Least used station rank: 323
Postcode: EX17 5JB
Ordnance Survey national grid reference: SX783988

"Where to this time?"

"Yeoford," I replied to the guard who I had seen earlier in the day, on the same Pacer.

A journey of just four minutes and I had reached the highlight of my day.

Yeoford opened in 1854 and was called, for a time, Yeoford Junction. The opposite platform is still very much evident with tracks still in situ alongside. It is also easy to make out what would have been the station yard. The other tracks, but not the platform, are still in use by the GWR service from Exeter to Okehampton, which currently runs on summer Sundays only. It is not possible to catch one of these services at Yeoford due to the fact the two tracks are in fact two distinct single lines, separating at Crediton, a little over 3 miles to the south.

The station lacks a plexiglass shelter; instead there is a real wooden hut, the age of which is difficult to guess: certainly not young. Walking in, I found a couple of bookcases filled with books, on the basis of 'feel free to take', or donate, as the individual sees fit. Unfortunately nothing there was on my wish list but still, it is always good to see books. Then it got better – at the other end of the hut I spied a hanging basket bracket in the shape of an Irish Setter, my favourite dog breed. Books in the waiting shelter, and a gun-dog shaped basket support; obviously people of discernment were nearby.

Back to Exeter and then home. Waving my train down I saw it was the Class 153 DMU again.

"Back to Exeter?" the guard said to me; this man not only remembered me, but seemed to know my schedule.

Settling into the train out of Exeter I reflected on my day. Four stops in a day, not bad at all. The pace was quickening, plans were forming, onwards and upwards.

Berney Arms, the stop that started my rail journey around Britain's mainland, seen on a gorgeous afternoon on 17 August 2017.

A Class 156 Super Sprinter DMU with the huge Norfolk sky in the background is about to call at Berney Arms on 17 August 2017. This train is the 17.47 Great Yarmouth to Norwich, and is only scheduled to call at Berney Arms during the summer months.

The northbound platform at Dilton Marsh on 16 February 2018. Since this photograph was taken the scene has altered greatly. All the original wood has been replaced with stainless steel, aluminium and plexiglass.

Dilton Marsh photographed on the 22 May 2019, looking north. Much has changed since my earlier visit. Passing is the 11.11 Westbury to Southampton Central formed of a Class 166 Networker Turbo Express DMU.

Thornford photographed on 13 March 2018. Despite the all concrete construction I found this a very attractive stop due to its very strong rural feel in what to me is typical Dorset countryside.

Yetminster, seen on 13 March 2018. It serves the lovely and quite busy village to which it is adjacent. The white building just past the waiting shelter is the former station building, and signs of the redundant second platform can be made out at the right of the picture.

Chetnole is situated a little over 3 miles to the south of Thornford, which is also constructed mainly of concrete and is very similar in appearance. Photographed on 13 March 2018.

Dockyard, which is less than 2 miles west from Plymouth, is surrounded by housing, seen here on 20 March 2018.

WHAT DO YOU MEAN CANCELLED? • 25

The 12.04 Penzance to London Paddington HST service passing Dockyard on 20 March 2018.

Exton seen on 22 March 2018. It is a beautiful spot on the Exe estuary with numerous waders and other birdlife out on the mudflats.

Lympstone Commando photographed on 22 March 2018, while taking care not to point my camera into the base, which is only a few metres to the right.

Lympstone Commando on 22 March 2018, and despite this rather stern warning, any passenger can get off the train here, although they cannot leave the station!

WHAT DO YOU MEAN CANCELLED? • 27

Umberleigh, photographed on 26 March 2018 looking north.

Morchard Road looking south on 26 March 2018. The old station buildings are now privately owned. Today's shelter can just be made out adjacent to the help point.

Copplestone looking north. Note the mini 'signal box' made as a home for insects, photographed on 26 March 2018.

The 14.53 Exmouth to Barnstaple comprising a Class 150 Sprinter DMU calls at Yeoford on 26 March 2018. The tracks on the right are not in fact part of the Barnstaple branch, but the line to Okehampton.

CHAPTER 3

THE JOY OF LISTS

I had now completed twelve stops, and with planning in full swing I felt I had made a pleasing start. Not everyone would agree with me, but I am of the firm conviction that it is not possible to over-plan: 'Perfect Planning Prevents Pathetic Performance' is definitely a motto to live up to.

One of the first things I decided on, after careful study of the appropriate map, was to divide the country into a total of twelve areas. This served two main purposes. Firstly, many of these tours were obviously going to involve overnight stays, therefore it made sense to locate myself centrally within each area in order to limit the number of nights away, as hotels can be expensive. Secondly, Rover tickets were to be extensively used, and these can usually be used to their best advantage if you are located centrally. Looking at a rail map of the whole of Great Britain, which showed just request stops, it was striking just how many are on the westward side of the country.[1] There are very few in the South East, just Bures on the Marks Tey to Sudbury branch which is some 53 miles north of London Liverpool Street, and another six stops in East Anglia.

The twelve areas I decided on, in the order I visited, were:

  Devon
  Cornwall
  South West Wales
  Heart of Wales
  Cambrian Coast
  North Wales
  Stratford-upon-Avon
  Manchester, Burnley, plus two others
  Cumbrian Coast
  North Scotland
  West Scotland
  East Anglia

Rail fares, as we all know, are most certainly not cheap, and always rising, but it is possible with some forethought and planning to keep costs to a minimum. Those who are old enough or, even better still, young enough, can obtain a railcard and save a third off ticket prices.

The more you use it, the more you save. Purchasing tickets in advance can be particularly beneficial for longer journeys and can produce surprisingly big savings, but the traveller needs to be wary of any applicable conditions. These tickets are often not flexible in their use and usually restrict travel to a specific train. The most useful tickets (in my experience) are the Rovers and Rangers of which there are many types. They always offer good value.[2] These tickets allow for unlimited travel in a specified area, but do be aware that many are limited to off-peak times. Check the National Rail Enquiries website (not to be confused with Network Rail) to see a full listing of what is available.[3]

Which stops are just by request only? That is clear to see in the timetable, as 'x' marks the spot. If you see a time written as 14x00, then that is a request stop. My own guide to what constituted a request stop was easy; I used the same Wikipedia list that I had copied in January 2018, making it a sort of datum point. My reasoning was that, clearly, anomalies do exist, therefore I needed a constant reference point. For instance, some stops are by request in one direction only, and others on the list when I started have since become mandatory stops. Heritage lines also have request stops, but only two of these stops are listed, although many others do exist; something for me to bear in mind for future adventures.

Lech-a-Vuie on the 'West Highland Line' is an abandoned platform not used since the 1970s, but it's still shown on the list, and to my mind required a visit. Something I was to be very glad of when I finally arrived, in that it instantly became a real highlight for me. Even to the extent that I am currently trying to find out everything that I can about this remote highland platform, information about which appears to be rather scant. One of the great joys of this odyssey has been how seemingly insignificant and forgotten places like Lech-a-Vuie can catch the imagination.

Because these excursions were to be enjoyable, not stressful, and thus memorable for all the right reasons, and not the wrong ones, planning had the upmost importance. Thinking about how to ensure all went according to plan did bring to mind two train travel stories from my younger years: how the pram went to Crewe and the tale of the King's Lynn express.

My father and I loved trains and train travel, my mother on the other hand loved buses and they were always her first choice. The thought of getting on a train filled her with dread. She had this firm conviction that no matter which train you got on, it never took you to where you wanted to go. This in her view was not a problem with buses, where you can always ask the driver 'does this bus go to wherever', and if he doesn't know then surely all is really lost. This belief, that trains would almost wantonly deposit you anywhere other than where you intended to be, while clearly much exaggerated, did in her case have some justification.

How the Pram Went to Crewe

A story often told by my grandmother explained just how a perambulator (that is pram or baby buggy to younger readers) made its way unaided from Southampton to Crewe and back again; a sort of homing pram? This pram had Victorian heritage, making it both grand and large, to the point I believe where Queen Victoria herself would have smiled approvingly on it, and as we all know she was not easily amused. The body bore a striking resemblance (I have seen photographs) to the hull of an ocean-going liner, very much in keeping with the port of Southampton, and finished in gleaming black with white detailing and the normal number of wheels – that is, four in total. These wheels consisted of two large ones at the front and two even larger ones at the rear, which I suppose in railway terminology would be described as a 2-2-0 wheel arrangement. An important point to note here is that my grandmother always told this story, never my grandfather, presumably because he generally got the blame for the whole sorry saga. Being a wise man indeed, he clearly understood the best course for anyone married to my grandmother was to keep your head down and speak when you're spoken to, for answering back would run the risk of having your pocket money stopped.

One sunny day my grandparents, who lived in Southampton, decided to have a day in Bournemouth. My mother, a year old at this time, was in the pram and proudly wheeled onto the platform. The pram being far too large to take onto the train resulted in my grandfather receiving instructions to ascertain from station staff the location of the Bournemouth train. This he did. Or thought he did. The baby was then removed and the empty pram loaded into the guard's van. No sooner had this been done and the door shut, the train began to move and despite their protestations would not, and did not, stop. The train and the pram then disappeared into the distance. Station staff were sought out and consulted, and the question asked of them, "Can you get the platform staff at Bournemouth to take our pram off the train and we will collect it when we arrive?"

To which the staff replied, "But that train's not going to Bournemouth it's going to Crewe."

Just how long before baby and pram were reunited I do not know, but it did somehow eventually happen, I have seen the photographic evidence. How long my grandfather remained in disgrace is also a mystery, although a not inconsiderable time would be my guess.

The Tale of the King's Lynn Express

As part of a single parent family, when I got home from school I had to fend for myself, a real 'latch key kid', something I coped with easily enough. My mother had a job in Reading at this time, about twenty minutes away by the dreaded train, and she typically got home about six-thirty, by which time I would have fed and watered myself. One day, six-thirty had passed and she had not arrived. I just sat watching TV and waited, then at about nine she finally arrived. She seemed most impressed that I had not got in to a state of panic, but I generally don't panic – nothing heroic, that's just me, I don't panic. At the time I was watching Inspector Lockhart unmask the villain in the latest episode of *No Hiding Place*, and was rather pleased to have missed *Coronation Street*.

The reason for her lateness? The explanation was simple enough: she went to the usual platform for the stopping train home, checked with the ticket collector that the train was going to Goring, and got an affirmative reply. What she did not understand however was that there were two trains on Platform 8 at Reading that evening, the local stopper (three stops and she would be home) and, in front, an express bound for King's Lynn. No prizes for guessing which one she got on. Nothing wrong with a jaunt to King's Lynn, I have been there and it is a perfectly nice place to visit, but on a damp and cold winter's evening, and after a day's work, perhaps not a good idea. After passing Tilehurst and then Pangbourne at speed, and suspecting there might be a problem, she decided to find the guard and see what the problem might be. Having found him he explained the situation, and added, "We sometimes stop at Oxford to water the loco. We might get you off there." A point to note here is that he said we *might* get you off, not you *can* get off.

While not exactly her lucky night, this luckily was one of the nights it did make a water stop at Oxford which was good, however the water tower was not on the platform, and this was bad. Salvation arrived in the form of several strong and willing railwaymen who lowered her carefully onto the tracks and escorted her up onto the platform. Only one thing remained for her to do now – await the next train back to Goring, after making sure it would actually stop there, something she managed to accomplish without further incident, arriving at Goring a couple of hours late and from the opposite direction, but home again nonetheless.

I determined there were to be no unexpected diversions or mystery tours for me. This I ensured by lots of time spent compiling a list of stops to visit by area, then a general look at the timetables to decide which were practical for day trips and which would require nights away. The full rail timetable can be purchased in book form, although it is not cheap and others are available free from local stations. However these do tend to be limited, only covering certain areas and lines. What I have found is that the NR website has links to the complete timetable and is free of charge.[4] It very quickly became apparent there would be quite a lot of nights that I would not be sleeping in my own bed, although at this stage I didn't realise quite how many. Only when I began to write this did I complete a final tally, and found myself somewhat shocked at the total of forty-eight nights, made up of forty-four in hotels and four on the Caledonian Sleeper. One day I intend to roughly cost that, after first making sure I'm sitting down.

Decision made, my first major tour would be of Cornwall, and the remaining five stops on the Tarka Line in Devon that I had not previously completed. Some serious and detailed planning would be needed, definitely not a problem but rather something I knew I would enjoy.

Several evenings were spent poring over timetables, maps and any other relevant information that I could find and a plan began to emerge. It transpired that by using a 'Freedom of the South West 8 in 15 Day Rover', I would be able to cover the area with mostly single day trips, and just one overnight stay in Penzance, 'the end of the line'. Incidentally this is a favourite ticket of mine, as it covers the whole South West from Swindon to Penzance, giving eight days of unlimited travel in a fifteen-day period (hence its name).

Seven day visits and one overnight into Devon and Cornwall would involve a lot of travelling and eight crossings of the Saltash rail bridge. It just got better and better, as much fun as it is possible to have with your clothes on, perhaps even more, who knows? All I knew was that it looked good and I wanted to get started.

It is not possible to overstate the value of and, for me, the pleasure of, spending time with the appropriate timetables before finalising any plans. This allowed me to fit the maximum number of stops into any single day, while still allowing for the minimum of one hour, ideally two, at each stop. The infrequency of services nearly always posed difficulties and in many cases it often worked best if I passed a stop, got off at the next and then caught the next train going back in the direction I had just come from, completing a line in a sort of to-and-fro movement. Suffice to say, following the rule of a few evenings spent engaged in serious planning, I produced plans that typically allowed visiting three or four stops on any one day, with a best effort of six.

While working on my first schedule I soon realised I was making a serious omission: being totally focused on making the best of the train times, I hadn't allowed myself time to eat. It might sound strange to say this, but when I am busy and on the move (and I do love to be on the move), then that is my focus, and having to stop for anything else is often simply forgotten or considered a waste of time and done somewhat grudgingly. Time spent at the stops themselves is the one exception to this and I always allowed sufficient time to savour the moment; after all I had often travelled a significant distance to be there.

Timetables were then revisited with eating time now included. Good use was made of a national pub chain, with convenient locations and reasonable prices. This then became the norm for all subsequent trips, and I managed to find one in almost every town, even the smaller ones.

For the journeys that would require overnight accommodation I used a mixture of hotel chains and small independent bed and breakfasts. The big chains are, in my experience, always safe in that you know exactly what you are going to get, in terms of service and cleanliness. With the small independents you can never be sure, but in all the forty-four nights I spent away there were only two, both at the same place, where the accommodation disappointed me. The general standard with all the others varied between good and excellent. There are various price comparison websites that were found to be useful and not only for getting the best price, but also for searching by location. This was a priority in my case, in that I was travelling only by public transport. The big question then was, how far is the hotel from the railway station? I found that, like long distance rail fares, the further in advance I could book a hotel the better, because prices and availability are directly linked. Something I learned to my cost when booking the two Scotland visits. Rooms were in short supply with prices on the high side, aggravated greatly by the simple fact Scotland is understandably very popular with tourists.

When finalised, the itinerary, for that is how my final plan for this expedition and all subsequent ones became known, was four pages long, very much a thing of great beauty. It was colour coded and contained much relevant information so that I could refer to the itinerary not only to check for timings, but also to learn exactly to where I would, or at least should, be at any given moment. A friend of mine, Gerald, was very interested in my progress, so I always left him a copy so he could track my whereabouts at any given time. Other important information also included on my itineraries was the last train times home (useful in the case of late running or the dreaded cancellation), local taxi firms and anything else that might be of use.

Itinerary apart, various other paperwork was always carried in my camera bag. Relevant timetables and maps – not only of the rail route and request stops, but also of the location of the local watering holes and any nearby second-hand bookshops, and a 'tick list' of my own design which allowed me to tick as correct, or amend when required, all arrival and departure times. This allowed me to easily update my records when I returned home. Other items carried at all times were waterproofs, my flask and a snack. Enough to keep me going until I reached civilisation and an evening meal. A cup of tea and whatever I could find in my bag to nibble, while listening to the breeze and the birdsong, soon became an important part of my request stop visits. Simple pleasures, and all the better for that.

CHAPTER 4

THE END OF THE LINE

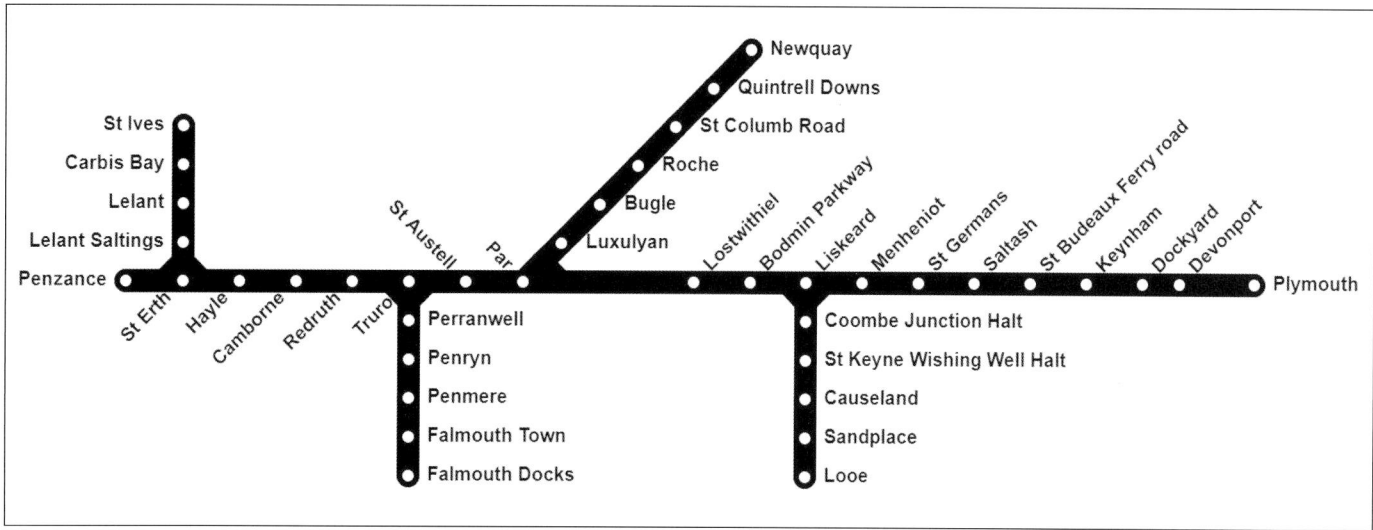

On the first day of my Cornwall and Devon expedition I started easily, going straight to Penzance and dropping my bag at the hotel, some 200 metres from the station. It was by this time late afternoon, and I passed some time photographing Penzance station. I had by this time decided that because visiting all the request stops on the British mainland would involve travelling to the four corners of the rail map, I should also include the four stations at the extreme compass points, with Penzance the most southerly, but not as some might think the most westerly.

Lelant
Annual passenger usage: 9,618
Least used station rank: 236
Postcode: TR26 3DS
Ordnance Survey national grid reference: SW547372

The next day, I boarded a Class 153 DMU at Penzance, the 08.44 to St Ives, calling at Lelant by request, and the only direct service of the day, with all the others requiring a change at St Erth. After 7 miles I stood on the platform at Lelant and watched the train rounding the sharp curve at the end of the station on its way towards St Ives.

Lelant is situated on the St Erth to St Ives GWR branch, known as the 'St Ives Bay Line'. When St Erth first opened in 1852 it was known as St Ives Road, a name it retained until the branch line opened in 1877. The St Ives branch has the distinction of being the last broad gauge branch to be built. A third rail added in 1888 converted the line to dual gauge, with the last broad gauge train running on Friday 20 May 1892.[1] A slipway once existed at the south end of the station, although little sign of it remains today, save for three granite level crossing gateposts and some rubble leading down to the water. Foundation stones from the otherwise vanished Lelant quay can still be seen at the north end of the platform, but I could not discern any signs of the siding that once ran onto it.

On my visit I found facilities to be quite basic, with an open bus stop-type shelter and a help point that was continually advising anyone who cared to listen, "Please wait your call is being connected."

The location is magnificent, situated on the west side of the Hayle Estuary and opposite the Royal Society for the Protection of Birds (RSPB) Hayle Estuary Reserve. The original wooden station building, painted in chocolate and cream, still exists, but is now a private house. It has been extended, but very much in keeping with the original building and, as Eric Morecambe might have said, 'you can't see the join'.

St Columb Road
Annual passenger usage: 18,858
Least used station rank: 94
Postcode: TR9 6QY
Ordnance Survey national grid reference: SW910595

Leaving Lelant and changing at St Erth, then at Par, my next point of call was St Columb Road, situated on the Par to Newquay branch, 14.25 miles from Par. The line is known as the 'Atlantic Coast Line' and is supported by the Devon and Cornwall Rail Partnership. The station here has been open to passengers since June 1876, although at that time it was called Halloon, being renamed in November 1878. The name Halloon means 'Hall on the Down', and it is mentioned in the Domesday survey. Halloon farm is a few minutes' walk away.

Despite what I took to be a lot of effort and presumably money put into installing rather elaborate blue railings, there was a rather forlorn feel to the place, made worse on my visit by the relentless rain. The old station yard is still discernible, but now stacked with shipping containers. There is the typical plexiglass and aluminium bus stop-type shelter, from which the abandoned second platform can be seen, standing isolated, devoid of its tracks and largely covered with brambles, now resigned to its fate and quietly dreaming of days gone by, when excited holidaymakers walked its length with their suitcases and bags.

Bugle
Annual passenger usage: 4,766
Least used station rank: 156
Postcode: PL26 8QP
Ordnance Survey national grid reference: SX017592

After putting my arm out to stop the next train going towards Par, I climbed on board a Class 153 DMU and began thinking of my next stop, Bugle, some 8 miles distant, but still on the Newquay branch.

Bugle is situated in the village of the same name and adjacent to the A391 which crosses the line at the Newquay end of the station. Bugle opened to passengers in June 1876, although freight services do predate this. The island platform now has just one face in use. It is still very easy to make out that an island platform existed here, and particularly obvious are the dual spans of the road bridge, the unused second span indicating the route of the now defunct freight-only Carbis Wharf branch.

The feel of a request stop is a little lost here due to the close proximity of modern housing on both sides, much of which has been built on former railway land. The station and its facilities are fairly typical and are kept both clean and tidy. Cleaning staff were in evidence during my visit, using a small cabin just off the platform for the storage of the necessary cleaning tools and materials. It is sad to say that some of the people living in the adjacent housing seem to have been using the railway that backs onto their gardens as a rubbish dump, a sharp contrast to the platform.

Menheniot
Annual passenger usage: 4,140
Least used station rank: 141
Postcode: PL14 3PJ
Ordnance Survey national grid reference: SX289612

The final stop on this, the first day of my 'Cornwall and Devon Rover', was to be Menheniot, therefore I made my way back to Par and a change of trains.

Menheniot was opened in May 1859 by the Cornwall Railway (CwallR), which amalgamated into the GWR in 1889. It is on the London–Paddington main line to Penzance, some 241 miles from London via Westbury or 262 miles via Bristol. As the station is on the main line it has two platforms, with access between them over a footbridge. Platform 1, the down or westbound platform, is very basic and has no shelter or seating. It does however have a help point and is the only entry/exit point, which means that Platform 2, the eastbound platform, has no access for the disabled because they would have to use the footbridge.

Platform 2 does have a rather lovely stone and wooden waiting shelter, in need of a little care perhaps, but charming nonetheless. Let's hope someone at NR does not, in the interests of progress, decide to replace it with a modern more functional plexiglass one. I am not opposed to progress or functionality, but the CwallR put this shelter here in 1859, which means that when I visited in 2018 it had already stood for 159 years – a real antique.

As I waited for my train to Liskeard and then on home, I reflected that not only had the day been good, but it had finished on a high. When I had arrived at

Menheniot the sun had come out and it was beginning to feel warm. I took some shots of the shelter, a real piece of railway history, and wondered how many things can be seen still in daily use that predate the original GWR. My train was due soon and on time, and my stopping arm was at the ready.

The next day I made an early start from home, this time to visit the 'Looe Valley Line'. Only 8 miles long, but a truly delightful journey which I have travelled before. Walking to Platform 3, the platform for the Looe Line, at Liskeard, it felt as if I had arrived at another station altogether. The branch line platform is situated across both a road and a car park, and is at right angles to the main line and at a higher level.

When the train leaves on its journey down the 'Looe Valley Line', it turns a complete circle, negotiating some very tight curves to face in the opposite direction, while dropping down almost 60 metres into the valley at Coombe. Even here it has not finished turning, and the driver has to change ends, allowing the train to reverse and finally head down the valley towards Looe. While it is true that all trains have to reverse at Coombe, most do not go into the station at Coombe Junction Halt and actually reverse short of the station itself, but tantalisingly in sight of it. Coombe Junction Halt is not a request stop, but with an annual passenger usage of only 156, it is the least used station in Cornwall and the tenth least used station in Great Britain. Also interesting to note is that while the term 'halt' has in the past been in very common usage on our railway system, today only two remain, both on the Looe line: Coombe Junction Halt and St Keyne Wishing Well Halt.

Causeland
Annual passenger usage: 1,834
Least used station rank: 91
Postcode: PL14 4ST
Ordnance Survey national grid reference: SX248591

When opened to passengers in 1879, Causeland was the only intermediate stop on the line and remained so until 1881, when Sandplace opened a little further down the line. Causeland then closed, reopening in 1888. Today it is served by GWR trains and promoted under the name Looe Valley Line.

This was my first experience of actually stopping at any of the three intermediate stops on this line, and Causeland most definitely did not disappoint. Beautifully kept, with spring flowers in wooden tubs, the timber shelter that I had seen in old photographs has been replaced with a more solid brick construction, but similar in style and appearance to the one in those old pictures. There is both a help point outside (which was working), and a payphone inside the shelter (which wasn't). Station signage and shelter were not only finished in chocolate and cream, the old GWR colours, but also in the appropriate style.

Nestled at the bottom of the Looe Valley and feeling almost enclosed, the atmosphere here could only be described as perfect. It was a gorgeous early spring day, with traces of mist rising as the sun warmed the damp ground after overnight rain. The valley seemed to have its own micro-climate. The only sounds were the tinkling of the adjacent brook, and birdsong. Butterflies were constantly flitting, seemingly unable to decide on the best place to settle, and a buzzard circled in the blue sky overhead. What more could I have wanted? It is true a small road does pass close to the station, but in the hour plus I spent there, no car went past.

Sandplace
Annual passenger usage: 1,780
Least used station rank: 88
Postcode: PL13 1PJ
Ordnance Survey national grid reference: SX248570

A little over 6 miles from Liskeard is Sandplace, which opened to passengers in December 1881, the line having been in use for freight since 1860. Sandplace derives its name from the once nearby wharf called Sand-Place, where sea sand was stored, in readiness for its use in soil improvement. Sandplace is mentioned in the 1919 poem by Bernard Moore, 'Travelling', in which he contrasts grimy London with the idyllic Looe branch line, mentioning all the stations by name. Although the poem is now over a hundred years old, it still retains its relevance today. Go there and you too will feel the tranquillity of the line he is describing for yourself.

Today Sandplace is still a rural idyll, but stepping from the train there I found a slightly different feel to the previous stop of Causeland. Here the snug fit of the valley is less evident, but this does not detract in any way from its charm, something it most certainly does have. The totems and other signs were again all finished in keeping with the old GWR, both in colour and style. The shelter is relatively modern, having been constructed in 1998, and of a fairly standardised design that I encountered in a number of other places.[2] Nevertheless this design is very sympathetic to its location and does look as if it naturally belongs there.

St Keyne Wishing Well Halt
Annual passenger usage: 1,302
Least used station rank: 67
Postcode: PL14 4SE
Ordnance Survey national grid reference: SX251610

Travelling just over a mile towards Liskeard, I had reached the final stop of the day, St Keyne Wishing Well Halt. It was opened in 1902 by the Liskeard & Looe Railway, making it the last station on the Looe Valley Line to have a passenger service and then known simply as 'St Keyne'. A nameboard once existed above the doorway of the shelter that read, 'St Keyne for St Keyne Well'.

The station is reminiscent of Sandplace with the same style of shelter, modern yet still in harmony with its surroundings. Here I felt the tranquillity of Causeland, due mainly to St Keyne's location snuggled at the bottom of the valley. Signs of the old Liskeard & Looe Union Canal are apparent, particularly the two arches of the road bridge. 'Sparse' would describe the traffic during my stay, with a solitary car passing.

Just behind the station is the Magnificent Music Machines Museum, and a ten-minute walk away is St Keyne Well itself. One of the legends surrounding the well is that 'husband or wife whichever drinks from the well first will have mastery in the marriage'. If only I had known that many years ago, I could have saved myself a lot of bother.

After taking my photographs and spending some time on the platform I decided to walk up to the well. On my return I encountered the only example of antisocial behaviour on my whole request stop odyssey. There was music in the air, getting louder with every step, and by the time I got onto the platform it was at concert level. The source was obvious, a young family with a man dragging a disco on wheels – that is, a sound system so large he had it mounted on a shopping trolley. After five minutes I went over and asked him if he could turn it down a bit; not off, but down. He immediately exploded into a rant about me denying his rights and suggested I call the police to see if I could get him arrested. Finding myself faced with a simple choice of getting into an escalating and pointless confrontation or walking away, I walked away.

By this time my train up to Liskeard was almost due, and the preceding down service had still not passed, so I decided to check using the help point, this being out of sight of the disco. The announcement came back "Trains for the rest of the day on the Looe line are cancelled due to a broken down train." I called the help line, a young man answered and confirmed the lack of trains and said he would call me a taxi.

"Is there anyone else waiting there?" he asked.

"No, just me," I replied.

A short while later my taxi arrived and off I went, wondering how long the disco people would wait before they realised something was not quite right; still they had their music to help pass the time. Thankfully this experience remained a one-off. I met many fellow passengers whose attitude and manner was the complete opposite, and railway staff who were always helpful, often interested in my journey and without exception a pleasure to deal with.

Lapford
Annual passenger usage: 1,498
Least used station rank: 76
Postcode: EX17 6QU
Ordnance Survey national grid reference: SS726079

Day three of the Devon and Cornwall foray saw me heading to the Barnstaple branch to complete two more stops, one of which is difficult due to the infrequency of services. Soon after leaving Exeter I asked, "Can you stop at Lapford please?" as I headed towards my next stop.

Lapford, opened by the NDevonR in 1854, originally had one platform on the north side of the A377. A second platform on the south side of the road was added later, and this has since been removed. The loop serving this second platform has also been removed, but it is easy enough to see signs of its previous existence. Goods sidings served the Ambrosia milk products factory. These have also been removed and the site is now used by a removal and storage firm.

The station is an attractive country stop with basic facilities including a bus stop-type shelter. It is cared for and the old station buildings, which are privately owned, still exist and are in good order. Access is via a set of twenty-two stairs from the road bridge, with no wheelchair access. Lapford is 16.25 miles and six stops out from Exeter St Davids, on the Tarka Line, and services today are provided by the GWR.

Portsmouth Arms
Annual passenger usage: 444
Least used station rank: 33
Postcode: EX37 9NB
Ordnance Survey national grid reference: SS630193

The service to Portsmouth Arms could be described as rather sparse, with only two trains a day in each direction on weekdays that are timetabled to stop; one early morning and another in the evening. This was the reason I chose to travel on a Sunday, when the station is positively busy with no less than four trains in each direction.

It is situated on the Tarka Line some 28 miles from Exeter St Davids and 10 miles from Barnstaple – the end of the line. I climbed aboard at Lapford and at the first opportunity I approached the guard.

"Can you stop at Portsmouth Arms please?"

"Portsmouth Arms? We never stop there," he replied, seeming genuinely shocked that I should even suggest such a thing.

Ten minutes later I was on the platform. The guard shut the passenger doors, looked at me from his open door and gave me a friendly wave, while no doubt wondering just what this strange man was going to do next. The train left and as it passed me the roar of the diesel engine built and then faded as the train receded into the distance. This was the first, but definitely not the last time of feeling the moment of a train leaving in quite this way. Seconds ago there was the train, the noise, then with a last glimpse it finally disappeared. I stood alone and for an all too short a while this became my world.

Opened in 1854 by the NDevonR, the station originally had two platforms. Only one is still in use today. The other still exists, with nature slowly reclaiming it. Facilities are limited and typical, with a platform level that has been raised in part by the use of plywood. A traditional style mile marker post exists on the platform advising us that we are 200 miles from London, and just behind the station there is a Pullman coach which is undergoing renovation.

Then it happened. While quietly looking along the line to see if my train was approaching, a fellow passenger arrived – at Portsmouth Arms! Now I hesitate to say he sneaked up on me, but I neither saw nor heard him approach. Two heavy thumps on the hollow-sounding wooden platform alerted me to the fact that I had company. Turning round I found myself face to face with a man who could only have been Gandalf's younger brother. Having seen *Lord of the Rings* I was in a position to make this assumption. He had it all: six-foot plus tall, ankle-length coat, the hair, a magnificent beard and a slightly unkempt look. The two thumps I had heard were the dropping of two large and heavy shopping bags. As the nearest shops are some way off, whatever did he have in his bags I wondered. It transpired they were full of what I assumed to be firewood, which he had foraged on the nearby hillside.

He said good afternoon and pleasantries were exchanged. At this point I thought to myself, best not, so I refrained from asking, "And how are things in the Shire?" A nice man, not your average perhaps, but then it has at times been suggested that I myself can be a bit different; long live the individual.

I made sure my arm went out first when the train came into view; after all, why else was I there, and anyway, I was doing him a favour, he had bags to carry. Doors opened and the same guard I'd had on the way up looked out. So much for *we never stop there* I thought. Twice in one day and with multiple passengers the second time, was this rush hour at Portsmouth Arms? It must have given him a story to tell when he got back to the railwayman's tea room.

Luxulyan
Annual passenger usage: 2,394
Least used station rank: 108
Postcode: PL31 2NW
Ordnance Survey national grid reference: SX047581

For the fifth day of the Cornwall and Devon Rover the decision had been made to only do one stop, Luxulyan. This left me with enough spare time to have a wander round the town of Liskeard before catching a train home. Furthermore, because of a poor train connection at Par, I saved time by going on to St Austell and from there catching a bus.

The line here was opened by the Cornwall Minerals Railway (CwallMinsR) in 1874, and a passenger service was introduced in 1876. Known as 'Bridges' when first opened, it became Luxulyan in 1905. Two platforms existed here, which were replaced by an island platform in 1910. This became a single-face platform with the removal of the goods yard in 1964.

The station is on the line from Par to Newquay, known as the 'Atlantic Coast Line', just one stop and a little over 4 miles from the main line at Par. Luxulyan has a small brick-built and pebble-dashed shelter painted white, most welcome not only as a respite from the ubiquitous plexiglass types but because it kept me dry on a day that became rather damp to say the least. The help point is solar powered, there is also a small car park and the platform is wheelchair accessible.

A single-coach Class 153 DMU took me back to Par where I changed for a train to Liskeard. As the train pulled into the platform I saw one of the new HST formations that GWR had only just started to introduce, comprising two power cars and four passenger coaches. Gone are the slam doors; instead there are button-operated sliders. GWR is calling these 'Castle Class'. I am someone who remembers when Castle Class meant copper-capped chimneys, so I do have some misgivings about the name, and hope they don't call one *St Mawes Castle*, my favourite steam loco and one I have personally worked on.

This was my first time travelling on one of the new HSTs, and they will, I am sure, be a very welcome improvement on some of the quite long distance DMU services into Cornwall.

Roche
Annual passenger usage: 4,674
Least used station rank: 154
Postcode: PL26 8LG
Ordnance Survey national grid reference: SW989614

The final day of my request stopping trip in Cornwall saw me firstly visiting Roche, my last stop on the Atlantic Coast Line. The village takes its name from the Norman–French word *roche*, meaning rock, as there is a twenty-metre high granite outcrop, with a ruined chapel, to the south side of the village.

This station is a delight. Clean and tidy with a freshly painted wooden shelter that has a sloping roof. Station lighting is modern but of a design that gives a nod to previous times and does not look at all out of place. I even found an original GWR boundary marker near the shelter, dated 1896. Access to the platform is through an entrance on the opposite side of the single track, which is crossed via a barrow crossing (a non-vehicular level crossing without gates at the end of a station platform). The less mobile can reach the platform, although one of the ramps is rather steep. A 'set down' point does exist but no actual car park.

When passenger services were introduced by the CwallMinsR in 1876, Roche went by the name of Victoria, being renamed in 1904. A second platform existed but became disused when the passing loop was removed in 1965. Now heavily overgrown, very little of the second platform is visible today. One part that does remain, and is in daily use, is the ramp leading from the station entrance, formed from the slope which would have been the end of the old platform.

Perranwell
Annual passenger usage: 31,504
Least used station rank: 435
Postcode: TR3 7JY
Ordnance Survey national grid reference: SW780398

Opened in August 1863 as Perran, by the CwallR, the name had to be changed six months later because it was often confused with Penryn, the next stop down the line. Today Perranwell is the first intermediate stop on the 'Maritime Line', that is, the 12-mile branch from Truro to Falmouth Docks. A request stop in April 2018, but not to all trains, some being scheduled to stop even in the absence of requests, the current (2019) timetable does indicate that it has now lost its request stop status with all services stopping.

It is a charming and cared-for little stop with several reminders of past times. The whole station underwent a refurbishment in the late 1990s, receiving one of the little brick shelters with the sloping roof I had seen at Sandplace. The adjacent goods shed is still there (now commercial premises) as is the old second platform, now overgrown of course. The undergrowth that day was alive with a profusion of spring butterflies and small birds. While I watched, two beautiful and colourful jays arrived, then proceeded to have the most terrible and long lasting fight, probably over territory; life is hard for a bird in springtime.

Towards the Truro end of the platform there is a hand pump, formerly used as a drinking fountain, and a marvellous metal nameboard, finished in chocolate and cream, quite possibly of GWR vintage. With Perranwell completed, I thought this a fitting note on which to leave Cornwall, with just three Devon stops to finish my first major request stop excursion.

Chapelton
Annual passenger usage: 188
Least used station rank: 13
Postcode: EX37 9DZ
Ordnance Survey national grid reference: SS580260

Chapelton is the last stop before Barnstaple on the Tarka Line and 34 miles from Exeter St Davids. The NDevonR opened this line in 1854 with passenger services commencing in 1857 at the station then known as Chapeltown. This station closed in 1860, reopening in 1875 with its present title of Chapelton.

On arrival I had the disappointment of seeing that I had not alighted alone; someone else had also disembarked, though he did do the decent thing and departed quickly enough. Another delightful rural spot, the only buildings nearby are the old station and a sawmill, and being a Sunday the mill was quiet. The owner of the old station house was busy tending his garden and called over, "Two people at Chapelton, a busy day."

This was certainly a valid comment, as the daily average usage at Chapelton is about half a person. He went back to tending his garden which was not only impressive, but maintained a timeless look as if still part of the station, even to the extent of including a vintage station nameboard.

As expected, the station had the usual basic facilities, with a brick-built shelter of a design that I had not seen before or since, and flowerbeds and tubs aplenty, aided I suspected, by the green fingers of the gardener from across the track.

Newton St Cyres
Annual passenger usage: 2,468
Least used station rank: 110
Postcode: EX5 5AP
Ordnance Survey national grid reference: SX880989

Safely settled on board, or at least as settled as it is possible to get on a Pacer DMU, the guard walked past.

"Back to Exeter?" he asked.

"No, Newton St Cyres please."

"Come to the front door and I'll help you down."

I am fully aware that I am no longer in the first flush of youth, but had I suddenly aged since I last saw this man to the extent he was now concerned about my health and wellbeing? Approaching Newton St Cyres I followed his instructions and moved forward. The train stopped and the door opened. Then his concern became clear; the step down could conservatively be described as significant. Advising him I could manage, while desperately hoping he would not try to hold my hand, I stepped forward like a skydiver making his first jump, ready to bend the knees and roll forward, but there was no need. My feet hit the platform, I had made it. Turning to the guard I thanked him with my best nonchalant air and waited for the Pacer to clatter off into the distance.

Passenger services began at St Cyres in 1851, with the Newton prefix being added in 1913. Local people maintain a station garden just behind the bus stop-type shelter, and this is in addition to the plant tubs on the platform and is a credit to them. This was obviously a much busier place in the past as there is an extensive former station yard evident, and a second platform complete with brambles and buddleia.

A two-hour stop had been scheduled here before it would be time to head north again and my final Devon stop. Consulting my itinerary I clearly had laid to rest the omission of allocating time to eat in my earlier planning. This one had the entry 'lunch at the Beer Engine, Devon apple and blackberry crumble with Devon cream'.

King's Nympton
Annual passenger usage: 6,640
Least used station rank: 189
Postcode: EX37 9EU
Ordnance Survey national grid reference: SS662169

Same Pacer, same guard. "Where to now?" he asked.

"King's Nympton thanks."

Twenty-one miles later, again I experienced that magical moment when the sight and noise of the DMU is finally gone, and one is left alone to explore the surroundings.

Originally named South Molton Road when first opened by the NDevonR in 1854, King's Nympton retained this name until 1951 when the nationalised BR renamed it to avoid confusion with the nearby ex-GWR station of South Molton. Allowing for the fact that much has been lost here (a signal box, three sidings and a second platform with passing loop have all gone), I could still feel that this place had once been of import. A clue was in the rather grand station building that encroached onto the platform. The shelter on the platform itself is the only real concession to modernity; its small blue-painted frame has been tucked rather discretely away, helping to preserve a scene of yesteryear. Standing there it was easy to imagine that I could have opened the door and walked into the waiting room to sit down. This I decided against; after all, the present owners might have set the dogs on me, and it had been a good day up to then.

Back on the Pacer, the same guard said nothing but gave me a quizzical look.

"Exeter please," I said.

"Exeter it is," he replied, and made his way on down the train.

Above: A general view of Penzance, Britain's most southerly mainland station, on 22 July 2019. Two Class 802 bi-mode five-cars sets form the 14.00 Penzance to London Paddington, which is about to depart.

Opposite above: Lelant looking towards St Ives seen on 10 April 2018. The site of the former quay is on the right of the photograph.

Opposite below: St Columb Road on a rather damp day, 10 April 2018. The end of the abandoned platform can be seen in the foreground.

Above: A somewhat unimpressive Bugle photographed on 10 April 2018, looking north.

Opposite above: Menheniot on 10 April 2018 with the 17.01 Plymouth to Liskeard, formed of a Class 150 Sprinter DMU set, passing the nineteenth-century shelter.

Opposite below: A Class 150 Sprinter DMU forming the 15.56 Plymouth to Liskeard approaching Saltash on 26 July 2019. While not a request stop itself, the train will in 14 minutes call, if requested, at Menheniot.

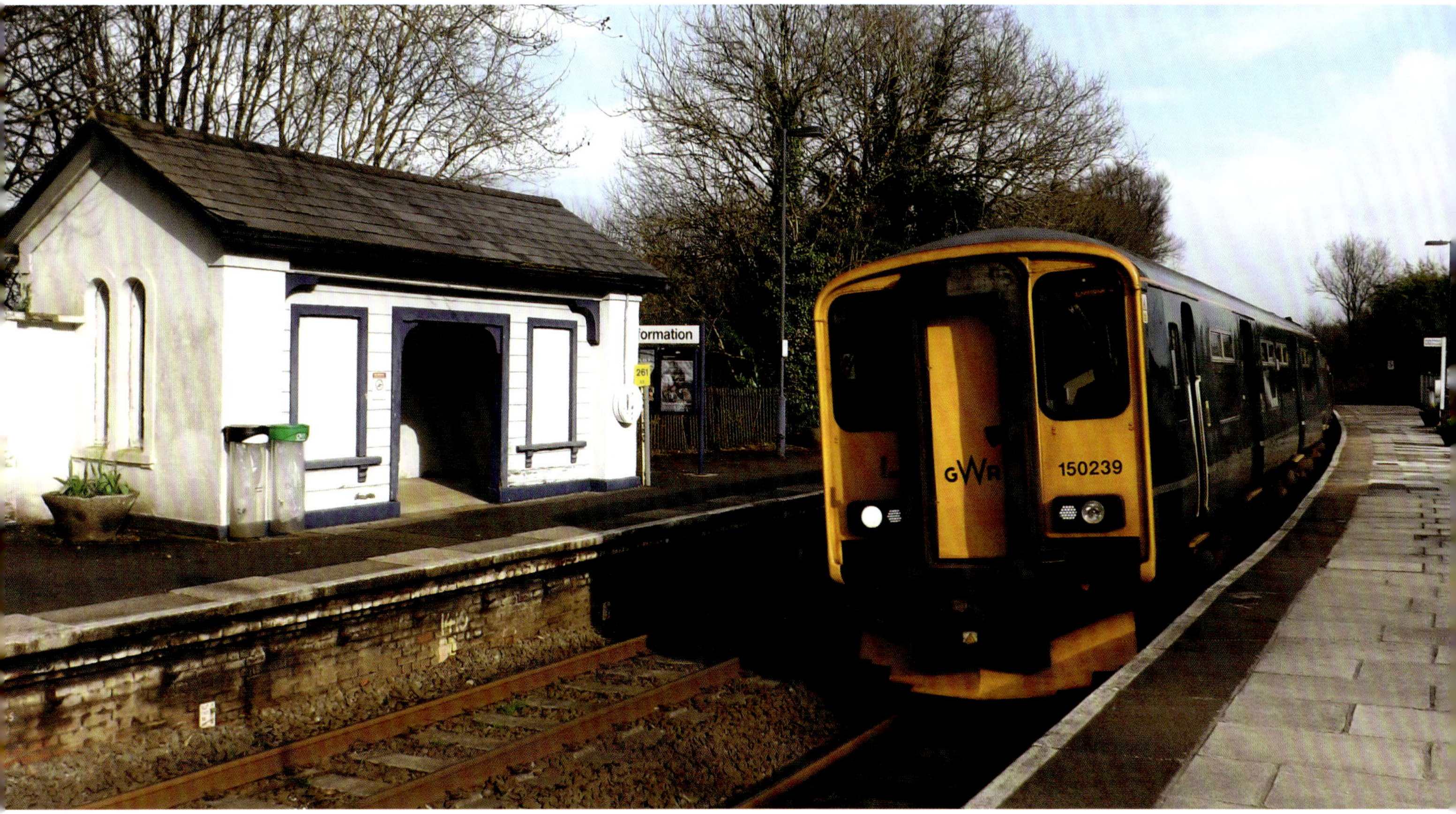
GWR
150239

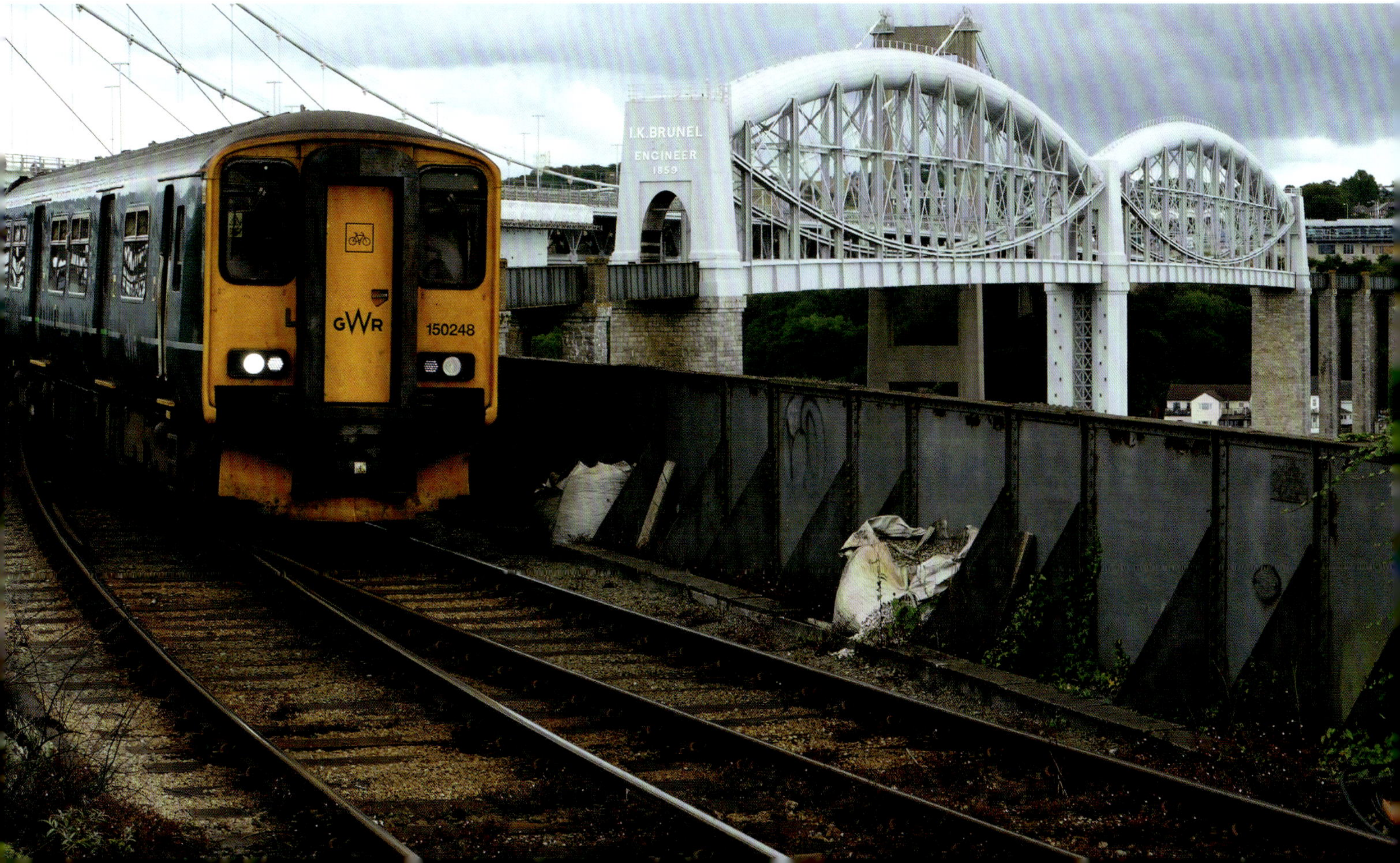
GWR
150248
I.K.BRUNEL
ENGINEER
1859

Causeland on 12 April 2018, looking towards Looe. After overnight rain the sun had penetrated into the valley causing the hillsides to steam.

A single coach Class 153 Super Sprinter DMU forming the 13.20 Liskeard to Looe service is seen approaching Causeland on 12 April 2018.

Sandplace looking towards Looe, photographed on 12 April 2018. The shelter here was constructed in 1988 and is a type that I encountered in quite a few locations.

St Keyne Wishing Well Halt, surely one of the best station names ever. Pictured on 12 April 2018 looking north. The second arch was for the former Liskeard & Looe Union canal.

The 14.50 Looe to Liskeard passing St Keyne Wishing Well Halt on 24 July 2018. This service comprises a two-car Class 150 Sprinter DMU set.

Lapford seen on a very damp 12 April 2018, looking towards Exeter.

Portsmouth Arms, one of the more northerly stops on the Barnstaple branch, photographed on 15 April 2018, looking towards Barnstaple.

Luxulyan, on the Newquay branch, is the first stop from Par. This photograph is looking south on 17 April 2018.

Above: The charming Roche, pictured on 20 April 2018, a gloriously sunny spring day.

Opposite above: Perranwell on the Maritime Line looking north towards Truro, which is the next stop, seen on 20 April 2018.

Opposite below: Photographed on 20 April 2018, the 15.51 Truro to Falmouth Docks, formed of a two-car Class 153 Super Sprinter DMU, passes the splendid metal station nameboard at Perranwell.

THE END OF THE LINE • 49

Above: Chapelton seen on 22 April 2018. The former second platform is clearly visible on the left of the photograph.

Opposite above: Newton St Cyres. This stop is on the Tarka Line and the first after leaving Exeter St Davids. Photographed on 22 April 2018, looking south.

Opposite below: Kings Nympton seen on 22 April 2018, looking south towards Exeter.

THE END OF THE LINE • 51

CHAPTER 5

THROUGH THE TUNNEL

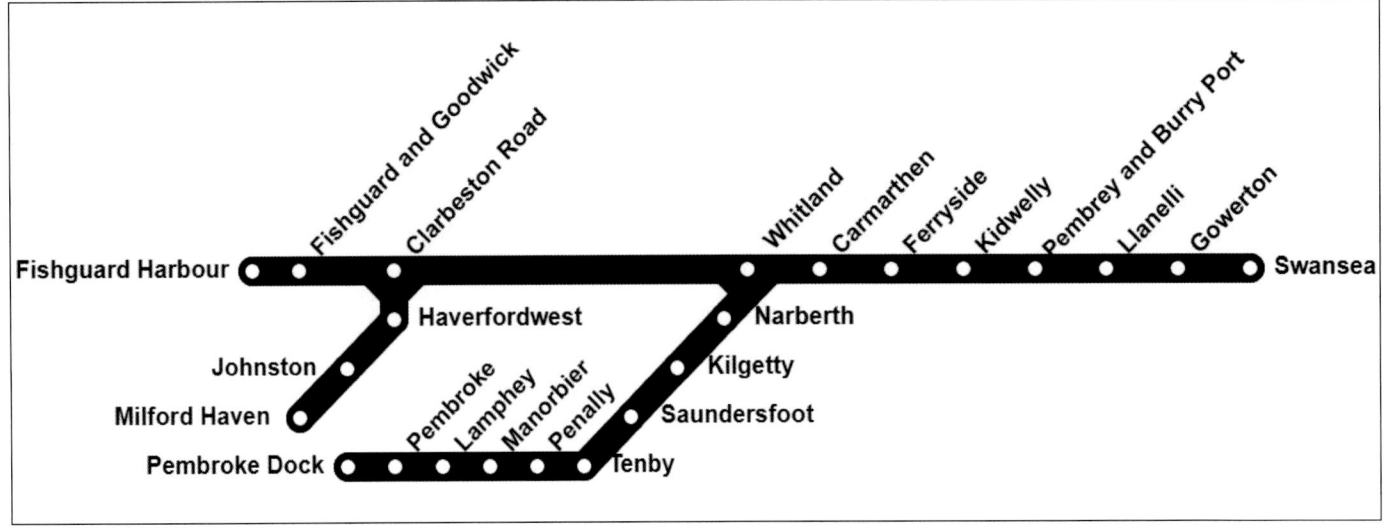

The South West had now been completed. My thoughts and planning turned to Wales, which with over sixty request stops required a total of five separate trips, all involving overnight stays of varying lengths.

My Welsh experience was what I'd expected – a good one. The people of Wales were warm and friendly just as I have always found them; and who could not like their accent? A lovely people especially given that history has often not treated them kindly. Swathes of South Wales were destroyed and polluted in the name of industry and progress. It is true that a little financial prosperity was the reward for breathing coal dust and fumes, and shortened lives. However, even this would not be allowed to last, when the process of abandoning the pits and industry begun by Margaret Thatcher (and continued to this day) left in its wake deprivation and urban decay. None of which prevented the Welsh people I met trying to help me with my utterly hopeless pronunciation of their place names, and do it with a smile.

To begin I had a four-night stay in Carmarthen, which allowed me to visit all ten stops in south-west Wales plus three on the 'Heart of Wales Line'. Travelling from Swindon to South Wales meant going through the Severn Tunnel. Living most of my life near the GWR main line, this to me has always been the 'way to Wales'. The tunnel opened in 1886, and at a little over 4 miles it became at that time the longest underwater tunnel in the world. I don't know when I first learned this, but I do remember Eddie, my old charge hand from Reading telling me, and he would have known as a true GWR man.

Ferryside
Annual passenger usage: 20,806
Least used station rank: 337
Postcode: SA17 5TD
Ordnance Survey national grid reference: SN366104

Half an hour after leaving Swansea, I arrived at Ferryside, my first Welsh request stop. It was opened in 1852 as a broad gauge line by the South Wales Railway (SWalesR), which amalgamated with the GWR in 1863.

Ferryside has two platforms with a footbridge connection. A brick shelter exists on each platform, and on my visit these were both painted in the Arriva Wales corporate aquamarine; a colour I personally found a little hard on the eye. The presence of double track does lessen the request stop feel here, but there is semaphore signalling and a real signal box and level crossing; oh joy. I have read that the signals are due to be replaced; perhaps they have already gone.

Kidwelly

Annual passenger usage: 28,188
Least used station rank: 410
Postcode: SA17 4UH
Ordnance Survey national grid reference: SN401064

Kidwelly is the next stop eastwards from Ferryside, and it also opened in 1852. In busier times this was the location of the junction for the Burry Port and Gwendraeth Valley Railway, the connection being to the east of the station. The branch line finally closed in 1996 and I was unable to find any trace of it in the vicinity of Kidwelly station.

Basic brick shelters and electronic departure/arrival screens are provided on both of the two platforms, with access between the platforms via the level crossing at the eastern end of the station. A signal box is adjacent to the level crossing but alas, colour-light signals have been installed. A plaque on one of the shelters commemorates the fact that the station gardens were landscaped by the Kidwelly Scouts and both shelters have murals on the back wall also courtesy of the Scouts.

My train to Carmarthen approached, I held out my arm and it stopped. On board I had no need to speak to the guard as Carmarthen is a 'normal' stop. A short walk followed to my hotel, which was my home for the next four nights. After a quick check of my room I headed back to the station, there being time for one more stop that day, Johnston on the Milford Haven branch.

Johnston

Annual passenger usage: 9,008
Least used station rank: 228
Postcode: SA62 3PL
Ordnance Survey national grid reference: SM932106

The SWalesR opened Johnston in 1856. The line here originally continued to Neyland and Johnston served as the junction for what used to be known as the Milford Haven branch. Neyland closed in 1964 making the section to Milford Haven the main line. The line was double tracked until 1988 when resignalling took place along with the removal of the second track, causing the abandonment of the other platform, parts of which can still be seen. Johnston has had several name changes over the years. It was originally called Johnston, then Milford Road in 1859, Johnston in 1863, Johnston (Pembroke) in 1928, Johnston (Dyfed) in 1976 and then finally back to Johnston again.

Facilities here are very basic but do include a brick shelter similar to the others I had seen earlier in the day. The help point was not working, but a fairly new electronic information display unit was, perhaps intended to supplant the help point. A customer service phone number is displayed on the noticeboard, and there is level access to the platform. A small car park is also available. Compact industrial units occupy the site to the west side of the station while to the east the land is occupied mainly by modern housing.

As I stood waiting for the train back I thought that apart from the cowslips on the grass bank this had not been the prettiest of stops. But at least it was still here, when so many small stations now only exist in fading black and white photographs and the fond memories of the passing generations. A Class 175 DMU came into view, I quickly raised my arm and moments later I was on my way back to Carmarthen, for an evening meal and then to bed, in readiness for tomorrow's four stops.

Clarbeston Road

Annual passenger usage: 7,828
Least used station rank: 211
Postcode: SA63 4UH
Ordnance Survey national grid reference: SN015209

Clarbeston opened to passengers in 1854, and was renamed Clarbeston Road in 1906 when the GWR opened a direct route to Fishguard Harbour. It was initially sited to the east of the road that crosses the line here, moving to the west side in 1914, although there is some doubt about this date.[1] Clarbeston Road is 245 miles from London Paddington and 16 from Fishguard Harbour.

As a station on the main line the track here is double with two platforms, both having bus stop-type shelters of the glazed and shiny aluminium variety. A help point is located on Platform 2, while some of the lamp posts have warning signs stating 'some trains pass at speed'. One post did have an additional board describing local walks. Passengers wishing to move between platforms are requested to use the ramps and road bridge. While scratching about in the undergrowth, something that I usually do, I came across a brick with 'Ammanford Colliery' embossed into the frog, and nearby a metal drain cover of GWR vintage.

The train that took me to my next planned stop was another two-car Class 175 DMU. I asked the guard for Clunderwen, and he replied, "Do you mean ... ?" suggesting a place name that sounded very different from what I'd said.

"Yes that's the one," I replied, hoping it was indeed the one.

Clunderwen
Annual passenger usage: 24,474
Least used station rank: 375
Postcode: SA66 7NG
Ordnance Survey national grid reference: SN119192

Clunderwen is another station that since its opening by the SWalesR in 1854 has undergone several name changes. It was first called Narberth Road for Cardigan and Tenby, and then in 1863 shortened to Narberth Road for Cardigan. It was renamed to Clynderwen in 1875, a name it retained until 1965 when it became Clynderwen Halt, and in 1969 it reverted to Clynderwen. Then in 1980 a final change was made to Clunderwen.[2]

Despite its location on the main line (and I say this because it has always been single track branch line byways that truly excite me), Clunderwen I found to be a pleasant stop. Both platforms have brick shelters, this time not painted in Arriva 'yuck' (aquamarine) but left in natural colours. Electronic information screens and a help point are both here to assist passengers, as too is a wheelchair-friendly car park. Platforms are wheelchair accessible, but the distance between them is approximately 300 metres, using access roads and a road bridge.

After spending some time wandering around the site of the old station yard, I located the bases and loading bays of several structures. I also found part of the platform that would have formed the bay platform for the Rosebush Line, and because there was a fence, albeit rather flimsy, I could do this without risk of trespass on the running lines themselves.

After spending two hours at Clunderwen I boarded a train bound for Carmarthen. My ticket was checked, no need to say anything, the guards on the main line didn't recognise me, due to the fact that these trains were going quite long distances and therefore I was not seeing the same guards twice. Still not to worry, Kilgetty and Narberth next, which are both on the single track Pembroke branch, and as they would say in Bristol, 'them be proper request stops me luvver'.

Kilgetty
Annual passenger usage: 16,402
Least used station rank: 306
Postcode: SA68 0UF
Ordnance Survey national grid reference: SN126072

A change of trains was required at Carmarthen and with time in hand I took the opportunity for a well-earned coffee and slice of cake. No need to walk into the town as the station had a more than adequate watering hole. The Pembroke train pulled in before time, and I made my way on board, advising the guard standing on the platform I required Kilgetty. I do like to request my stop sooner rather than later, because there is always the worry of what happens if we are approaching the stop I want and I can't find the guard. A missed stop; unthinkable as that would throw my itinerary into disarray.

Kilgetty and Begelly opened in 1866 when the Pembroke & Tenby Railway (P&TR) extended its line from Tenby to join the GWR main line at Whitland. The new station name of Kilgetty came into effect in 1901. Only one platform has ever existed here as the line has always been single and with no passing loop.

Kilgetty at first glance appeared to be a proper request stop. It is very much a part of the village and not at all remote, but it did still fit the bill. The platform is over 40 metres long and more than adequate for the two-coach Class 150 DMU that I had just alighted from. Facilities are typically basic with a brick shelter that has been left, mercifully, in a natural stone finish. Not so the general station fittings, which were all Arriva aquamarine: why they picked this colour I do not know. Perhaps B&Q had an extra special, once in a lifetime, end of season, never to be repeated, today only offer, who knows? Just my opinion, I am sure there are people who think it's a great colour, aren't there? I note that Transport for Wales now has this franchise, so let's hope they have plenty of paintbrushes.

The platform is separated from an adjacent residential caravan park by a metal railing fence supplemented by a high and rather impressive hedge. I'm not sure if this is because the passengers don't like the look of the residents, or because the residents don't like the look of the passengers, and the Arriva aquamarine. But the hedge is planted on the caravan park side of the fence.

Next was Narberth, only one stop up the line. I took no chances. After the train stopped at Kilgetty and the guard had opened his door I got on and, passing him, said, "Narberth please."

"You've got a Rover ticket haven't you?"

"I have," I replied, thinking to myself, now this is more like it, real branch line service.

Narberth
Annual passenger usage: 18,966
Least used station rank: 330
Postcode: SA67 8TY
Ordnance Survey national grid reference: SN120147

Ten minutes after leaving Kilgetty I had arrived at Narberth, which the P&TR opened in 1866. Sidings that served cattle pens, stables and an oil tank were once here along with a loading bank.[3]

My immediate impression on arrival was that I liked this stop but also that it seemed to be a station of two parts. At the northern end it's clear people have tried to make the station a more welcoming place, with a nod to past times; possibly locals, as I saw very little sign of the corporate hand, or its paintbrush. There is a brown wooden shelter, which in my request stop experience is of a unique type, and on the outside of this is a noticeboard giving tourist information concerning Narberth and the surrounding area. Alongside the shelter is a well-tended garden and standing among the plants is a station nameboard, made of wood. Although not very old, it would not have looked out of place had it been here when steam was the norm.

At its southern end the station is made up of the original and substantial building, now used by a joinery and woodworking business. This building backs directly onto the platform and the original and imposing awning is still in place, most unusual for a small country stop. Apart from the fact that the second track is now gone and what remains of the opposite platform is now hidden in the undergrowth, this part of the station has, in all probability, changed remarkably little in recent years. To the north side of the approach road, what would have been a goods shed is still standing and this, like the main building, is also used for commercial purposes.

There is no car park, but a drop-off point is available and the platform has step-free access. An electronic departure/arrival screen is situated on the platform.

Saundersfoot
Annual passenger usage: 8,002
Least used station rank: 216
Postcode: SA69 9BG
Ordnance Survey national grid reference: SN123061

On the third day of my south-west Wales exploration I left Carmarthen to head south on my way to Saundersfoot, my first call of the day. In doing this I passed through both Kilgetty and Narberth.

The P&TR opened Saundersfoot in 1866. The station at that time was located a little under a mile to the south of its present location, and moved northwards in 1868. A passing loop with a second platform existed here until the mid-1960s. It is located 16 miles from Pembroke Dock, which is the end of the branch line, and 245 miles from London Paddington.

After watching the train that I had just alighted from depart, I became struck with the feeling of how big and empty a space this felt. Not only is the platform of a length that suggests an importance that is now lost, but it is also quite deep. This feeling of openness is due in part to the fact that the limited facilities are all located very much to the rear and away from the platform edge. The wide approach road leads right onto the platform, with only a row of bollards separating the station from the public road. A brick shelter, bench seat and noticeboards are all provided, with up-to-date train information on an electronic display.

As my train came into view my thoughts turned to the last two stops of the day, Lamphey and Penally, also on the Pembroke branch. If they lived up to the photographs that I'd seen of them then it would be a case of leaving the best to last. My stopping arm was out.

Lamphey
Annual passenger usage: 4,868
Least used station rank: 158
Postcode: SA17 5NR
Ordnance Survey national grid reference: SN014003

Lamphey opened in 1863 along with the other stations on the Pembroke to Tenby section of this line. It was built with a single platform and no passing loop.

Once the train had departed on its way to Pembroke and the quiet had descended I began to take in my surroundings and Lamphey most certainly did not disappoint. There were houses nearby, most notably the old station house, but I still had not the slightest doubt in my mind that I had set foot in rural Wales. A delightful station, it has a brick shelter that I had encountered before in this part of the world, again left unpainted. Two plaques are affixed, one of which states that the 'Lamphey & District Women's Institute' look after the gardens and the other advises that 'Mr Lee McCartney' has adopted the station. All these people are to be congratulated on an excellent job. The platform is fairly long but the HST stopping boards are still located some way past the platform ends. These do look a little out of place here, but are actually needed as at the time of my visit there was a summer Saturdays HST departing at 15.08, arriving into London Paddington at 20.30.

I sat for a while enjoying the glorious spring sunshine. Behind me was a field full of sheep and lambs (well I was in Wales) and in front of me a hedgerow full of small birds, blue tits mostly, and other species that were difficult to identify. The thought occurred to me that I needed pocket binoculars. Time passed all too quickly as it always does in locations like this. I waved my train down. The guard who I had seen before didn't ask for my ticket.

"Where to next?"

"Penally thanks."

Obviously curious she then enquired, "Are you visiting all the stops?"

"No, only the request ones," I said.

She smiled. "Oh I see,'" she said, and went on her way, presumably deciding that as I did not look the violent type, her best course of action would be to humour me.

Penally
Annual passenger usage: 5,168
Least used station rank: 163
Postcode: SA70 7PS
Ordnance Survey national grid reference: SS118990

The P&TR opened Penally station in 1863, and it has been closed and reopened several times in its history. Closed for the first time in 1964, it then reopened in 1970 but only for the summer months. It repeated this in 1971, before opening again in 1972, this time permanently.

It is a lovely little and cared-for stop, with the original station building easily discernible as a now much altered private home. There is an unmanned level crossing at the end of the platform and a little further on there are HST stopping boards. On summer Saturdays only, the HST service will stop not only here if it's requested, but also at Lamphey, Kilgetty and Narberth. It also stops at Saundersfoot, which for this service only is a mandatory stop. Today's station has the usual facilities plus a wooden shelter of a different style to the others I have encountered. There is an adjacent car park and, most unusually, toilets. Both appeared popular, not with railway passengers (I was the only one of those), but with passing walkers.

Penally is situated on the coast and very near the Pembrokeshire Coast Path. At the time of my visit people were leaving their cars and using the level crossing at the end of the platform to walk to the coast. This was something I later did myself, encountering lots of small birds in the reeds alongside the path. They were probably reed warblers but I couldn't be sure, reminding myself again to get some binoculars. About three-quarters of a mile to the south west of the station, on the higher grassy slopes, there is what seems to be some sort of earthworks. Not ancient though: they are what remains of the training trenches used for recruits before they were sent to that slaughter which became known as the Great War. Personally I fail to see what is great about the needless deaths of so many brave young men.

I returned to Carmarthen, having completed 'West Wales'. The next day I aimed to visit three 'Heart of Wales Line' stops.

The next morning, the last day of my first Welsh trip, I was waiting at Llanelli for the train to Ammanford on the Heart of Wales Line. There are thirty-one stops between here and Shrewsbury on this line, sixteen of which are request stops travelling in a northerly direction and even more, a total of twenty-one, if travelling south. The first request stop on the line, if travelling south, is Broome, and the last is Bynea, a distance of 85 miles with twenty-one request stops: one every 4 miles. Request stop heaven? The journey from Llanelli to Shrewsbury is 110 miles with a journey time of over four hours, making the average speed 27mph, all in a single-car DMU. This is fantastic I thought, I must take this journey again soon.

The station speakers burst into life and announced my train, all thirty-one stops. Then the request stops were repeated, advising passengers to tell the guard if they wished to alight, then finally a warning to stand back from the platform edge; this is all in Welsh. The whole thing was then repeated in English. Total time taken? About three minutes. Absolutely marvellous, without a doubt my favourite station announcement of all time.

Ammanford
Annual passenger usage: 19,934
Least used station rank: 336
Postcode: SA18 2DD
Ordnance Survey national grid reference: SN623126

When opened in 1841 Ammanford was known as Duffryn and has undergone five name changes in its history. It became Tirydail in 1889, then Ammanford and Tirydail in 1960, then BR added the suffix 'halt' in 1965. It then reverted to Ammanford and Tirydail in 1969, and finally became Ammanford in 1973. The platform was moved from the north side of Station Road to the south around the year 1900.

Ammanford is like several other stations on the Heart of Wales Line, a request stop but only for trains travelling south. The shelter is of an aesthetically pleasing design and on the platform is a wheeled coal tub that once would have seen service in one of the local pits. This has been put to good use, and is now a flower planter. A help point and information screen are both present along with noticeboards. Overall a very agreeable station albeit quite busy when I visited, but considering the size of the town this was hardly surprising.

Llangadog
Annual passenger usage: 5,578
Least used station rank: 174
Postcode: SA19 9LU
Ordnance Survey national grid reference: SN699285

On leaving Ammanford for Llangadog there was no need to put my arm out, seeing as Ammanford is not a request stop for trains travelling north. Once on board I did have to request Llangadog, and this I did in my very best Welsh accent, which I had been practising in my mind, but not out loud and perhaps more importantly not on actual people. The guard repeated back to me the name I'd said or at least what I had tried to say, but only after she had stopped laughing. It always amazes me how tolerant the Welsh are of people completely destroying their language.

The Vale of Towy Railway (VoTR) opened Llangadog station in 1858 when it was called Llangadock, becoming Llangadog Halt in 1965 and then simply Llangadog in 1969. A signal box, passing loop and second platform did exist but have all now been removed.

This is another well-presented stop. Facilities are typical, with a brick shelter similar to that at Ammanford, however this one did have something extra special: swallows nesting in the roof. Not only that but they continued to hunt and fly in and out of the shelter even with me sitting in it, a remarkably pleasant way to spend an hour. Access to the platform is wheelchair-friendly. The usual noticeboards and information screen are to be found adjacent to the car park.

The train that would take me to the delightfully and intriguingly named Sugar Loaf, the last stop of the day and of this particular trip, was approaching. While I waited the swallows continued to swoop all around me, at times giving the impression they might collide with me or perhaps even each other; however, their airborne agility is truly amazing and any chance of mishaps unthinkable. Perhaps they were just saying goodbye to someone who had gladly sat with them, thankful to have shared their company for the last hour.

Sugar Loaf
Annual passenger usage: 1,846
Least used station rank: 93
Postcode: LD5 4TE
Ordnance Survey national grid reference: SN844438

The Central Wales Extension Railway (CWalesExR) reached Sugar Loaf in 1868. The station, then called Sugar Loaf Summit, was opened in 1899 by what had now become the London & North Western Railway (L&NWR). There once existed on this site a group of railway workers' cottages, and the station was provided mainly to allow the children of the workers to travel to school. It closed in 1965 and then reopened as Sugar Loaf in 1984. The suffix 'halt' appears on tickets but does not seem to be used in the timetable or elsewhere.

Having researched all the stops previously, I had high expectations of what Sugar Loaf would be like and these were about to be exceeded. The guard had already advised me she could only open the front door due to the length of the platform. Stepping down from the train I thought, oh yes, this place really is tiny, a sort of Berney Arms with hills. Located in a deep cutting approximately 50 metres from the A483, not only is it invisible from the road but no other sign of human habitation can be seen. Could it be that Sugar Loaf is hiding here, hoping that the drivers careering along the road above do not become aware of this oasis of calm and peace, because after all if they did they might stop, and break the secluded peace.

After the train had departed and calm had returned, I saw a red kite circling above. Not only is this my favourite British bird of prey it also features on the logo of the publicity for the Heart of Wales Line. The surrounding trees and bushes were alive with small birds and unknown small creatures scurried through the undergrowth.

As I expected the facilities were limited, only a help point, noticeboard and an open bus stop-style shelter. Access is down a steep and rather long flight of stairs which could be a real challenge for the less able-bodied. Something it did have that I had not seen before nor since was a visitor's book, with a recent entry from a Wiltshire person that read, 'There is nothing here, how wonderful!' Who could disagree with that? Just to the south of the station is a trackside board that reads: 'Sugar Loaf summit 820 feet (250 metres) above sea level'. I also noticed that some of the chairs (that is, the mountings that are screwed onto the wooden sleepers which in turn hold the rails) were marked BR (W), that is, 'British Railways Western Region', and an even older type were embossed 'GWR'.

Becoming totally immersed in the moment and my surroundings, time passed unbelievably quickly. The train south, which would eventually take me home to Swindon, was approaching: and the time to say goodbye to Sugar Loaf had come, but I shall go back. When the door opened the guard, who seemed genuinely pleased to see me, looked out and said, "Wow, I've never stopped here before."

That really did make my day.

Ferryside photographed on 1 May 2018. The platforms themselves did not have much to offer, but there were semaphore signals, although sadly these are scheduled to be replaced. This view is facing westwards.

Kidwelly looking towards Carmarthen on 1 May 2018.

Johnston is one of only two stops on the Milford Haven branch, here looking back towards Clarbeston Road on 1 May 2018.

Clarbeston Road, the junction for the Milford Haven branch, which can be seen in the distance, veering away to the left. Photographed on 2 May 2018.

Clunderwen photographed from Platform 2 on 2 May 2018. The platforms here are staggered and the second platform can be seen on the left. Photographed looking towards Swansea.

The Pembroke branch has five request stops. Here is Kilgetty looking south-west on 2 May 2018.

Narberth was in need of a coat of paint, but has managed to retain its platform canopy. Here seen looking here towards Whitland, 2 May 2018.

Left: Saundersfoot on the Pembroke branch, photographed looking north towards the main line on 2 May 2018.

Opposite above: Another view of Lamphey, this time looking towards the west on 3 May 2018.

Opposite below: Penally, one of my favourite West Wales stops, photographed on 3 May 2018, facing towards Pembroke.

I felt some of the request stops west of Swansea were a little bland. Not so with Lamphey, a delightful place full of the sounds and smells of the countryside. Pictured here looking east on 3 May 2018.

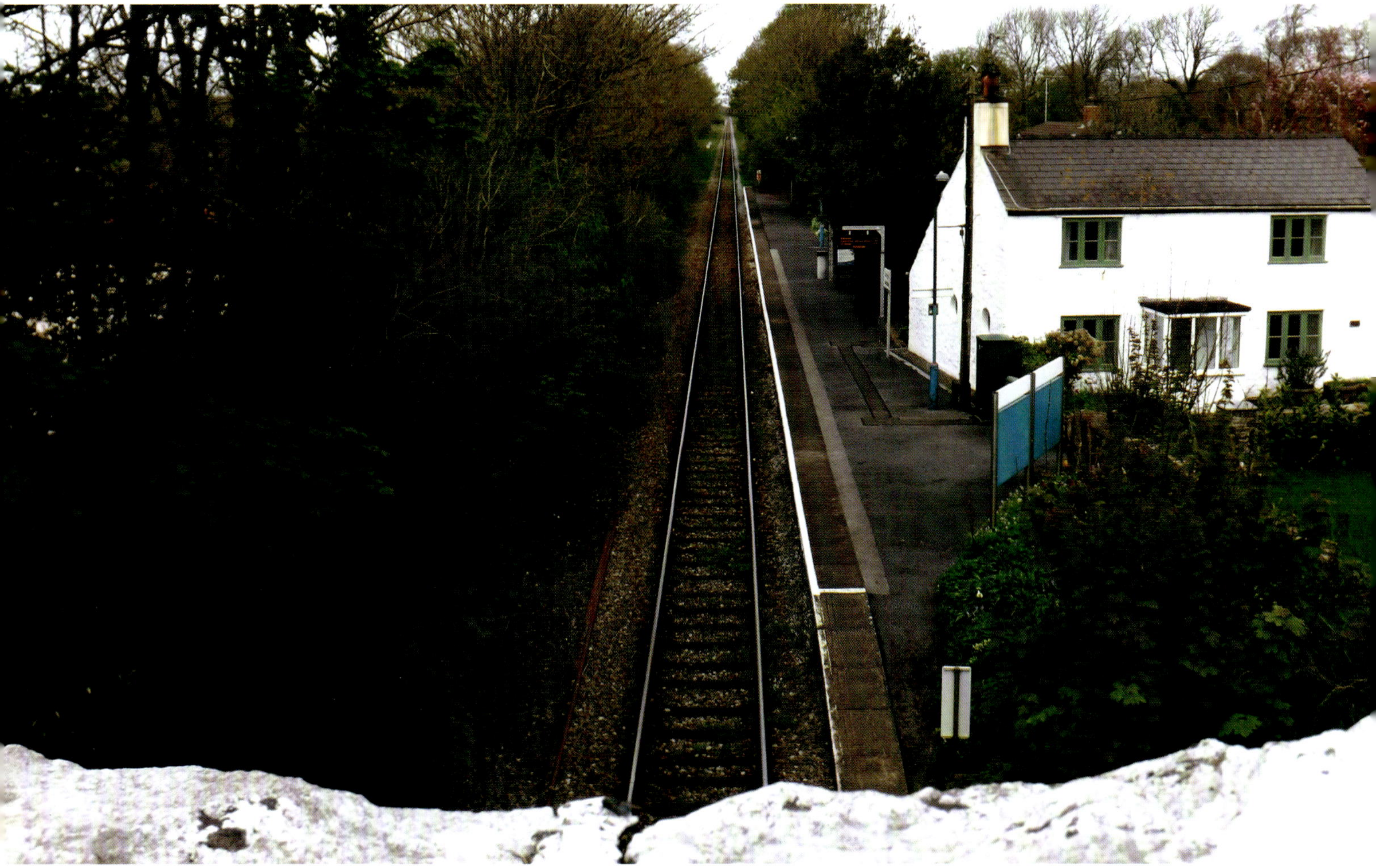

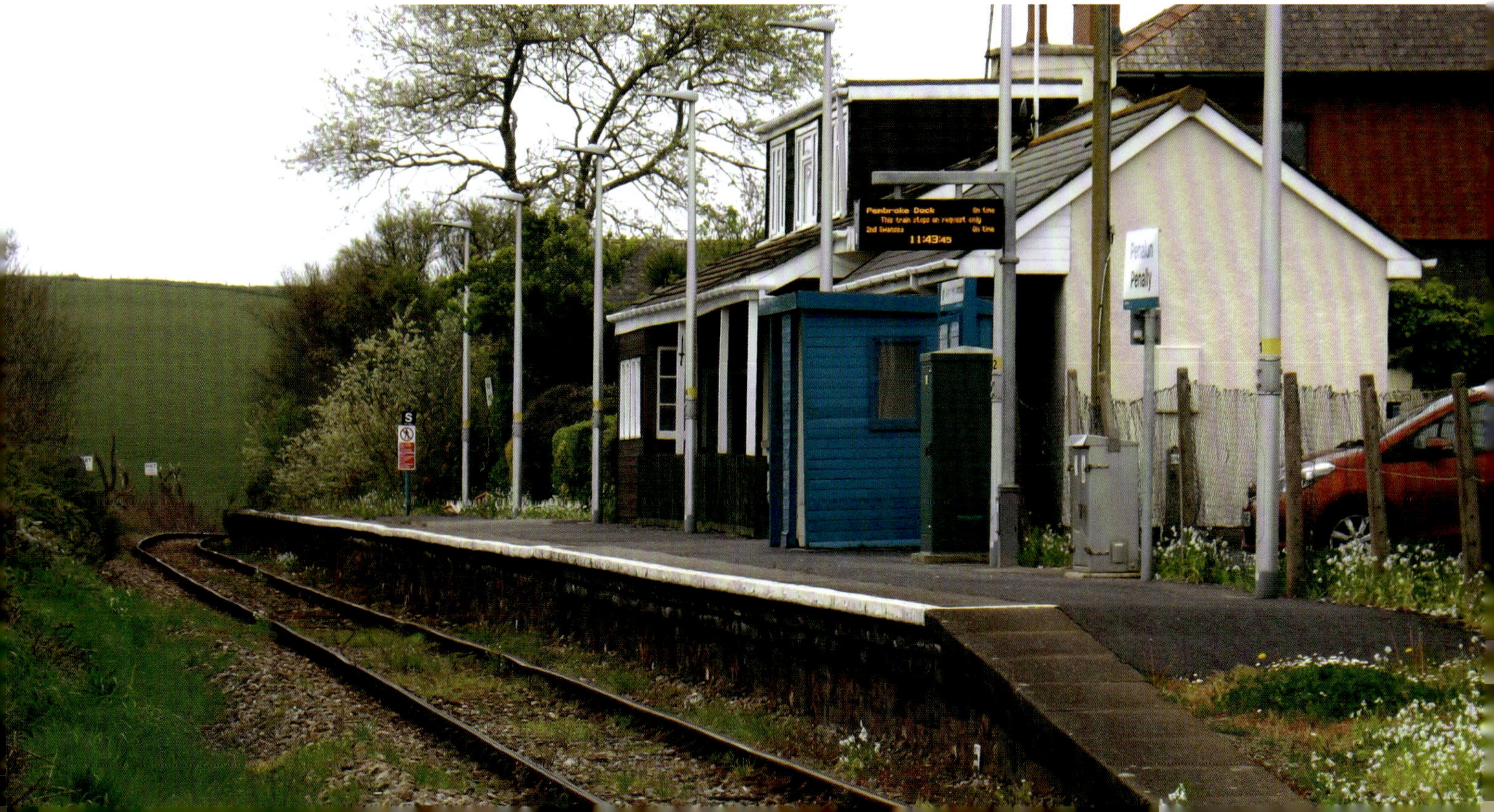

THROUGH THE TUNNEL • 63

Ammanford looking south on 4 May 2018. The old coal tub now being used as a flower planter is, I think, a nice touch.

Llangadog, a well-kept and nice-looking stop, photographed on 4 May 2018.

The 10.09 Shrewsbury to Swansea service comprising a single car Class 153 Super Sprinter DMU passing Sugar Loaf on 4 May 2018.

Sugar Loaf looking towards Swansea on 4 May 2018.

Sugar Loaf was so good I fitted in a second visit during my next trip on the Heart of Wales Line. Here the 10.09 Shrewsbury to Swansea formed of a Class 153 Super Sprinter DMU is about to stop at Sugar Loaf, just for me, on 10 July 2018.

CHAPTER 6

REPEAT AFTER ME, CYNGHORDY

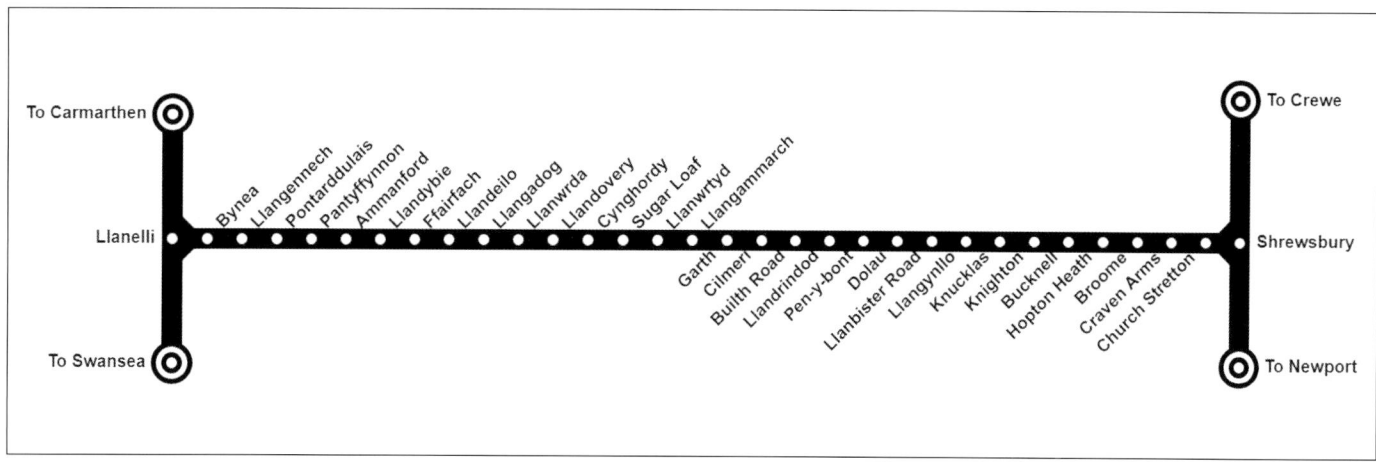

Back home in Swindon I had a few weeks before my next foray into request-stop land, and I got down to some more serious planning. My focus was now on completing more of the Heart of Wales Line which I decided would require two trips, basing myself at different locations each time. Firstly would be a two-night stay in Knighton. From there I intended to visit six stops in Wales and three at the north end of the line which are actually in England. Knighton is a small market town with the claim to fame that not only does Offa's Dyke run through it, but so too does the England / Wales border.

Llangennech
Annual passenger usage: 3,350
Least used station rank: 128
Postcode: SA14 8UY
Ordnance Survey national grid reference: SN563012

I arrived at Llangennech by taxi from Llanelli, to begin my Heart of Wales Line adventure. This was the first time I had done this and one of the few occasions that I did not arrive and leave by train. This allowed me time to fit in a second stop that day, before heading to the hotel in Knighton.

When first opened by the Llanelly Railway & Dock Company (LR&DC) in 1840, Llangennech station was located a little further to the south, moving some time around 1910 to its current location on the north side of the level crossing.[1] In common with many other small stations it did for a time have the title 'halt' applied, becoming Llangennech Halt between 1959 and 1969. In past times two signal boxes along with sidings were present, but I didn't see any traces of either.

The line here is double track and both platforms have relatively new wooden shelters that have been left in a natural wood finish. Access between the platforms is by use of a barrow crossing that forms part of the level crossing. There is a help point near the entrance/exit and both platforms have an information screen. Wooden flower tubs with the name Llangennech cut into them are on both platforms. It has fine views to the River Loughor, which is only a short walk away, although stout footwear might be advisable for anyone contemplating walking down to its banks.

Bynea
Annual passenger usage: 2,228
Least used station rank: 105
Postcode: SA14 9TL
Ordnance Survey national grid reference: SS549991

After a couple of hours at Llangennech a Class 153 single-car DMU came into view. I made sure to request Bynea when I boarded, for this, my final stop of the day, was less than 2 miles to the south, and according to the timetable only three minutes' travelling time away.

The LR&DC opened Bynea in 1840. Bynea has in the past been a much busier place than it is today. Not only did it have a signal box and to the south some sidings, but the Yspitty branch curved away eastwards at the north end of the station.[2] This branch served a tinplate works, steelworks and several other industrial complexes. Bynea also had the suffix 'halt' for a time, becoming Bynea Halt in 1959 before reverting to its original name in 1969.

My first impressions once alone on the platform at Bynea were of a rather urban yet open space, compounded by the double track passing through the station and a busy road bridge crossing the line a few metres away. A car park is available next to Platform 1 and a help point is on Platform 2. Access is on the level although the distance from the car park to Platform 2 is approximately 400 metres, via the road bridge and Station Road. Both platforms have basic metal shelters with opaque 'glazing' that is reinforced with metal crosshatching (not very attractive). A fairly large and planted garden surrounds the access path from Station Road, but sadly it seemed rather unloved with grass strangling most of the plants.

My time here passed and I boarded my train, a single-car Class 153 DMU, and in around two hours and thirty-nine minutes I was in Knighton where I would spend the next two nights. Leaving Knighton station, which is actually in England, I walked to the hotel and was back in Wales, because the town straddles the border.

My stay in a local pub proved to be most comfortable, and the food was of restaurant quality. This was something I realised even before I had even taken the first mouthful of my vegetable wellington, but how you might ask? Simple: it looked good but more than that, it wasn't served on a plate but on a piece of irregularly shaped Welsh slate. Lucky I hadn't ordered gravy I thought to myself. Walking into the breakfast room on my first morning I noticed two people were already there. The mandatory good mornings were exchanged, then, save for the clanking of knives and forks on plates, silence returned.

After breakfast I made my way to the station. It was a glorious summer morning. The train, some twenty minutes late due to signalling problems, rolled into the platform and stopped. A couple of minutes later I was on my way to Bucknell, the next stop north and the first of the three request stops on the Heart of Wales Line that are in England.

Bucknell
Annual passenger usage: 4,234
Least used station rank: 146
Postcode: SY7 0AD
Ordnance Survey national grid reference: SO355736

Bucknell was opened to passengers in 1861 by the Knighton Railway (KtnR), later to become part of the L&NWR. A second platform remained in use until the 1960s and to the east side of the station there once existed a goods yard and shed.

On my visit I found a pretty little stop, with a shelter of the type I had seen at Causeland, brick-built with a sloping roof and support columns at the front, a recent design but not at all out of place. There is a help point, an information screen on the platform and a payphone in the shelter. Access to the platform is by ramp. The second platform, although no longer in use, is nonetheless still very much evident, and has been turned into a very colourful garden, which during my time there was alive with several species of butterfly. Despite the fact that by this time I possessed pocket binoculars, positive identification proved impossible due to my woeful butterfly spotting skills.

After passing an extremely pleasant hour, the train that would take me south and back into Wales came into view. By this time I had been joined by a fellow passenger, a little old lady with a shopping trolley, who then proceeded to wave the train down before I had a chance. I decided not to object because she had said a friendly "good morning, lovely weather" to me and, after all, she had arrived on foot. I conceded this gave her the right as a local, over me the rather strange interloper.

Pen-y-Bont
Annual passenger usage: 1,824
Least used station rank: 90
Postcode: LD1 6RE
Ordnance Survey national grid reference: SO097648

The Central Wales Railway (CWR) opened Crossgates, as it was known in 1865, and the L&NWR changed the station name to Penybont. In 1980 it became Pen-y-Bont, courtesy of BR. The station is situated between the villages of Crossgates and Penybont, although it is nearer the former. It is located 62 miles north of Llanelli.

After a journey of around thirty-five minutes and a distance of slightly more than 20 miles from Bucknell the train pulled up at Pen-y-bont, just for me. The first thing that struck me was the naturalistic garden that runs for most of the platform length, alive not only with butterflies but also honeybees. I decided to sit in the very warm June sunshine for a while, before I explored the station and took my photographs. The sun was on me, I had a cup of tea, and apart from the buzzing of the bees, total silence. High in the blue sky a pair of red kites were circling, no doubt glad to feel the warmth of the sun on their feathers. This is why I am here I thought, what more could I possibly want?

On the platform is a small wooden shelter, and inside is a plaque telling us that the station has been adopted by the Cooke family. On the wall is a dispenser containing Heart of Wales Line timetables. Outside is the expected information screen; also on the platform is a wooden bench dedicated: 'In fond memory of Bill Smith 1938–2014, railway enthusiast and dedicated station volunteer'. There is a car park and access to the platform is through an entrance/exit gate and across a barrow crossing. The now abandoned second platform is very clearly visible and still has a station nameboard present. Curiously the station nameboards, some of which are Arriva corporate signs and others older, all have the name Penybont, while the sign at the access road, and the timetable, both say Pen-y-Bont.

It always amazed me how quickly time passed at some of these stops, and all too soon I was saying goodbye to Pen-y-Bont and getting ready to wave down the next train going north and over the border into England.

Broome
Annual passenger usage: 1,150
Least used station rank: 60
Postcode: SY7 0NT
Ordnance Survey national grid reference: SO399809

Heading north for forty-five minutes took me to Broome in Shropshire. Situated 23 miles south of Shrewsbury it is the last request stop on the Heart of Wales Line in a northerly direction.

First made available for passenger use in 1861 by the KtnR, John Marius Wilson's *Imperial Gazetteer of England and Wales* (1870–1872) mentions the name 'Broom and Aston' railway station.[3] A goods yard and sidings existed until the 1960s, but this area is now a light industrial site. Other changes made around this time were the removal of the signal box and singling of the track.

Facilities here are the basic norm, with a wooden shelter containing a non-working payphone. The platform has a Harrington Hump, a raised platform section, so called because this inexpensive and easily fitted device was first used at Harrington on the 'Cumbrian Coast Line'. The platform at Broome can only be reached by a fairly long and steep path, which in wet weather could be muddy. Opposite the platform the undergrowth is rather thick and I could not see any sign of the one-time second platform.

I did however spent a most enjoyable hour watching the various hedgerow birds darting to and fro, while I sat in the still glorious June sunshine that I had enjoyed earlier in the day. My itinerary showed one more stop for the day, at Builth Road.

Builth Road
Annual passenger usage: 7,458
Least used station rank: 204
Postcode: LD2 3PY
Ordnance Survey national grid reference: SO024532

Builth Road station is approximately 2.5 miles from Builth Wells – the town from which it gets its name. It opened in 1866 and was one of two stations that once existed here, the other being Llechryd, later called Builth Road Low Level. The two stations formed an interchange between the CWalesR and the Mid-Wales Railway (MwidR). Builth Road was renamed Builth Road High Level in 1950, and reverted to its original name in 1969 after the closure of the low-level station.

When my train had departed I immediately sensed that this would not be one of my favourite stops. The shelter is a glazed aluminium type and the basic facilities all exist. Entrance to the station is by a short alleyway through the former station buildings. Once on the platform these station buildings, now bereft of the canopy of old, and exposing a fairly large expanse of bland brickwork, gave me an impression that was more inner city than request stop. On the west side of the track is Railway Terrace, which is a row of former railway workers' cottages. Much of the goods yard and all of the second platform have been swept away, leaving what can only be described as waste ground. The goods shed is still there, now isolated and alone at the far end of its now non-existent yard, contemplating why it has been left forlorn and abandoned.

As the time for my train back to Knighton for the night approached, a family joined me on the platform. Only one intended travelling, the others were on waving-off duty. Normally my ideal stop is one I have to myself, but this time was different, because they had an Irish Setter with them. I walked past them and he wanted to say hello, not a surprise, after all that is what Irish Setters do, and it would have been mean to disappoint him, so I obliged; definitely the highlight of the Builth Road visit.

Hopton Heath
Annual passenger usage: 1,006
Least used station rank: 55
Postcode: SY7 0QD
Ordnance Survey national grid reference: SO380774

After my final night in Knighton, I headed to the station. Two stops had been planned for the day before returning home. There would be a final stop on this Rover ticket, but I intended to complete that on a day trip from Swindon.

Hopton Heath, which is spelt Hoptonheath on some older Ordnance Survey (OS) maps, was opened in 1861 by the KtnR. The second platform, goods yard and shed that the station once boasted are now all gone, and so too have the sidings. It was the least used station in Shropshire when I visited, a title that it has since swopped with Broome, the next stop up the line – how neighbourly is that?

The extensive former station buildings are now privately owned, and give the impression that Hopton Heath was, during its history, a much more important place than it is today. Accommodation for today's passengers is a wooden shelter similar to others on this line. This one however was sorely in need of a fresh coat of paint. There are noticeboards here but no help point. Access to the platform is from the road above and down a flight of twenty-five stairs, definitely a challenge for those with mobility issues. It would be possible to approach the station using a footpath from the nearby caravan park, but although it is on the level the path is narrow, grass covered and it is a long walk; still a challenge perhaps?

Overall, Hopton Heath did not disappoint, the only sound, apart from the nearby rookery, was that of a single farm tractor and trailer clanking over the road bridge, and even that seemed to be in total harmony with the place and moment. Being able to spent time watching a squirrel nibbling a nut and becoming fully absorbed in the moment brought me an inner calm and quiet. This was what I was really seeking; and the sight of those tracks disappearing into the distance.

Dolau
Annual passenger usage: 1,372
Least used station rank: 69
Postcode: LD1 5TG
Ordnance Survey national grid reference: SO139670

Twenty miles south from Hopton Heath is Dolau, opened by the CWR in 1865. It was renamed to Dolau Halt in 1965 before reverting in 1969.

Dolau is not only one of the best kept stations I have seen, it probably is *the* best; the Dolau Station Action Group, which looks after it, does an amazing job. The gardens are immaculate and the attention to detail extraordinary. Period signals, two flagpoles, lights in the style of gas lamps and a rail trolley – I could go on as there is so much to see there. Too much, leaving me with the feeling that I'd walked into the midst of a display of some sort, and not a quiet, rarely used railway station. The Queen visited Dolau as part of her Jubilee tour in 2002 and unsurprisingly there is a plaque she unveiled (she really does do a lot of unveiling) to commemorate the occasion. More references to this event are evident to the extent that I felt I could be walking down Windsor High Street past some of the many souvenir shops. Dolau – definitely a case of royalists one, republicans nil.

The very comfortable wooden shelter, complete with station clock had, I suspected, been provided by the Station Action Group. Inside are dispensers of local leaflets and on the walls various award certificates the station has won. A help point, noticeboards and an information screen are all there to aid the traveller. The second platform remains cared for, to the extent that if someone relaid the missing track, trains could start using it straight away.

After a four hour stay I waved my train down. Dolau is one of the stops that is not a request stop for northbound services, but I was going south, and making the three hour, seventy-six mile journey to Swansea, and then on home to Swindon.

Cynghordy
Annual passenger usage: 1,170
Least used station rank: 63
Postcode: SA20 0LY
Ordnance Survey national grid reference: SN802406

My itinerary for the 23 June 2018 showed the following: Swindon departing 08.08 for Swansea, then Cynghordy and return, arriving Swindon at 21.19. This allowed me one and three-quarter hours at Cynghordy, on a day trip which entailed travelling for thirteen hours and covering 320 miles; this all sounded perfectly normal to me.

As I always saw a different guard on this line I was not recognised as the 'man with the Rover ticket', but that did not prevent them from being helpful and friendly. I asked the guard for Cynghordy, thinking that the 'Cyn' might be pronounced a bit like cyan. She repeated the name correctly and, trying to get it right, I then followed suit. Still not right, an impromptu Welsh language pronunciation lesson followed, then on my fourth attempt I got it right or perhaps she decided that was the best I could do and she went on her way, chuckling.

Very little remains to be seen of the Cynghordy opened in 1868 by the CWalesExR. The station building, signal box, yard and passing loop have now all gone. Unlike Sugar Loaf station 4 miles up the line and hiding in its valley, Cynghordy stands proudly in the open, quietly relishing its remoteness. The heat of a blazing June day was on me and the silence so complete even the birds were not evident, saving their energy for later in the day. There is a house at the bottom of the approach road it is true, but the isolation is still tangible.

A metal shelter, noticeboard and help point comprise the facilities here. Going into the shelter I found that someone had made cushions for the hard metal seats; what a lovely thing to do. My thoughts immediately turned to my beautiful daughter, with her skills as an art teacher, and love of all things textile. I could easily imagine her doing that under similar circumstances. I am sure she will want the previous sentence removed, but if I am allowed to misquote Hollywood film mogul Darryl F. Zanuck 'the kid stays in the book'.

Llangennech photographed on 20 June 2018 looking south.

Bynea, the first request stop on the Heart of Wales Line out of Swansea, looking south on 20 June 2018.

Bucknell, despite being on the Heart of Wales Line, is one of three stops that are actually in England. Photographed on 21 June 2018 looking towards Shrewsbury.

REPEAT AFTER ME, CYNGHORDY • 73

A single car Class 153 Super Sprinter DMU forming the 09.34 Swansea to Shrewsbury service, stopping at the lovely Pen-y-Bont on 21 June 2018.

Broome on 21 June 2018, with the 14.05 Shrewsbury to Swansea arriving. This service was a single-car Class 153 Super Sprinter DMU. This appeared to be the norm during my journeys on the Heart of Wales Line.

Builth Road, looking north on 21 June 2018. The old goods shed can be seen in the distance.

The extensive former station buildings at Hopton Heath. Today passenger comfort is provided by the blue wooden hut to the left of the photograph, taken on 22 June 2018.

A Class 153 Super Sprinter DMU at Hopton Heath with the 10.09 Shrewsbury to Swansea arriving on 22 June 2018.

The immaculately kept Dolau photographed on 22 June 2018, looking north.

The marvellous Cynghordy, photographed facing towards Swansea on 23 June 2018. This to me is how a request stop should look, sound and feel.

CHAPTER 7

RAILWAY MINDFULNESS

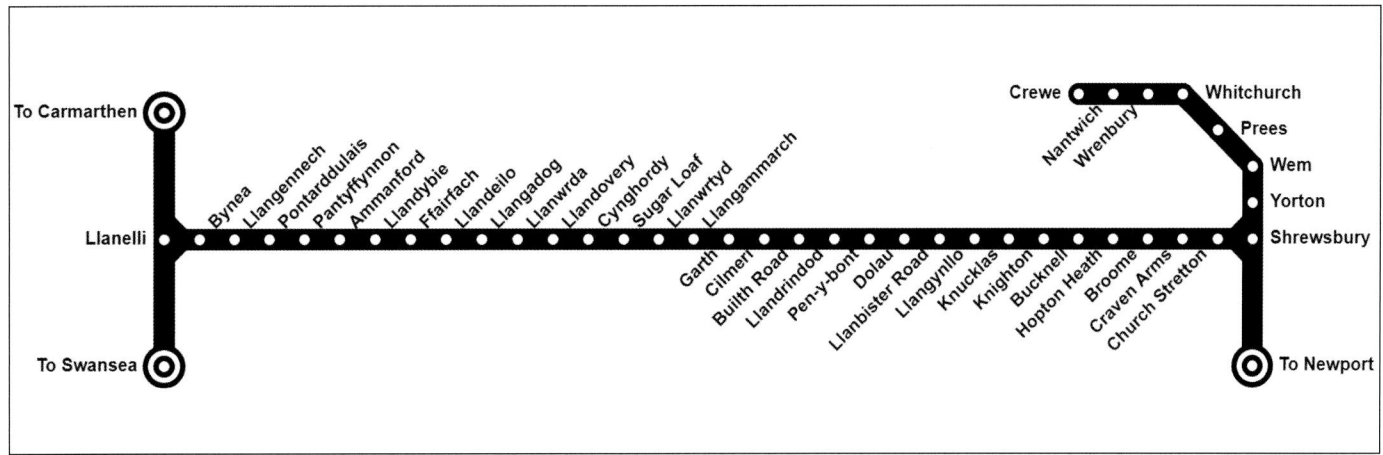

On my return from Cynghordy, several busy planning evenings were needed because I had already booked a hotel for the next outing beginning in only two weeks' time. The planning was not only essential, but as always for me a most satisfying process. It always felt particularly good when my computer printer pushed out the final draft of my latest itinerary. This trip completed the Heart of Wales Line plus the three request stops on the 'Welsh Marches Line', thirteen in total.

At this time I acquired a copy of *Tiny Stations* by Dixe Wills. In this book he describes visiting a selection of request stops in Great Britain. When I first opened the book I immediately went to the chapter on Sugar Loaf. There he describes 'concentrating on the moment', often known as 'mindfulness'. At the risk of sounding over-dramatic it really was a lightbulb moment – I suddenly realised that this was exactly what I had been doing at some stops – not consciously, but it had been happening.

A long wait at a railway station can be a bit stressful for anyone, especially if the train is delayed and you are relying on a connection. Visiting a request stop is different, for me at least. My time there might be anything up to five hours, but this is what I had planned, I wanted the time to explore and be a part of a place. This allowed me to relax, to not only see my surroundings with new eyes, but also to listen anew.

Listening to the wind rustling the reeds and not tiring of the sound, watching a butterfly for ten minutes, wondering if it will ever settle. I found myself becoming totally absorbed in the moment and my surroundings. I realised how time passed so quickly, remembering how after two and a half hours at Berney Arms I still wanted more. I had been immersed in the moment; nothing else mattered, just being alive and being there.

Llangammarch
Annual passenger usage: 1,782
Least used station rank: 89
Postcode: LD4 4EE
Ordnance Survey national grid reference system: SN935473

Opened in 1867 by the CWalesExR, Llangammarch had the suffix Wells added to its name in 1883, and then removed in 1980. Despite the modern timetables and other official sources showing plain Llangammarch, all the on-site station signs say Llangammarch Wells.

It is a tidy station with a small car park, level access and the usual noticeboards and information screen. Although no formal station garden exists there are a good number of nicely maintained flowerpots. The shelter is of a modern brick design with pillars. No trace remains of the original station building which was demolished in 1980.

Pontarddulais
Annual passenger usage: 4,820
Least used station rank: 157
Postcode: SA4 8TH
Ordnance Survey national grid reference: SN587040

'Pontarddulais', as it was known when first opened by the LR&DC in 1840, became Pontardulias Halt in 1965. BR removed the suffix in 1969, before finally renaming it Pontarddulais in 1980.

Boarding my train at Llangammarch I had a journey south of eighty minutes, plenty of time to silently practise my pronunciation, before I made my request, which was not perfect, but I gave myself seven out of ten. Pontarddulais has CCTV coverage and an information screen; there are also railway noticeboards and 'Heritage Boards' give details of the station and the surrounding area. The shelter is of the aluminium and plexiglass type. The now single platform is very wide and given over to a gravel area on the eastern side, evidence of the existence of the former direct Swansea line. Little other suggestion of its previous history remains to be seen. Gone are the goods yard, the signal boxes, the four platforms and the diverging direct line to Swansea Victoria, along with all the branches that served the many industrial sites nearby. Just to the east side of the station is the rather grandiose goods shed, now a garage, the only former station building that I could see.

Llandybie
Annual passenger usage: 10,756
Least used station rank: 250
Postcode: SA18 3UN
Ordnance Survey national grid reference: SN619154

Boarding a northbound service at Pontarddulais I didn't have to ask for my next destination, Llandovery, for it is not a request stop, a shame as it is one that I can actually pronounce. This is where I stayed for the next three nights. After booking into the hotel I headed back to the station and the final stop of the day, Llandybie.

Opened in 1857 by the LR&DC, the station was first known as Llandebie, changing to Llandybie in 1971. The site once occupied by a signal box is now a private home and the former small goods yard has become a modern housing estate.

The platform has step-free access via a steep ramp, an information screen and noticeboards. There is a very solidly constructed stone shelter of an unusual design, and from an old photograph I have seen, it clearly is a part of the original station. It is much modified now, having had a flat roof and windows added, but the basic structure is still there. Interestingly someone had dumped an old three-piece suite in it. I speculated on how it got there: "Saver to Llandybie please, one adult and an old three-piece suite." The station seemed to me a little tatty, grimy and unloved. It is in the village itself and being close to a populated area can mean an accumulation of dirt and rubbish, as I noted earlier.

Walking back to my hotel in the evening I called into the local Co-op and managed to find a copy of the *Morning Star*, my daily newspaper of choice, which not all shops stock. I made a point of returning during my stay.

Llanwrda
Annual passenger usage: 2,052
Least used station rank: 100
Postcode: SA19 8EH
Ordnance Survey national grid reference: SN714310

Studying my timetables in the evening I came up with a plan. I was going to deviate from my itinerary. This is not a decision I would normally take lightly but this time an exception could be made, as it would allow a second brief visit to Sugar Loaf. By catching the 07.28 I could have half an hour there before boarding my intended first train of the day train at the same station, instead of Llandovery. I would then still arrive at Llanwrda, my planned first stop, on time.

The VoTR opened Lampeter Road in 1858, which later became Llanwrda, then in 1965 it was renamed to Llanwrda Halt, with the suffix being removed in 1969.[1] A goods yard, sidings and a second platform were once sited on the north side of Station Road. The platform still in use today is on the south side, with a level crossing in between. The abandoned and now overgrown second platform can still be seen.

This is a clean and cared-for stop, with a nice looking modern shelter, an information screen and noticeboards. Access is by a ramp, but there is no car park.

While enjoying the surroundings and the early morning summer sunshine with a cup of tea, I heard the sound of running feet coming up the entrance ramp, nearly two hours before the next train. Why the hurry, I thought. Then a man in his late forties, in T-shirt and shorts, flashed past me, turning his head long enough to say good morning. He carried on to the far end of the platform, which is surprisingly long at Llanwrda, and on reaching the end he proceeded to do various bend- and stretch-type things before he about-turned and headed back. After touching base at the entrance gate he headed down the platform and repeated the whole procedure. When he passed me on the sixth turn he was going noticeably slower, which allowed him more time to speak.

"They'll probably find me dead at the end of the platform one day."

"If you're not back in ten minutes I'll call an ambulance," I responded. He did make it back and disappeared down the road, still jogging.

Garth (Powys)
Annual passenger usage: 1,032
Least used station rank: 57
Postcode: LD4 4AF
Ordnance Survey national grid reference: SN953494

The train that would take me the 20 miles to Garth arrived on time, as they mostly did, and stopped without a request. Llanwrda is another of the stations that is only by request in a southerly direction. I asked the guard for Garth, quietly confident this time that my pronunciation would be perfect, and indeed it was.

Garth was opened by the CWalesExR in 1868, and apart from the overgrown and now abandoned second platform I could see no sign of any old railway infrastructure. Gone are the goods sidings that were once to the south of the station, along with the branch that led into the brick and drainpipe works.

On the platform is a brick-built shelter along with all the facilities that appear to be normal for this line. The small station car park has level access making it easy for wheelchair users. Overall, a nice visit. Although my stay had to be slighter shorter than most, I was able to spend some time watching the very busy blackbird, sparrow and robin population in the hedgerow growing on the old platform opposite.

Ffairfach
Annual passenger usage: 2,694
Least used station rank: 115
Postcode: SA19 6UL
Ordnance Survey national grid reference: SN629212

Ffairfach is 29 miles south of Garth and was my third stop of the day. Opened in 1857 by the LR&DC, it was between the years 1961 and 1969 called Ffairfach Halt.

The guard said, "I saw you last week didn't I?"

"Quite possibly," I replied, and stepped onto the platform.

He gave me a wave and I returned the compliment, the doors shut and the train moved off. I liked Ffairfach. It has a fairly busy road crossing close to the end of the platform, but I still liked it. There is a small wooden shelter that is just shabby enough to look right, containing noticeboards, both official and local. On the opposite side of the track there is an open space with two derelict and nondescript brick buildings, but no sign of the sidings or the gasworks that once occupied the site. I was also unable to locate any trace of the siding that once ran from the south side of the station to the Co-operative Wholesale Society Creamery.

Knucklas
Annual passenger usage: 3,454
Least used station rank: 134
Postcode: LD7 1PN
Ordnance Survey national grid reference: SO254740

For the final stop on the second day I headed to Knucklas. Opened in 1865 by the CWR, between the years 1956 to 1969 it was called Knucklas Halt before reverting to its original name. The station was built on the side of a hill overlooking the village, and to the west is the magnificent Knucklas viaduct, built with crenelated towers and parapets, giving the appearance of a medieval castle.

The station was very much what I had come to expect, with a brick-built shelter, information screen and noticeboards. There is no car park, just a drop-off point with access to the platform via stairs or a ramp. At the east end of the platform it is still possible to see a substantial former railway building now privately owned, and the extent of the former goods yard can also be made out.

The Welsh weather was still being most kind to me and with a full two hours before my train I had good opportunity to put my binoculars to use. What better way to spend an hour than sitting in the warm sunshine watching the small birds that call the undergrowth opposite their home, going about their business, apparently oblivious to my presence?

Cilmeri
Annual passenger usage: 1,436
Least used station rank: 75
Postcode: LD2 3NU
Ordnance Survey national grid reference: SO002511

On the third day of this Welsh trip I intended to complete the final three stops on the Heart of Wales Line, and was greeted by glorious weather when I arrived at Cilmeri. Known originally as Cefn-y-Bed when first opened by the CWalesExR in 1867, this was a short lived name as it became Cilmery in 1868. It then became Cilmery Halt in 1939 before losing the suffix in 1969 when it reverted back to Cilmery, finally becoming Cilmeri in 1980.

Cilmeri is 39.5 miles from Craven Arms, and there is a milepost on the platform that tells us precisely that. Other facilities are the norm for this line with a couple of exceptions. There is a rather nice cast metal station name board complete with the Heart of Wales Line red kite logo. The shelter is of an unusual wooden design. Its age I could not ascertain, but I have seen it in photographs taken there in the 1960s and it looked as though it had already been there for a while, and in worse condition than it is today. A bonus for the shelter is that it had several swallows' nests in it, and due to the low roof these were only just above head height. These amazing birds must be very tolerant to human presence because people must use the shelter. True, passenger numbers are low, an average of only four a day, but each time they share their world with us; if only we humans could be that tolerant, another world would be possible.

Llangynllo
Annual passenger usage: 806
Least used station rank: 45
Postcode: LD7 1SY
Ordnance Survey national grid reference: SO209730

Llangynllo is another station that since its opening in 1865 by the CWR has undergone several name changes. Originally named Llyncoch it became Llangunllo and then in 1965 Llangunllo Halt. The suffix was dropped in 1969, and it finally become Llangynllo in 1980.

Llangynllo afforded me a pleasurable stay, with its brick shelter and typical amenities. It is a stop that from the platform feels like it has quietly merged into the surrounding countryside. Oddly, the entrance/exit begins as a narrow path that opens out past some houses (ex-railway) and via a five-bar gate onto the road. This gave me the feeling that I was walking through people's gardens, which in fact I was. I could find no sign of the water tower, or the siding that previously existed, however the second, disused, platform is still very visible.

Llanbister Road
Annual passenger usage: 992
Least used station rank: 54
Postcode: LD1 5UW
Ordnance Survey national grid reference: SO174716

Llanbister Road is 69 miles from Llanelli and was opened by the CWR in 1865. Like many other stations on this line it has been subjected to renaming, in this instance to Llanbister Road Halt between 1964 and 1965.

The final stop of the day was also the last on the Heart of Wales Line. My time there was more than two hours, which turned into a real joy. There was nothing strikingly different here, the usual station fittings with the sort of brick shelter I'd seen before, but with additional birds' nests, belonging to an impossible (for me) to identify species. The old station building and second platform are both easy to recognise at Llanbister, but not the signal box, siding or goods shed, all traces of these having been obliterated.

Sitting quietly and taking in the tranquillity of the place, I found myself suddenly treated to a marvellous sight. A male great spotted woodpecker settled on an electricity pole opposite me and proceeded to do the most damage to said pole as possible. I know that these beautiful birds are often on the covers of 'garden bird', books and yes some fortunate people do get them in their gardens, but I don't, and for me this was a real treat.

He remained for ten minutes and left before returning a little later. This he did several times, spending in total at least twenty minutes with me. What a perfect way to complete the Heart of Wales Line.

I visited Yorton on the 'Welsh Marches Line' during my journey home, then Prees and Wrenbury on the same line as a separate day out from Swindon, shortly afterwards.

Yorton
Annual passenger usage: 7,686
Least used station rank: 209
Postcode: SY4 3EP
Ordnance Survey national grid reference: SJ504237

Leaving Llandovery on the final morning and I began the journey home, travelling first to Shrewsbury, then Yorton on the Welsh Marches Line, next to Newport and finally to Swindon.

Yorton was opened in 1858 by the Shrewsbury & Crewe Railway (S&CreweR). The station had two small sidings, but these have now been removed. Nevertheless it is still possible to see where they were once located.

The station has two platforms and access between them is by use of the road (no footbridge here): two sets of stairs for Platform 1, and a ramp for Platform 2. The original station building is still in use on Platform 1, although judging by the amount of dust on the seats not very often. That aside it is always good to see an older building still serving its original purpose. On Platform 2 the station buildings are still there, but now privately owned. Seeing the small painted metal shelter provided for today's travellers I tried to think of a kindly description. The best I could manage was that it would keep the rain off.

Prees
Annual passenger usage: 7,374
Least used station rank: 200
Postcode: SY13 2DW
Ordnance Survey national grid reference: SJ537337

Opened in 1858 by the S&CreweR, Prees has at times provided more of a service to local people than the daily commuter train of today. Two sidings, a goods yard and shed were once here, now long gone. These were adjacent to the station house, which still exists but is no longer railway property.

Today Prees still has two platforms and both are in good order. The usual facilities are all here and both platforms have a metal shelter similar to the one at Yorton, only bigger, but no more attractive. Access between platforms is via the use of ramps and the level crossing, which is controlled by automatic barriers.

Wrenbury
Annual passenger usage: 11,744
Least used station rank: 266
Postcode: CW5 8EX
Ordnance Survey national grid reference: SJ601470

Wrenbury is in many respects similar to Prees, 9 miles to the south. It too was opened in 1858 by the S&CreweR and had a yard and goods shed. The yard is now used by a construction company. The original station building on Platform 2 still exists but has been much altered and is now a private house.

Regular non-stop passenger and freight trains pass both of the two platforms at Wrenbury, undermining the request stop ambience. The shelters on both platforms are similar to those at Prees, although here some of the plexiglass panels have been left clear and unpainted, giving the whole thing a less dank and dark feel. Other facilities are as to be expected. Movement from one platform to the other is by use of ramps and the level crossing, with its automatic barriers.

I noticed on the up platform face a set of signal pulleys, still with pieces of wire attached. A sad reminder of the signal box and semaphore signals that were once here, at a time when the signalman who worked the crossing gates could see the people crossing, probably waving as he recognised their familiar faces. Now there are automatic barriers, efficient, noisy, safe and secure, but no people, save the person monitoring a screen in Cardiff 130 miles away. If you do happen to walk over this crossing, give a wave to the camera, because if anyone happens to be looking they might see you and wave back; but how will you know?

The timetable says Llangammarch, but the station signage clearly states Llangammarch Wells, looking north on 9 July 2018.

Once a busy junction, today Pontarddulais has just one platform, photographed looking towards Swansea on 9 July 2018.

Evening sunshine appears to be making life difficult for the driver of this Class 153 Super Sprinter DMU, forming the 18.21 Swansea to Shrewsbury service as it approaches Llandybie on 9 July 2018.

Llanwrda looking south towards Swansea, photographed on 10 July 2018.

Garth (Powys) seen on 10 July 2018. All signs of the original station have been removed here, with modern housing now occupying the old station yard.

The 14.35 Swansea to Shrewsbury Class 153 Super Sprinter DMU arriving at Ffairfach on 10 July 2018.

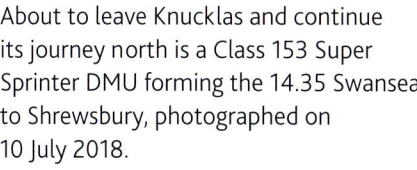

Ffairfach looking north on 10 July 2018. The shelter contains an additional noticeboard detailing seasonal 'Rambler' services.

About to leave Knucklas and continue its journey north is a Class 153 Super Sprinter DMU forming the 14.35 Swansea to Shrewsbury, photographed on 10 July 2018.

Cilmeri, seen here looking south on 11 July 2018. At a distance of 60 miles to Shrewsbury this is close to the halfway point on the Heart of Wales Line.

The very attractive Llangynllo, looking north on 11 July 2018.

Llanbister Road was my last request stop on the Heart of Wales Line and made for a very pleasant visit on a warm summer evening. Viewed from the road bridge facing north on 11 July 2018.

A two-car Class 150 Sprinter DMU set at Yorton on 12 July 2018. The 14.24 Crewe to Shrewsbury service is about to stop, as requested, by me.

Prees looking towards Crewe, photographed on 16 July 2018.

Wrenbury seen on 16 July 2018 looking south towards Shrewsbury.

CHAPTER 8

RETURNING TO THE SCENE OF THE 'CRIME'

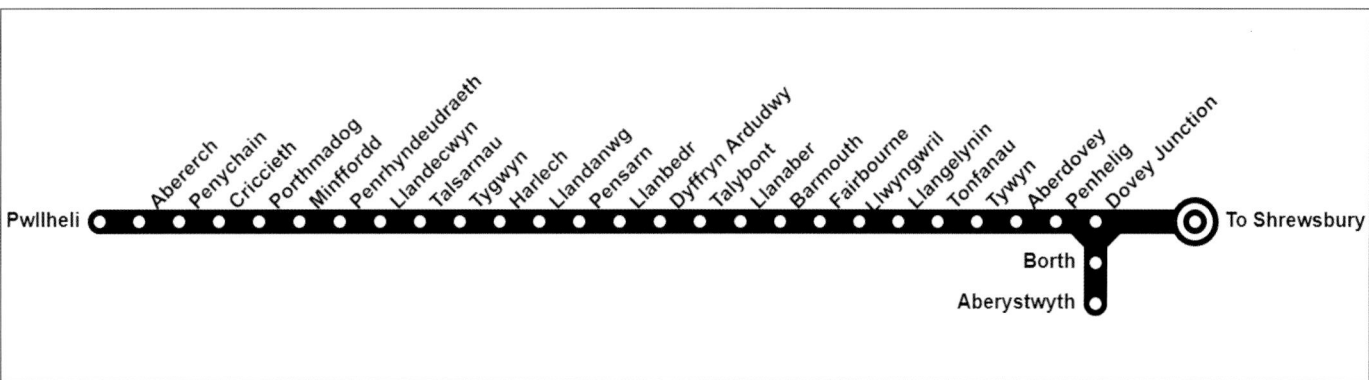

With a little over two weeks having passed since my last trip and maintaining a busy summer schedule I now planned a four-night stay in Barmouth, which would allow me to visit all fifteen stops on the 'Cambrian Coast Line'. I was rather looking forward to staying in Barmouth again, having spent a night there once before. Working on the railway as a 15-year-old I had an allowance of free tickets which could only be used in the Western Region, with Barmouth about the farthest I could possibly go.

Arriving into Barmouth early one evening in 1962 and some hours after the last train home had left, I bedded down on the beach for the night, which apart from a visit from a local bobby proved uneventful enough. I obviously didn't look too much like a desperado so after the torch in the face routine and a quick look in my bag, he told me, "That was a bloody silly thing to do," and not to go into the town, and I was left in peace; happy days.

Today, as I had to pass through Dovey Junction, I factored in an hour-long stop. Although not a request stop, Dovey Junction is remote, having no access other than by rail or on foot. In fact it only exists because the line from the direction of Machynlleth splits here: one direction going to Aberystwyth the other to Pwllheli. I also took the chance to spend some time watching the ospreys, whose nest could be seen from the platform end.

Morfa Mawddach
Annual passenger usage: 11,434
Least used station rank: 260
Postcode: LL39 1BQ
Ordnance Survey national grid reference: SH628141

Morfa Mawddach was originally called Barmouth Junction when opened by the Aberystwith (*sic*) & Welsh Coast Railway (A&WCR) in 1865, taking on its current name in 1960. It is a shadow of what it once was, in that there were once three signal boxes and four platforms, and it was at one time the junction with the line to Ruabon and the short lived Arthog Tramway.

Morfa Mawddach is in a beautiful location, with views of the estuary, mountains, Barmouth Bridge and the town itself, yet the station is now unrecognisable from when I passed through here in 1962. The usual facilities, including a non-working payphone, are present, and a metal shelter painted green, not Arriva 'yuck', despite this being in Arriva territory – super. Old platform remains are easily seen and accessible, with the disused trackbed forming the start of the Mawddach Trail. There is a large car park which is popular with walkers using the trail.

Penhelig
Annual passenger usage: 8,570
Least used station rank: 222
Postcode: LL35 0LU
Ordnance Survey national grid reference: SN620961

Despite the A&WCR opening the line here in 1863, Penhelig did not open until 1933, by which time it was under GWR ownership.[1] Originally Penhelig Halt, the suffix was dropped in 1968.

Located on a relatively short stretch of track between two tunnels, and on the side of a hill overlooking the sea, Penhelig feels as though it is part of some full size model railway layout. Watching my train disappear into the tunnel, then standing alone on the platform, I could easily have been one of those figures people dot about on their model stations to add realism. In my case I would be the one with a bag just setting off on another journey.

Penhelig has all the modern facilities expected at a request stop, including a shelter – a *magnificent* shelter. Recently and sympathetically renovated, it is the original GWR building, built from timber and with a pagoda-style roof. Resplendent in a colour scheme of two-tone cream and green paint externally, it has red benches inside. The shelter is divided into two distinct parts with separate entrances, with only one side open for public use. The ticket window has been left in place but is painted over on the public side. On my visit in 2018 the door to the other non-public side was locked, but peering through the window I could see some of the old ticket office paraphernalia still in place.

Llwyngwril
Annual passenger usage: 28,560
Least used station rank: 417
Postcode: LL37 2JS
Ordnance Survey national grid reference: SH589097

Llwyngwril was opened in 1863 by the A&WCR, and survives to this day albeit in much reduced circumstances. Gone is the second platform, although it is still visible, no doubt patiently watching the other platform while awaiting its own passengers who will never come. The signal box has also vanished and so too has the water tower, but then it's been a long time since locomotives paused here to quench their thirst.

The station today has a car park, noticeboards, an information screen and a metal shelter. There is also a Harrington Hump installed on the platform. The old station building is evident as a private house. Something that sets Llwyngwril apart from any other station is that the village is home to a group of 'yarn bombers' who have not only applied their skills and efforts to the village but also to the station. 'Yarn bombing' is a type of street art that employs yarn rather than paint. On my visit the station boasted a life-size porter, a bicycle (I kid you not) and Paddington Bear with his suitcase. There was also a lot of knitted luggage on the platform; great fun.[2]

Llanbedr
Annual passenger usage: 11,340
Least used station rank: 259
Postcode: LL45 2LR
Ordnance Survey national grid reference: SH579268

After my first night in Barmouth, I had a busy day planned with the timetable allowing me to visit five stops in a day. First up was to be Llanbedr, some 7 miles north and 25 miles from the end of the line at Pwllheli.

Although the line had been opened by the Cambrian Railways (CAMR) in 1867, it was not until 1923 that the GWR opened the station, then called Talwrn Bach Halt. It became just Talwrn Bach in 1968 before finally being renamed Llanbedr in 1978.

It is quite an open spot and the station is only half a mile from the village. Despite this it still manages to have a rural and isolated feel; even the traffic using the level crossing is sparse. A metal shelter and an outside bench are provided for passenger comfort along with the ubiquitous information screen and noticeboards. Modern lighting has been installed, with parts of the old lighting columns left in place to quietly rust away. In my two hours there I identified reed buntings and reed warblers close to the platform. The male bunting in particular is a very handsome little bird. I also saw a steady flow of gulls, black-headed mostly, but some larger types, steadily criss-crossing overhead.

Pensarn
Annual passenger usage: 2,736
Least used station rank: 117
Postcode: CW5 8EX
Ordnance Survey national grid reference: SH578279

Situated on the river Arto and close to the wharf, Pensarn was opened by the CAM in 1867. Eighteen years later in 1885 the CAM re-named it Llanbedr and Pensarn, a name it retained until 1978 when it became simply Pensarn. Only a single platform has ever existed here but in the past there was a passing loop, a siding and a goods yard.

There is a metal shelter similar in design to others on this line, this being one of the bigger examples, with the plexiglass panels left clear and not painted over. A small car park is adjacent and all the other usual facilities are available. The platform is rather long, and the farthest end has become weed covered. All signs of the signal box and the other buildings previously on the platform have vanished. The area once occupied by the goods yard is now heavily overgrown, hiding evidence of its former life. The only exception to this is a loading gauge standing as a lonely sentinel at the very far end of the yard.

Llandanwg
Annual passenger usage: 4,312
Least used station rank: 145
Postcode: LL46 2SB
Ordnance Survey national grid reference: SH570286

Leaving Pensarn I had to quickly make sure the guard knew that I wanted to alight at Llandanwg, it being only two minutes distant. "Llandanwg please," I said. He just gave me a quizzical look. I said, "The next one up the line thanks," and this did register with him and he repeated a name that was quite as alien to me as my attempt must have been to him. Still, we got it sorted and we moved off.

When opened by the CAM in 1867 Llandanwg had a railway line but no station, for that it had to wait until 1929 when the GWR built Llandanwg Halt, and so the name remained until 1968 when it lost the suffix. It has always been a wayside halt with minimum facilities, and a single platform. A platelayers hut once stood opposite the platform, of which no trace is discernible today.

My first glimpse of Llandanwg told me that this would be another for my favourites list. It has everything that for me makes a great request stop. Access to the station is through a gateway on the road overbridge, and down a long ramp. Once on the platform, there are noticeboards, an information screen, a bench seat and a plant tub but no plants. There is a shelter, small and constructed from a mix of corrugated iron and wooden boards, reminiscent of the one I had seen at Cilmeri, but with a major difference – here there were swifts nesting in the roof space. They were squeezing through the ends of the corrugations and into the roof void. How lucky I was to be able to sit and watch these gorgeous birds popping their heads out of the roof before flying off, and when inside the shelter to be able to hear the young clamouring to be fed. Forgive me for saying this, but my time there flew by.

Tygwyn
Annual passenger usage: 1,580
Least used station rank: 79
Postcode: CW5 8EX
Ordnance Survey national grid reference: SJ601470

The GWR opened Tygwyn Halt in 1927, some sixty years after the CAM had built the line, and it was later renamed Tygwyn in 1968.

It is a quite basic little station. There is a house close by but no other sign of human habitation can be seen from the platform, and this gives it a very rural feel. There is a level crossing at the end of the platform and I wondered if the house once served as a crossing keeper's cottage. Just inside the station entrance gate are a help point and noticeboards, and on the platform there is an information screen. Access is by use of a ramp. The shelter is made of metal with large plexiglass panels and is completely open at the front. While this might not be too good for keeping the rain off, it does give the shelter a light and open feeling. Outside is a bench on which is displayed the wording, 'This Station is Adopted by Twenty Thirteen Friends Club' – the name of a local group who look after the stop. It is thanks to this group that Tygwyn is the pretty stop that it is – there are wooden flower tubs and the shelter has been stencilled with various flower and wildlife motifs.

Talsarnau
Annual passenger usage: 5,400
Least used station rank: 168
Postcode: LL47 6UA
Ordnance Survey national grid reference: SH609361

After studying the local map at Tygwyn station I realised the distance to Talsarnau by road is only 1.5 miles, a comfortable walking distance. The decision was quickly made and thirty minutes later I arrived at Talsarnau on foot: a rare event.

Talsarnau was opened by the CAM in 1867, the same year it took the line over from the A&WCR. Between 1877 and the 1890s the name was spelled Tal-sarnau.[3] A small siding ran to the rear of the main station buildings, entry being controlled by a ground frame located towards the south end of the platform.

The former main station building, now a private dwelling, is still very much in evidence, but I could see no trace of the siding or any of the other buildings that were once here. A help point, noticeboards and the usual information screen are all in evidence. Platform access is via a ramp and a Harrington Hump has been installed. There is a green shelter of what seems to be the standard style on the Cambrian Coast Line, which has a working payphone and a mural painted by local children, which makes it somewhat more attractive.

I waved down my expected train, a Class 158 DMU, and boarded. The guard asked me where I was going, but not for my ticket, for we had met earlier in the day. I settled in for my thirty-five minute journey to Barmouth, thinking to myself that in the first two days of this trip I had completed over half the stops on this line; most satisfactory.

Llanaber
Annual passenger usage: 3,318
Least used station rank: 127
Postcode: LL42 1AZ
Ordnance Survey national grid reference: SH598180

My first request stop on day three of the Cambrian Coast Line expedition was Llanaber. Only 1.5 miles north of Barmouth, it instantly became a favourite of mine.

Officially opened in 1914 by the CAM and called Llanaber Halt, it had however been open on an occasional seasonal basis since 1911, with details only publicised locally.[4] BR renamed it Llanaber in 1968. Despite its proximity to Barmouth the feeling of remoteness is palpable. The station is perched precariously on a ledge below the village and just above the Irish Sea. On my visit the sea was calm but it is easy to imagine what it would be like here during a storm. At the north end of the station there is a lineside board warning drivers of the possibility of waves washing over the track. During 2014 the line remained closed for five months due to the track being washed away just north of the station.

Access to the platform is by a steep track surfaced with stone chippings, but once there I found an information screen, noticeboards and a payphone. Painted half in Arriva colours and half in red rust is a metal shelter, the rust no doubt due to the constant actions of the sea. A stop with a real feeling of bleakness, and all the better for it.

Tonfanau
Annual passenger usage: 9,292
Least used station rank: 123
Postcode: LL36 8LP
Ordnance Survey national grid reference: SH563038

The CAM opened Tonfanau in 1895. A siding and a level crossing were once both here. To the south of the station a tramway led to the Tonfanau Quarry, which closed in 1998. During the Second World War an army base was established to the west of the station. This closed in 1966, reopening briefly in 1972 when it became a centre for Ugandan Asian refugees.

Just a single platform exists today and access to it is by the use of a gated barrow crossing and ramp. There are the usual basic facilities including a metal shelter and a bench on the platform. All signs of the buildings that used to be on the platform have been swept away. Apart from a single house close by, which looks to be the rebuilt stationmaster's cottage, there is no sign of any other human activity nearby. A few minutes' walk from the station, going past the ruins of the old army base, is the beach, and during my time there it was deserted as far as the eye could see in both directions.

Dyffryn Ardudwy
Annual passenger usage: 16,636
Least used station rank: 309
Postcode: LL42 2EU
Ordnance Survey national grid reference system: SH581233

First opened by the CAM in 1867 as Dyffryn, Dyffryn Ardudwy became Dyffryn-on-Sea in 1924 and then Dyffryn Ardudwy in 1948. The station buildings were substantial, with two platforms and a platform-mounted signal box. A siding was also present.

On my visit I found what was for me a 'real' request stop, although it was busier than most I had seen, with at least six people getting off with me. The first thing I noticed was that the level crossing had a crossing keeper – not flashing lights or an automatic barrier, but a real person. I wondered how long it would be before he is replaced by flashing lights and a siren when the station is finally dehumanised. The old station buildings have been converted into a private dwelling. The second platform is still intact if a little overgrown. Platform 1, which is in use today, is reached by a ramp from the level crossing. A metal shelter, which is painted green, contains both a payphone and a mural painted by local schoolchildren. There is an additional bench nearby. The usual information screen and noticeboards are also present.

Very little birdlife was apparent in the vicinity, possibly due to the heat at that time of day, but butterflies were plentiful. I even managed to get a very acceptable photograph of a Wall brown, something that pleased me because I do find butterflies very difficult to photograph in that they are constantly on the move.

Talybont
Annual passenger usage: 26,936
Least used station rank: 404
Postcode: LL43 2AQ
Ordnance Survey national grid reference: SH586214

Talybont was first opened by the CAM in 1914 as Talybont Halt, a name it retained until it became just Talybont when BR dropped the suffix in 1968.

After leaving Dyffryn Ardudwy I had a short trip south to Talybont, which is in fact only a little over a mile away. Stepping down from the train I was the only person alighting (arriving in true request stop style), but to my amazement about thirty or forty people were waiting to climb aboard. What I hadn't realised was that there are several large caravan parks in the vicinity. Holidaymakers who want a change from a day on the nearby beaches can hop on the train to Barmouth, which is only ten minutes away, which makes Talybont quite a busy station during the summer months.

The station is not particularly inviting, with lots of recent steel mesh fencing, used to channel people to and from the platform. This is no doubt due to safety concerns about the relatively small platform, and as I have already said it can get quite busy. The shelter gives quite an impression, with a semi-circular plexiglass roof mounted on four pillars and an internal metal screen enclosure, the first of this type I had seen. There is no car park, but a drop-off area is available. From here people are channelled quite literally onto the platform, past the steel fencing. There is a payphone in the shelter but no help point, however information screens and noticeboards are both available.

Llandecwyn
Annual passenger usage: 1,886
Least used station rank: 95
Postcode: LL47 6YL
Ordnance Survey national grid reference: SH618379

Llandecwyn was opened by the GWR in 1930. Originally Llandecwyn Halt, it lost the suffix in 1968, and survived a closure attempt in the 1990s. The station today is a very modern, clean and functional place having been completely rebuilt in 2014 as part of a project to replace the Pont Briwet Bridge.

Situated next to a busy road with access to platform level by use of a ramp or stairs, it has a metal and plexiglass shelter and the usual other facilities. Despite (due to its modernity) not having the request stop feel of others, it is fortunate that it is still there at all, having survived both a closure attempt and a complete rebuild. Turning my back on the road, I realised that what it does have is a magnificent view, across the Dwyryd Estuary to the town of Penrhyndeudraeth on the other side. During the hour-plus I spent here the tide was out and I made good use of my binoculars to watch the various waders feeding on the mudflats in the evening sunshine. While identifying waders is certainly not a strong point for me, I did manage a few, notably oystercatcher, common sandpiper and little ringed plover.

Abererch
Annual passenger usage: 2,506
Least used station rank: 111
Postcode: LL53 6PJ
Ordnance Survey national grid reference: SH403360

On the morning of my fourth and last day on the Cambrian Coast Line, I travelled north, this time to Abererch, some 30 miles away, and only 2 miles from Pwllheli at the end of the line. I had also reached a milestone in this request stop odyssey because my previous stop, Llandecwyn, was number seventy-six, and Abererch would take me past the halfway point.

The CAM opened Abererch in 1867 and it became Abererch Halt in 1956, losing the suffix twelve years later in 1968 to become Abererch once more. An OS map from 1963 shows a small siding on the west side of the station, once the site of a camping coach during the summer months. There was also a crossing keeper's cottage adjacent to the station.

It is a typical request stop, with an information screen, noticeboards and a help point. There is no car park or drop-off point other than using the adjacent road. The shelter is rather strange in that it is open on three sides. It has a roof and back only, with the front facing the Irish Sea 150 metres away. My advice to anyone visiting in stormy weather is to wear a mac.

Penychain
Annual passenger usage: 4,126
Least used station rank: 140
Postcode: LL53 6HJ
Ordnance Survey national grid reference: SH428364

Opened as Penychain Halt by the GWR in 1933 with a single platform, the station saw considerable use during the Second World War by personnel from the nearby naval shore establishment. Some time after the war ended, the navy base became Pwllheli Butlin's holiday camp. In 1947 the station became Penychain with the dropping of the 'halt' suffix. The increasing numbers of people arriving and leaving at the beginning and end of their holidays saw the addition of a second platform. A signal box was sited at the eastern end of the station, and I have seen a photograph which shows a station nameboard that states 'Penychain for Pwllheli Holiday Camp'.

I did have a fellow passenger when I arrived, but he quickly disappeared leaving me alone standing outside a huge stone-built shelter more akin to a barn. This and the very long platform were both signs of much busier days when people arrived for their holidays by train rather than by car. The entrance/exit is by a series of fenced ramps zig-zagging up to the road. There is a payphone in the shelter, and an information screen on the platform but there is no help point.

Morfa Mawddach was once called Barmouth Junction, and traces of the old platform and line to Ruabon can be found behind the shelter. Photographed looking north on 31 July 2018.

Penhelig, with its beautifully restored shelter, photographed facing towards Dovey Junction on 31 July 2018.

The old station buildings and modern shelter at Llwyngwril. Note the knitted ticket collector and luggage, seen on 31 July 2018.

Left: Llanbedr looking towards Pwllheli, photographed on 1 August 2018.

Opposite above: Llandanwg is to me another request stop that has it all. It even had swifts nesting in the roof of the shelter. Seen here on 1 August 2018 looking south.

Opposite below: Tygwyn looking south on 1 August 2018. A beautifully maintained stop, and a credit to the work of the local volunteer group.

Pensarn seen on 1 August 2018, facing south.

RETURNING TO THE SCENE OF THE 'CRIME' • **97**

The 17.42 Pwllheli to Machynlleth service comprised of a two-car Class 158 Express Sprinter DMU arriving at Talsarnau on 1 August 2018.

Llanaber is only 1.5 miles from Barmouth, but nonetheless still had a feeling of remoteness when I visited. Looking north in August 2018.

The Class 158 Express Sprinter DMU appeared to have a monopoly of Cambrian Coast Line services during my visit. Here, one is arriving at Llanaber forming the 14.56 Dovey Junction to Pwllheli on 1 August 2018.

The 11.37 Pwllheli to Machynlleth passing Tonfanau on 2 August 2018. This service comprised a two-car Class 158 Express Sprinter DMU.

Left: Tonfanau proved to be a good spot for butterflies, with at least four species noted. I find butterflies very difficult to photograph as they never settle for long, but this gatekeeper did give me just long enough to capture it on 2 August 2018.

Opposite above: Talybont looking towards Pwllheli on 2 August 2018. The station suddenly became very busy shortly after my arrival with people from nearby caravan parks going to Barmouth for the day.

Opposite below: The very modern and utilitarian Llandecwyn photographed looking south on 2 August 2018.

Dyffryn Ardudwy on 2 August 2018 and the 10.55 Machynlleth to Pwllheli service, here formed of a Class 158 Express Sprinter DMU, is about to stop.

Above: Abererch seen on 2 August 2018. Less than 2 miles behind the camera is Pwllheli, the last stop on the Cambrian Coast Line.

Opposite above: Penychain with its barn-like shelter, now hardly used since holidaymakers mostly arrive at the nearby camp by car. Looking north on 4 August 2018.

Opposite below: A Class 158 Express Sprinter DMU passing Penychain on 4 August 2018. This service is the 09.34 Pwllheli to Birmingham International.

RETURNING TO THE SCENE OF THE 'CRIME' • 103

CHAPTER 9

THE SOGGY WALKERS

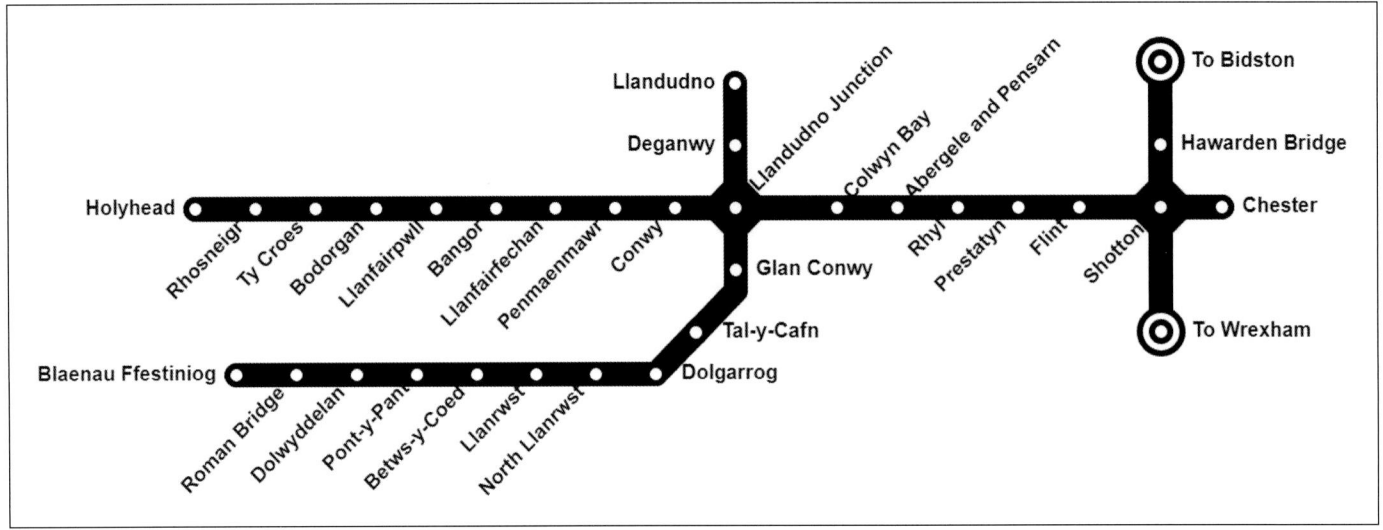

By September 2018 I still had one major trip for the year, involving a four-night stay at a pub in Llandudno Junction. This allowed me to complete North Wales and the Conwy Valley Line, a total of seventeen stops. I was really looking forward to this because I had never travelled over some of these lines before.

My stay in Llandudno Junction turned out to be most agreeable, with a very pleasant landlady, excellent meals and a room both comfortable and immaculately presented. The wi-fi code of 'Killers' did give me slight cause for concern, and I went to bed on the first night hoping that this implied nothing more than someone was a fan of the rock group The Killers, and nothing sinister. After all I didn't want to wake up in the morning and find myself dead.

Llanfairfechan
Annual passenger usage: 14,040
Least used station rank: 288
Postcode: LL33 0BP
Ordnance Survey national grid reference: SH677751

Llanfairfechan was opened by the L&NWR in 1860, although the line had been in existence since 1848. The current station is much changed since its early days. Gone are the signal box, station buildings and the goods yard which closed in 1964. The station buildings were demolished in 1987, to allow work on the adjacent A55.

Both platforms have information screens and noticeboards, and solidly built stone shelters. These shelters date from the remodelling that took place in 1987. Platform 1 has a payphone and there is a car park on this side. The only original structures still remaining are the platforms themselves, and a footbridge.

Penmaenmawr
Annual passenger usage: 11,692
Least used station rank: 264
Postcode: LL34 6AT
Ordnance Survey national grid reference: SH718765

First opened by the Chester & Holyhead Railway (C&HR) in 1849 and known as Penmaenmaur, this was changed to Penmaenmawr in 1860. It was once a very grandiose station with impressive buildings. On the north side were transfer sidings used to accommodate the traffic of stone aggregate from a local quarry.

The old station building is still intact on Platform 2, and is now privately owned. There is a bench seat but no shelter. The original station canopy is still in place and provides adequate cover. Platform 2 has a metal shelter with plexiglass panels, although most of these were missing when I visited. The original building has gone but part of the facade does still stand. Both platforms have the usual information screens and noticeboards, plus Harrington Humps. A footbridge links the platforms and there is a payphone near the station entrance. The sidings are still in place, but now overgrown, and the signal box, built in 1950, is still extant at the northeast end of Platform 2.

Llanfairpwll
Annual passenger usage: 20,604
Least used station rank: 343
Postcode: LL61 5UJ
Ordnance Survey national grid reference: SH525715

My last stop on my first day in North Wales was Llanfairpwll, also known by its other title Llanfairpwllgwyngyllgogerychwyrndrobwllllantysiliogogogoch, the longest station name in Great Britain. The Fairbourne Miniature Railway did for a time have a stop with an even longer name when it renamed 'Golf Halt' Gorsafawddach aidraigddanheddogleddollonpenrhynareurdraeth ceredigion, but this reverted to Golf Halt in 2007.

When Llanfairpwll was opened by the C&HR in 1848 it served as the terminus for the line from Holyhead until the Britannia Bridge opened. The turntable, sidings and goods yard that were once here have all disappeared. BR closed the station in 1966 but reopened it in 1970 with a single platform when it again acted as the terminus for the line from Holyhead, after the Britannia Bridge temporarily closed due to fire damage. It closed again in 1973 for a short time to allow for the addition of a second platform, and the station was brought up to its current standard.

During my time there it became quite busy for a request stop with at least ten people waiting for a train going in the Chester direction, and as it was about 18.00 I presumed these were people going home from work. Both platforms have bus stop-style shelters, the usual basic facilities and that long station sign that all tourists have to do a selfie in front of. The old station building on Platform 1 is now under private ownership. The platforms are linked by the recently refurbished footbridge, and a little to the east is the signal box immediately adjacent to a manned level crossing.

Bodorgan
Annual passenger usage: 5,552
Least used station rank: 173
Postcode: LL62 5BL
Ordnance Survey national grid reference: SH386701

In 1848 the C&HR opened Bodorgan, which previously had a goods yard and water tower. The quite extensive station buildings on Platform 1 incorporated the stationmaster's house and a signal box was situated on Platform 2.

On my arrival I found the main station buildings on Platform 1 still intact but privately owned. Incorporated into this building is a shelter with benches. The other platform has a stone-built shelter complete with swallows' nests, but due to an impending storm and very strong winds, no birds were flying. Arrival/departure screens, noticeboards and a payphone are all available. A drop-off point provides level access, but the second platform can only be reached by use of a barrow crossing.

While taking my photographs a local man approached me and asked why I was interested in Bodorgan, so I explained about my project to visit and photograph all the request stops in Great Britain. He told me he remembered using this station in his childhood when his mother would take him to visit relatives. He said he had been taking photographs here every time any changes had been made, and had pictures going back to the 1960s when the goods yard still existed. Then he took me on a full tour of the site, showing me the extent of the yard, the site of the signal box and which doorways in the station building led to the waiting room, toilets and other points of interest. A lovely man and such a nice thing to do, but then I felt he was very proud of 'his' station.

Conwy
Annual passenger usage: 57,006
Least used station rank: 616
Postcode: LL32 8LD
Ordnance Survey national grid reference: SH770784

Initially known as Conway when opened by the C&HR in 1848, that name was retained for more than 100 years. In keeping with its status of a historic walled town, extensive station buildings on both platforms were constructed in a mock-Tudor style, with a footbridge linking the platforms. Conway closed as part of the Beeching cuts in 1966, and shortly afterwards all the station buildings were demolished. The station reopened in 1987 with the name Conwy.

The station was quite busy during my visit, and it was hard to imagine any train passing through without having to stop. In fact, with a passenger usage of over 57,000 annually, it is the busiest request stop in Wales. Facilities are the expected information screens and noticeboards, with stone shelters and step-free access on both platforms. Connection between the two is via a road bridge. Trains coming from the east make a grand entrance into Conwy by passing through a magnificent crenelated archway.

Valley
Annual passenger usage: 17,742
Least used station rank: 295
Postcode: LL65 3EW
Ordnance Survey national grid reference: SH291791

Some 118 years after being opened by the C&HR in 1848, Valley, like many others, fell to the Beeching axe and closed in 1966. Sidings once existed at the western end of the station that served a nearby corn mill and cattle pens. In 1962 new sidings were constructed approximately 250 metres to the east of the station to service the nearby Wylfa nuclear power station. These were converted to a triangle in 1989 to allow the turning of locomotives. Valley reopened to passengers in 1982.

Today, Valley has two platforms with step-free access to both by use of the level crossing. The original station building on the eastbound platform is still intact although it does look a little sad and uncared for. No shelter or seating is provided on this platform, and the only escape from the elements would be to huddle under a small canopy that is part of the old station building. Noticeboards and an information screen exist on the westbound platform along with an aluminium and plexiglass shelter. There is a signal box which controls the nearby siding and the level crossing with semaphore signals. It's good to see an original wooden signal box still in use, although by its appearance I can only think NR ran out of paint several years ago.

I had seen very few signs of bird life on this trip, because of the very strong wind. I did however manage to find a shaggy inkcap (or lawyer's wig) fungus. Although not rare, this was a particularly good specimen and rather early in the season.

Ty Croes
Annual passenger usage: 4,292
Least used station rank: 143
Postcode: LL63 5HX
Ordnance Survey national grid reference: SH348723

Built in 1848 by the C&HR, Ty Croes had two staggered platforms separated by a road. In 1872 a signal box was added. A warehouse and a goods yard were situated at the west end of the station, which closed in 1964.

Arriving at Ty Croes I found a brick-built signal box still working with semaphore signals. The level crossing gates that separate the two platforms are still operated by hand. The eastbound platform has step-free access, and a small metal shelter which contains a payphone. Some brick foundations of the old station buildings are still clearly visible near the shelter. On the west side of the station it was possible on my visit to see the extent of the former goods yard. The westbound platform has a stone-built shelter, but this would not be accessible to wheelchair users due to a narrow entrance gate. Noticeboards and information screens are located on both platforms. There is no car park, just a passenger drop-off point.

The high winds were still discouraging most of the bird life from flying, but as compensation I was able to spend five minutes watching a common toad ambling along the inside of one of the rails.

Rhosneigr
Annual passenger usage: 11,558
Least used station rank: 262
Postcode: LL64 5QZ
Ordnance Survey national grid reference: SH328737

Rhosneigr was opened by the L&NW in 1907. The original station buildings were made of wood but replaced by concrete at a later date.[1] The station was closed for the whole of 1917/1918, reopening on 1 February 1919.[2]

The old concrete station building on Platform 1 is still intact but not in use, having had all the doors and windows sealed up, but a small brick shelter offers refuge to the modern traveller. On Platform 2 there is a typical aluminium and plexiglass shelter. Information screens and noticeboards are provided and so is a payphone. A small car park is available with access between the platforms via the road under the railway line. The station is step-free, but it is advised on the National Rail Enquiries website that wheelchair access is not possible because the 'paths are not compliant'.

Glan Conwy
Annual passenger usage: 3,166
Least used station rank: 121
Postcode: LL28 5ED
Ordnance Survey national grid reference: SH802761

Opened by the Conway & Llanrwst Railway (C&LlR) in 1863 as Llansaintffraid, in 1885 the station was renamed Glan Conway. Succumbing to the Beeching axe and closing in 1964, it reopened in 1970. In 1980 a final renaming made it Glan Conwy. A small siding was once located at the southern end of the station.

Day three of my North Wales trip, and I had now moved on to the 'Conwy Valley Line', with Glan Conwy my first stop, 1.5 miles from Llandudno Junction. It is a charming spot on the banks of the River Conwy and with expansive mud flats when the tide is out. It's a great place to observe waders, but not on the day I visited. 'Storm Ali' had arrived with a vengeance and winds of over 80mph were blowing up the river. A few gulls were out but most of the bird life had obviously taken whatever shelter it could find.

The former stationmaster's house still exists behind a white picket fence and now a private home. There is a bus stop-type shelter with a payphone, together with posterboards and an information screen on the platform to assist passengers. The car park has step-free access to help the less mobile gain access to the station, while the extensive raised section of the platform will assist the less agile with boarding/alighting.

Pont-y-Pant
Annual passenger usage: 842
Least used station rank: 46
Postcode: LL25 0DQ
Ordnance Survey national grid reference: SH752536

Pont-y-Pant was opened by the L&NWR in 1879. In 1904 it became Pontypant, and then in 1956 the hyphens were restored.[3] Sidings existed at the north end of the station and were used in part to load slate that had come from the nearby Rhiw-goch quarry.

Despite a rather wet and windy day I did enjoy my visit. I found the privately owned original station building to be immaculately maintained. There were flower planters and a metal framed wooden slatted bench with 'Pont-y-Pant' in relief on the back. The shelter has a green and cream metal frame with plexiglass panels and a payphone. Although access to the platform is step-free it would not be suitable for wheelchairs due to a narrow gate. An arrival/departure screen and noticeboard are all present. The extent of the one-time sidings can be made out, but it is hard to imagine slate being loaded in what is now a quiet rural backwater.

Tal-y-Cafn
Annual passenger usage: 1,148
Least used station rank: 60
Postcode: LL28 5RR
Ordnance Survey national grid reference: SH787717

The C&LlR opened Tal-y-Cafn in 1863. It has been known for most of its years as Tal-y-Cafn & Eglwysbach after it was renamed thus in 1885. In 1974 it reverted to its original name Tal-y-Cafn. There were two platforms with a passing loop and a siding at the southern end of the station, and a ground frame controlling the signals that protected the level crossing.

Storm Ali was in full swing when I arrived, but at least the rain had stopped, which allowed me to enjoy my visit. The station is maintained by local volunteers, and the disused second platform is now a garden, complete with an old wooden board still proclaiming that this is Tal-y-Cafn & Eglwysbach. There are posterboards, plus an information screen and a payphone. The original station building is mostly privately owned, but NR do maintain an office here for use by the crossing keeper, as the gates are manually operated. The crossing keeper invited me into his inner sanctum for a brew and a chance to get out of the wind; you don't get that at Paddington or Waterloo. The shelter is without doubt the strangest one I had encountered anywhere, suitable only for one, two if very close friends, or three if you are prepared to risk legal action – the small size is due to the fact that this hut once housed the ground frame before it was taken out of service.[4]

Roman Bridge

Annual passenger usage: 942
Least used station rank: 50
Postcode: LL25 0JE
Ordnance Survey national grid reference: SH712514

The L&NWR opened Roman Bridge in 1879, later adding a goods yard, which closed in 1956.[5] It is another attractive station situated in a beautiful location in the Lledr Valley. The original station building remains, with some very nice details, including a bench painted in green and red with the station name on it, and a small canopy with the supporting columns again in green and red. A modern shelter, similar to the one at Pont-y-Pant, along with the usual noticeboards, complete the platform facilities. There is also a set-down point with step-free access.

After a short while in this isolated place the rain began in earnest, forcing me to retreat into the shelter. Some thirty minutes later it suddenly became standing room only, as I found myself surrounded by a group of soggy walkers looking for somewhere out of the rain to have a snack break. One of them spotted a badge on my bag – this lady, like myself, was the secretary of a local Unite Community branch. A general political discussion took place, covering among other things the merits, or not, of Margaret Thatcher (the 'Lady' did feature on my badge) and even though it was raining I was at least among friends.

North Llanrwst

Annual passenger usage: 1,942
Least used station rank: 97
Postcode: LL26 0EG
Ordnance Survey national grid reference: SH795622

Opened as Llanrwst by the C&LlR in 1863 it was at that time the terminus for the line from Conwy. The station was re-sited in 1868 to allow through traffic with the continuation of the line southwards. Renamed Llanrwst and Trefriw in 1884, it then reverted to Llanrwst in 1974. In 1989 it became Llanrwst North which allowed a brand new station, built closer to the town, to take on the name Llanrwst. Finally, in 2004, it changed again to North Llanrwst.

Stepping down I found a station of rather grand proportions with the buildings on both platforms intact, although sadly all the doors and windows were boarded up. Aside from that, the station is very attractive with detailing on the canopy and benches picked out in red and green. There are no modern shelters, the existing platform canopies providing any necessary shelter. The footbridge that once existed is gone, with access between platforms now via a barrow crossing. At the northern end of the station is a signal box and there are working semaphore signals. The large goods yard is gone, the site having become a light industrial estate. Station access is step-free but National Rail Enquiries advise that the entrance is not suitable for wheelchairs. Arrival/departure screens and timetables are all available.

The rain had stopped and I had nearly two hours on a fairly large station, with impressive architecture and semaphore signals. Not only that, but I had it all to myself – North Llanrwst belonged to me. When the time neared for the arrival of my train the signal arm moved to the off position, and in doing so it made that wonderful 'clunk' sound, once commonplace but sadly now nearly extinct. All this and railway mindfulness; I really couldn't have asked for more.

Dolwyddelan

Annual passenger usage: 3,442
Least used station rank: 132
Postcode: LL25 0TJ
Ordnance Survey national grid reference: SH737521

Dolwyddelan was opened by the L&NW in 1879 and renamed some time around 1880 as Dolwyddelen at the request of Lady Willoughby, reverting to Dolwyddelan in 1980.[6] The station had a passing loop with an island platform, an extensive goods yard with shed and a footbridge which led from the platform end onto the road.

On the 19 November 1909 the *North Wales Weekly News* reported that a David Evans had been in court charged with alighting from a train while in motion at Dolwyddelan. The stationmaster said he saw the defendant alight from a train travelling at 15mph; he called after the defendant who he said he had warned before. Whereupon, David Evans gave a false name. In court Evans apologised and was fined two shillings and sixpence (£15 in 2018) plus costs.[7]

This station has extensive gardens which are maintained by volunteers. A disused rail trolley, presumably from a local mine, rests on the platform. The goods yard is gone and because the platform is no longer an island, this has allowed the footbridge to be removed while still allowing step-free access to the road. All the usual modern facilities are in place, including one of the better looking bus stop-type shelters.

After boarding the train the guard recognised me and simply asked where I was going.

She then said, "Didn't I see you on one of my trains yesterday?"

"That's quite possible, I have been about for a few days," I replied. She then went off towards the front of the train, returning a few minutes later to say, "The driver has just asked me, who is that man that keeps waving us down?" I explained what I was doing and she went off again only to return to say, "The driver says he wishes he had the time to do that himself." It seemed he was a rail fan. Maybe for his next holiday he will stop driving and go rovering?

Hawarden Bridge
Annual passenger usage: 3,296
Least used station rank: 124
Postcode: CH5 1PY
Ordnance Survey national grid reference: SJ311695

On my fourth day in North Wales I made an early start, travelling by train to Shotton Low Level, followed by a short walk to Shotton High Level and then by train onto Hawarden Bridge.

Opened as Hawarden Bridge Halt in 1924 by the London & North Eastern Railway (LNER) it retained this name until 1953 when the suffix was dropped. The station is situated on the 'Borderlands Line', 13 miles north of Wrexham Central, and on the north side of the River Dee. I found Hawarden Bridge to be a rather run down and unloved place, with metal shelters on both platforms, and the usual information screens. Access to both platforms is step-free, but movement between them would entail the use of a barrow crossing. To the northern end of the station is a working signal box with colour-light signals, and to the southern end is the rather magnificent Hawarden Bridge itself.

Deganwy
Annual passenger usage: 10,940
Least used station rank: 253
Postcode: LL31 9EJ
Ordnance Survey national grid reference: SH779790

I decided to walk from Hawarden Bridge to Shotton Low Level where I could catch a direct train to Deganwy. That way I could walk across the actual bridge, and have a close up look at the structure.

The only intermediate stop between Llandudno Junction and Llandudno is Deganway, as it was first known when opened by the L&NWR in 1866, before being renamed Deganwy in 1882. A pier and sidings were built to accommodate the loading of slate coming from Blaenau Ffestiniog. These sidings were removed in the 1970s and the pier area has now been redeveloped with a marina and housing.

Deganwy is a fairly busy station serving a small but busy town, in a picturesque location on the banks of the River Conwy. There are two platforms connected by a footbridge and a bus stop-type shelter on both. Arrival/departure screens and posterboards are also present. The platforms are quite long at over 300 metres. At the northern end is a signal box, semaphore signals and a level crossing.

Dolgarrog
Annual passenger usage: 612
Least used station rank: 38
Postcode: LL26 0YR
Ordnance Survey national grid reference: SH782670

Dolgarrog was opened by the L&NWR in 1916. Slightly to the north there was once a standard gauge siding and line leading to an aluminium works a mile distant. This line closed in 1960. Dolgarrog itself closed briefly between November 1964 and June 1965.[8]

Despite having to don full wet-weather gear due to the heavy rain which fell during the whole of my time there I still enjoyed my visit. Dolgarrog has that isolated feel, and the honour of being the least used station in Wales, with an annual passenger usage of 612. Facilities are basic but do include a metal and plexiglass shelter similar to the others on this line, an information screen and a timetable posterboard. There is also a payphone. A perfect little stop, almost hidden in the surrounding greenery, known only to a few locals and any passing traveller lucky enough to momentarily glimpse it through a train window.

Dolgarrog was not only my last stop of this Welsh trip but I had now completed all sixty-one stops in all Wales.

Having just stopped at Llanfairfechan the 14.36 Holyhead to Cardiff Central service formed of a Class 175 Coradia DMU departs, heading towards Cardiff on 17 September 2018.

Penmaenmawr photographed on 17 September 2018 looking towards Holyhead.

Shown in the timetables as Llanfairpwll, the station nameboards however display the rather longer version of the place name. Personally I would not even attempt to say this aloud without an extra layer of Fixodent in place. Photographed on 17 September 2018.

The 17.31 Holyhead to Chester formed of a Class 158 Express Sprinter DMU calls at Llanfairpwll on 17 September 2018.

Left: Bodorgan on 18 August 2018, and a Class 150 Sprinter DMU forming the 09.23 Holyhead to Birmingham New Street is about to stop.

Opposite above: Valley, with the original station buildings seemingly in need of some care and attention, photographed on 18 September 2018 looking west.

Opposite below: The signal box at Valley which was still in use when photographed on 18 September 2018. Passing is the 09.25 service from Birmingham New Street to Holyhead, formed of a Class 158 Express Sprinter DMU.

Conwy looking east on 18 September 2018.

THE SOGGY WALKERS • 113

This Class 175 Coradia DMU is the 14.36 Holyhead to Cardiff Central service, which is here passing Ty Croes at speed on 18 September 2018. The westbound platform can be seen but the eastbound is behind the camera.

Rhosneigr seen on 18 September 2018, facing west. The main station buildings are fully sealed up, leaving only the small brick shelter available for passenger use.

Glan Conwy on the banks of the River Conwy, looking north towards Blaenau Ffestiniog on 19 September 2018.

The well cared-for former station building at Pont-y-Pant with the modern waiting shelter visible further down the platform. Photographed on 19 September 2018 looking towards Llandudno Junction.

Tal-y-Cafn looking south, seen on 19 September 2018.

The abandoned platform at Tal-y-Cafn on 19 September 2018, with an old station nameboard still in place and nicely tended gardens.

Looking south at Roman Bridge on 19 September 2018.

A two-coach Class 150 Sprinter DMU forming the 14.57 Blaenau Ffestiniog to Llandudno arriving at Roman Bridge on 19 September 2018.

Above: The lovely North Llanrwst photographed on 19 September 2018, looking towards Llandudno.

Opposite above: Dolwyddelan photographed on 19 September 2018, facing south.

Opposite below: Hawarden Bridge with the bridge forming a backdrop, seen on 20 September 2018.

THE SOGGY WALKERS • 119

120 • A COMPREHENSIVE GUIDE TO RAILWAY REQUEST STOPS: A PERSONAL ODYSSEY TO VISIT EVERY ONE IN BRITAIN

The 08.30 Wrexham Central to Bidston formed of a Class 150 Sprinter DMU seen here passing Hawarden Bridge on 20 September 2018.

Deganwy is the only intermediate stop between Llandudno Junction and Llandudno. This photograph is looking towards Llandudno on 20 September 2018.

Dolgarrog photographed on a very wet day, 21 September 2018. This was my final request stop in Wales.

CHAPTER 10

WHAT NO CHIPS?

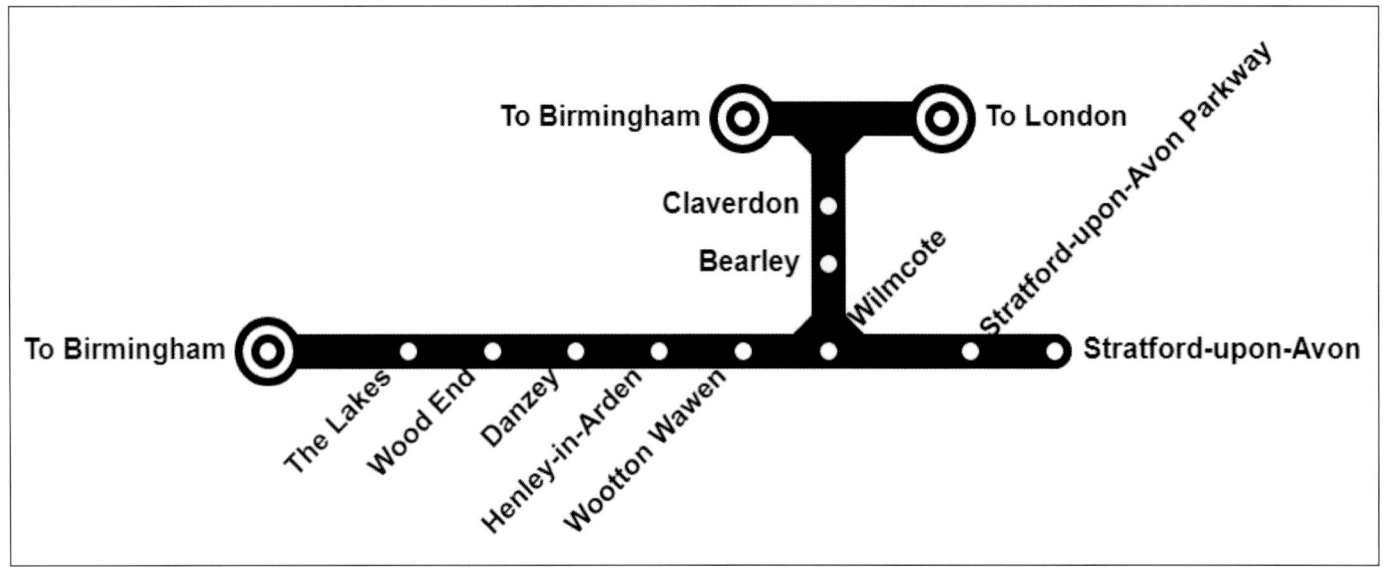

Wales and the West Country were both now completed, and with autumn closing in I made the decision to concentrate on fourteen easy stops, most of which could be done as simple day trips, while awaiting the arrival of spring. I started with the six stops in the area around Stratford-upon-Avon, which were all done in a single day.

Bearley
Annual passenger usage: 1,106
Least used station rank: 59
Postcode: CV37 0EU
Ordnance Survey national grid reference: SP171607

Opened by the Stratford on Avon Railway (SoAR) in 1860, Bearley originally had two platforms, a passing loop, a goods yard with a weighbridge and a shed.[1] In 1876 it became the junction for the Alcester branch and remained so until the closure of the branch in 1951. Between 1965 and 1968 it was called Bearley Halt.

Walking up the approach road to the station the first thing I noticed was the old stationmaster's house, and to the left the entrance to what would have been the goods yard. On the platform is a metal shelter with a payphone, noticeboards, a help point and an information screen. The disused second platform is clearly visible but little else remains of busier days at Bearley.

Claverdon
Annual passenger usage: 2,782
Least used station rank: 118
Postcode: CV35 8PE
Ordnance Survey national grid reference system: SP208643

Approximately 3 miles north of Bearley is Claverdon, opened in 1860 by the SoAR with a single platform located on the north side of the road bridge. A siding was provided later, then converted into a passing loop, and a loading bank was added. In 1938 the GWR doubled the line and the station moved to the south side of the road bridge.

At road level I found the original GWR booking hall and the parcels office still in existence, but boarded up and unused. Walking down the ramp and onto the platform I found it to be very much what I'd expected: a metal shelter freshly painted in brown, with a payphone, a help point and posterboards. Overgrown and abandoned, the old, unused platform is nonetheless still a visible reminder of grander times. Summer had now definitely passed, but I still spent an enjoyable hour in the autumn sunshine in what is a very sheltered place, watching two squirrels busy collecting nuts, no doubt to stock their winter larder, and listening to the cacophony from a nearby rookery.

When it was time for me to leave, a Class 165 DMU came into sight. I didn't have to signal, this being a Chiltern Trains service, and unlike West Midlands Trains both Bearley and Claverdon are treated as mandatory stops. After changing at the recently opened Stratford-upon-Avon Parkway my next call would be The Lakes. From there I planned to work my way down the line towards Stratford-upon-Avon.

The Lakes
Annual passenger usage: 26,936
Least used station rank: 280
Postcode: B94 5SE
Ordnance Survey national grid reference: SP106734

The Lakes Halt was opened by the GWR in 1935, renamed to The Lakes in 1968. It was built as a very simple station with two short platforms, each with its own wooden shelter.[2]

I arrived at The Lakes to find it not substantially altered since it was first built. The platforms are still very short, although both have been provided with Harrington Humps and the shelters are now of the modern bus stop-style. Step-free access is available to both platforms from the road bridge and down a ramp of about 40 metres in length. Movement between the platforms involves using this road bridge. One of the shelters has a payphone and both platforms have arrival/departure screens and noticeboards.

Wood End
Annual passenger usage: 11,740
Least used station rank: 265
Postcode: B94 5DS
Ordnance Survey national grid reference: SP106718

Opened with the name Wood End Platform in 1908 by the GWR, the suffix was dropped in 1924. Situated in a cutting with basic facilities it once catered for parcels traffic.[3] The station buildings were made of wood and a footbridge, which survived until 2014, linked the two platforms. Access to both is now via stairs and footpaths from the road.

Wood End sits at the bottom of a cutting with a tunnel at the southern end of the station. There is a feeling of seclusion, as though it's hiding in a world of its own. Having said that, there's not an awful lot to interest the visitor. Both platforms have brick shelters that are basic, but kept in good order and with help points; one also has a payphone. Information screens, noticeboards and Harrington Humps are provided for both platforms. Direct passage between platforms is not possible, and each has its own entrance route from the road, down a long footpath and then a long flight of stairs to platform level. Not only do these stairs present a challenge due to their number (fifty at least), but they are rather ugly, finished in galvanised steel with yellow handrails. On the plus side, two freestanding station nameboards from a previous era do remain. I wondered what they would have thought watching their old friend, the footbridge, who had stood with them through the years, being dismantled and unceremoniously taken away like a pile of rubbish that had served its purpose, perhaps even thinking it would be their turn next.

Danzey
Annual passenger usage: 8,198
Least used station rank: 220
Postcode: B94 5BE
Ordnance Survey national grid reference: SP122696

The GWR opened Danzey for Tanworth in 1908, and it was subsequently renamed Danzey by BR in 1968.[4] A goods yard existed, as did a signal box, and buildings on both platforms which were constructed from asbestos sheeting.

A striking feature of Danzey today is the fact that both platforms have a row of substantial coniferous trees, leaving the platforms covered with a carpet of pine needles and a scattering of fir cones. There is a car park with level access to Platform 2, but Platform 1 can only be reached by use of a footbridge. There is a single help point; information screens and painted brick built shelters exist on both platforms. It is easy to make out the extent of the old goods yard from the concrete footbridge, which interestingly still has a Tilley lamp bracket in place on one of the parapets.

Wootton Wawen

Annual passenger usage: 11,128
Least used station rank: 255
Postcode: B95 6BJ
Ordnance Survey national grid reference: SP147631

Originally called Wootton Wawen Platform when opened by the GWR in 1908, this station retained that name until 1974 when BR dropped the suffix.[5] Arriving at Wootton Wawen, my last stop of the day, I had reached another landmark: 100 request stops visited in eight months, and I was still having fun.

The corporate hand is very evident here, in that the station is very similar to the other stops on the 'North Warwickshire Line'; this is not a complaint, for it is good these places still exist. There are two relatively long platforms, both with basic painted brick shelters, help points and arrival/departure screens. Access to both is step-free using ramps from the road underbridge, where noticeboards are located. A GWR style mile-post is on the up platform confirming that it is 15.25 miles to Tyseley South Junction.

Four in Lancashire

In November 2018 I had a two-night stay in a Blackburn bed and breakfast, which allowed me to complete four stops north of Manchester. I said earlier that if you have booked online you can never be sure just what you will find until you arrive, but every place I stayed in was a credit to the proprietors, with just one exception: Blackburn. Plumbing in the bathroom took the form of plastic piping laid loose across the floor, and a hole in the ceiling was the result of past water damage. I won't go on. At least the mattress seemed clean and looked quite new; be thankful for small mercies, as they say.

Travelling up from Swindon through Manchester and then towards Blackburn enabled me to make the first stop of the trip at Entwistle.

Entwistle

Annual passenger usage: 12,852
Least used station rank: 274
Postcode: BL7 0NG
Ordnance Survey national grid reference: SD727177

Entwistle was first opened in June 1848 as a temporary station, to the north of its present location, by the Bolton, Blackburn, Clitheroe & West Yorkshire (BBC&WyorksR) railway. Originally called Whittlestone Head, the station was relocated and renamed Entwistle in August 1848.[6] It was once a much busier place than now, with an extensive goods yard and a signal box that straddled the running lines. Interestingly the OS 6-inch map of 1912 shows a tramway running between the station and Know Mill Print Works, which would have generated extra freight traffic.

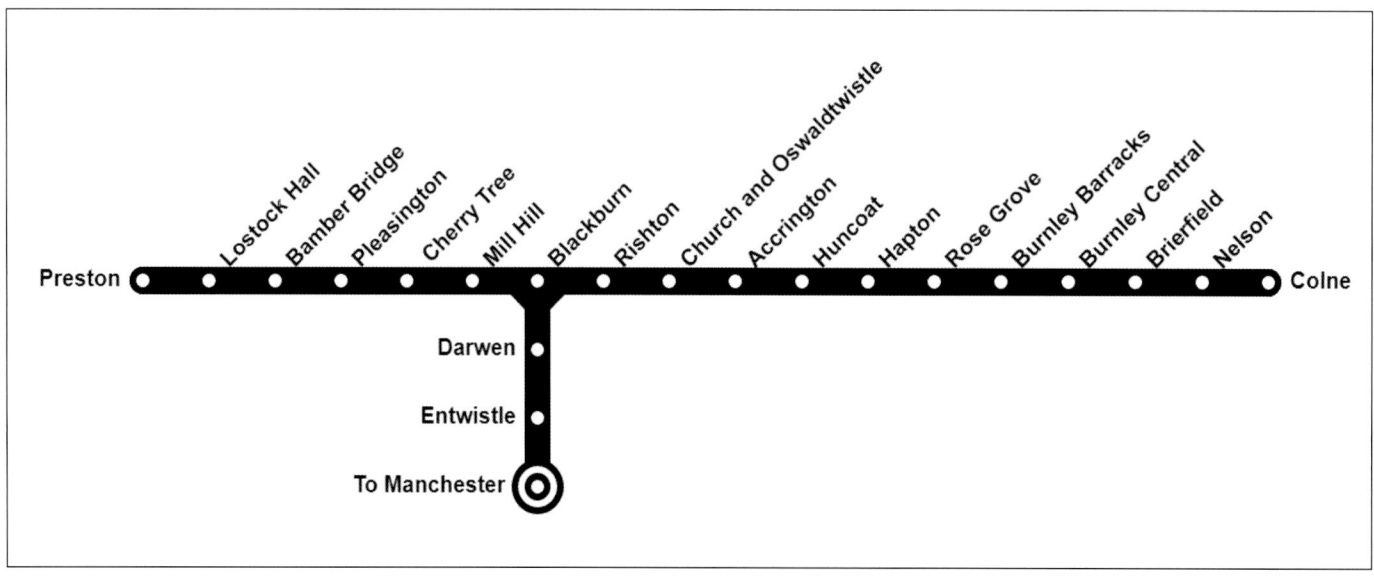

Situated on the 'Ribble Valley Line' some 8 miles south of Blackburn, Entwistle is now a shadow of what it once was. The entrance to the station is step-free and down a long ramp from the road. Near the entrance I found an original Lancashire & Yorkshire Railway (L&YR) boundary marker which predates the railway grouping of 1923. A brick shelter with a payphone is provided, but no help point or information screen; station upgrade work was in progress so perhaps these might be put in place at a later date. In addition to the usual noticeboards, a series of boards depict walks and wildlife in the surrounding area.

Pleasington
Annual passenger usage: 9,362
Least used station rank: 234
Postcode: BB2 5JQ
Ordnance Survey national grid reference: SD642262

Opened by the L&YR in 1846, Pleasington only acquired its current request stop status in 2012. At the eastern end of what is now Platform 2 once stood a signal box which was tall enough to allow the signalman to see over the adjacent road bridge. Two small sidings, also at the eastern end of the station, once ran into an industrial sandpit.

Pleasington is on the 'East Lancashire Line' and has two platforms with a bus stop-style shelter on both. There are public address speakers but no information screens. A payphone is located in the shelter on the westbound platform. Access is step-free using ramps from the road. A community art and horticultural project involving local college students, vulnerable adults and a local family group (among others) has enhanced the station's ambience and made it a more pleasant place to visit and wait. This has been done by installing various artworks around the station and by the use of flower tubs and other plantings.

Hapton
Annual passenger usage: 16,544
Least used station rank: 308
Postcode: BB12 7LG
Ordnance Survey national grid reference: SD791317

The L&YR opened Hapton in the early 1860s, but the station's once substantial buildings were all demolished in the late 1970s. A signal box, sidings/goods yard, and a branch line into Hapton chemical works were once all located at the eastern end of the station.

Hapton is on the East Lancashire Line and is halfway between Blackburn and Colne. There are two platforms and a payphone, but no information screens or help points. There are newly glazed shelters on both platforms and on my visit high-tech ticket machines were being installed. When working they may be able to give train running information. Access to both platforms is from the footbridge at road level and down ramps. Abandoned sections at the western end of both platforms give a clear indication that they were once longer than they are today.

Burnley Barracks
Annual passenger usage: 22,130
Least used station rank: 363
Postcode: BB12 0HG
Ordnance Survey national grid reference: SD831327

Burnley Westgate, as it was originally named, had a short life. It was opened by the East Lancashire Railway (ElancsR) in September 1848 to act as its temporary terminus while the extension towards Colne was completed. It closed in February 1849, and reopened as Burnley Barracks in September 1851.

My immediate impression of Burnley Barracks was a place of gloom and decay, compounded by the fact that the station sits in a hollow bounded on one side by a major road and the M65 on the other. Then, as if to add insult to injury, the line is crossed at each end of the platform by damp and dark road overbridges. Access is from the road above via a ramp. There is no help point nor information screen, a timetable posterboard is available and public address speakers are in evidence. Ticket machines of the type I had seen at Hapton were undergoing installation. A not very pretty blue metal shelter is on the platform, and the now defunct second platform is visible.

An Essex/Suffolk One-off

One bright and frosty morning early in January 2019 I headed to Bures on the Essex/Suffolk border, my first stop of the year which I completed as a simple day trip from home.

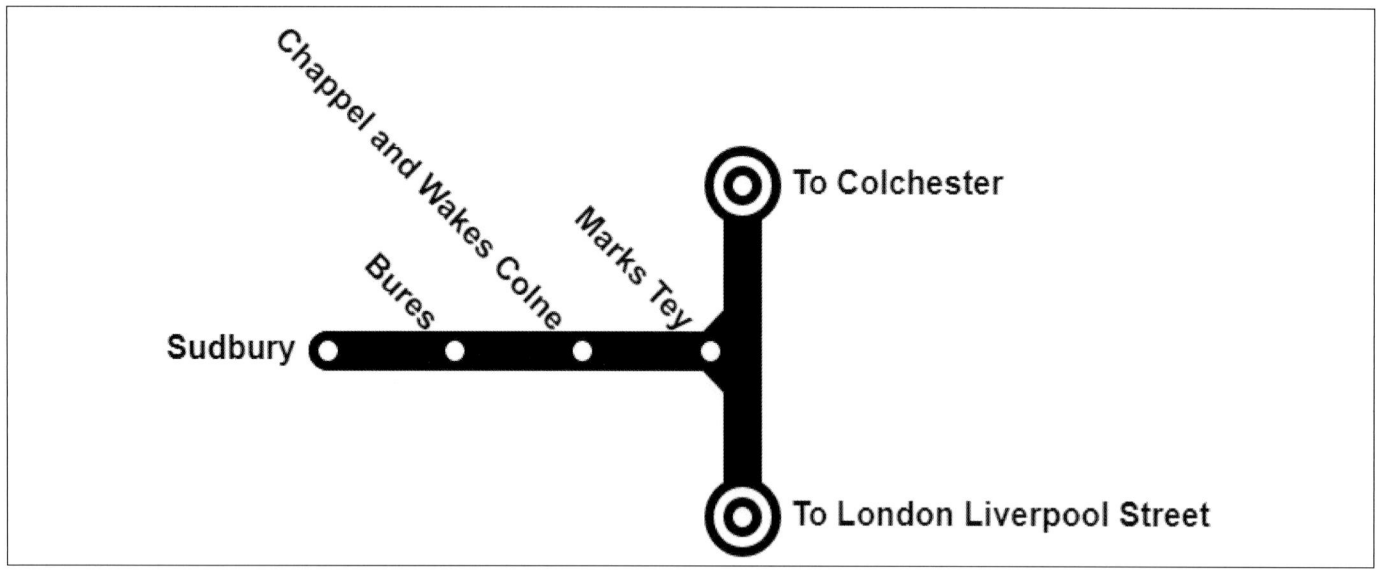

Bures

Annual passenger usage: 58,680
Least used station rank: 626
Postcode: CO8 5HS
Ordnance Survey national grid reference: TL903338

First opened by the Eastern Union Railway in 1849, Bures has survived one significant closure attempt in its history, in 1966, when the Minister for Transport, Barbara Castle, refused closure permission.[7] A signal box and goods yard were once to the south of the station, with further sidings to the north that served a malthouse and a brickworks. Freight services ceased in 1964, and the signal box was demolished in 1965, with the main station buildings following suit in the 1980s. Bures became a request stop in December 2017, then reverted to a mandatory stop in May 2019 after only eighteen months as a request stop.

Bures has step-free access, noticeboards, a ticket machine, a help point and an information screen. The shelter is a wooden construction of indeterminate age, but I have seen a photograph circa 1950 which shows it already in place. Inside the shelter is a mini-gallery of local scenes and posters, while outside is a panel depicting the history of the station. To the front is a nicely maintained and planted garden, to which various railway relics have been added to good effect.

Two in Greater Manchester

I had been eagerly awaiting the chance to visit Reddish South and Denton, which are on the line between Stockport and Stalybridge, for some time. Both were problematical due to a very limited service, with only the 08.46 Stalybridge to Stockport, and 09.45 return service on Saturdays. Not only that but the RMT union had been in dispute with Northern Rail (NRT) over the issue of driver-only trains and consequently had been on strike every weekend for almost a year. In February

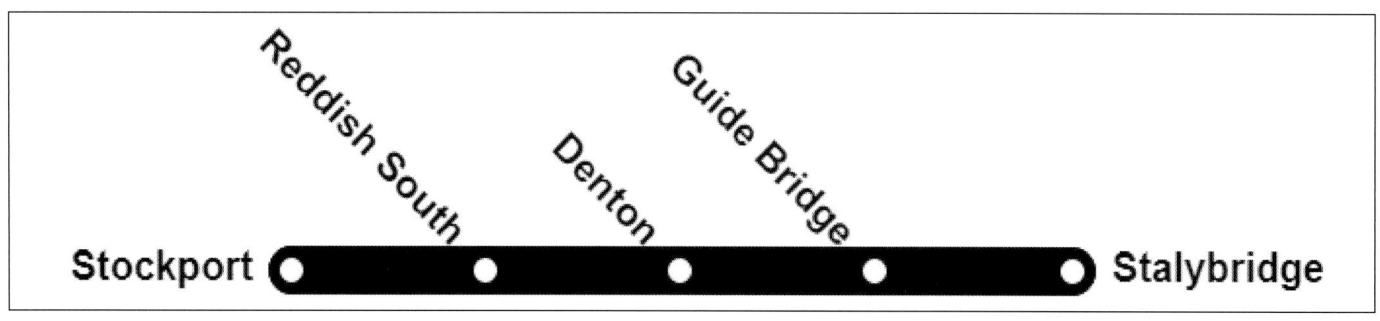

2019 talks to resolve the issue began in earnest and the strikes were called off. On Saturday 16 February 2019 and after a local overnight stay I was on the platform at Reddish South.

Reddish South
Annual passenger usage: 104
Least used station rank: 7
Postcode: SK5 6TU
Ordnance Survey national grid reference: SJ895932

Known simply as Reddish when opened by the L&NWR in 1849, the station did not become Reddish South until renamed by BR in 1952. By the early 1900s it had two island platforms with a booking office. There also existed an extensive siding serving the nearby engineering works, a signal box and an engine shed.

Today's Reddish South is very much reduced, with just a single platform and facilities that comprise a timetable noticeboard and nothing else. No lighting is installed nor is there a shelter, a seat or anything else to aid the weary traveller, just a platform accessed by a flight of stairs. Part of the now disused platform can still be seen and the extra, and vacant, archway under the road bridge indicates the location of the now missing tracks. Overall I rather liked Reddish South, but then perhaps I am a bit unusual in that way. Getting ready to put my stopping arm out and wondering whether the train would actually arrive (after all it was almost a year since the last one), I was joined by four other passengers (how dare they …). Arrive it did and on time. Boarding I found the train, while not full, quite busy with enthusiasts, which was not really surprising considering that this is quite an obscure passenger line, and this was the first chance to travel it in almost a twelve months.

There is a 'Friends of Reddish South Station' group who maintain the station garden, and have painted a mural on a nearby wall. They have a website and are campaigning for better services at Reddish.[8]

Denton
Annual passenger usage: 70
Least used station rank: 3
Postcode: M34 3NS
Ordnance Survey national grid reference: SJ914956

The OS 6-inch map of 1848 shows a small station on the L&NWR line at Denton. The line was quadrupled with two island platforms in 1889 and the OS map of 1910 reflects this. A booking office was at road level with stairs leading down to the platforms, and to the south of the station were sidings and a signal box.

Alighting at Denton a dozen of my fellow passengers stepped down with me for a photo opportunity. After a few minutes I was the only one left on the platform and the guard called to me, "Are you getting on?" When I replied in the negative he closed the doors and they were away. Watching the faces of my ex-fellow passengers at the train windows looking out at me standing alone at Denton, I did allow myself the thought, yes I'm a proper request stopper; I actually alight or board at every stop, I don't just look out of the window and say done it; that would be far too easy.

I liked Denton. It has managed to retain one of its island platforms and it has the facilities of a timetable noticeboard and a seat to enable the weary traveller to take the weight off their feet. After all, if you have just missed your train you may have a wait of over 167 hours. There is no shelter or lighting and access is down a flight of stairs. One side of the abandoned platform is visible but now overgrown, while the bridge abutment has a signal wire pulley and telegraph insulators still in place.

There is a 'Friends of Denton Station' group which has provided flower tubs and generally maintain the station. They are also campaigning to get services here improved, and have their own website.[9]

Fishy Business in Lincolnshire

Another long day to complete only one stop. I left Swindon station at 06.12 arriving back at 20.29, and all this to sample the delights of New Clee.

New Clee
Annual passenger usage: 1,236
Least used station rank: 65
Postcode: DN32 5GR
Ordnance Survey national grid reference: TA286103

Opened by the Great Central Railway in 1875, New Clee is 2.5 miles from Cleethorpes, which is the end of the

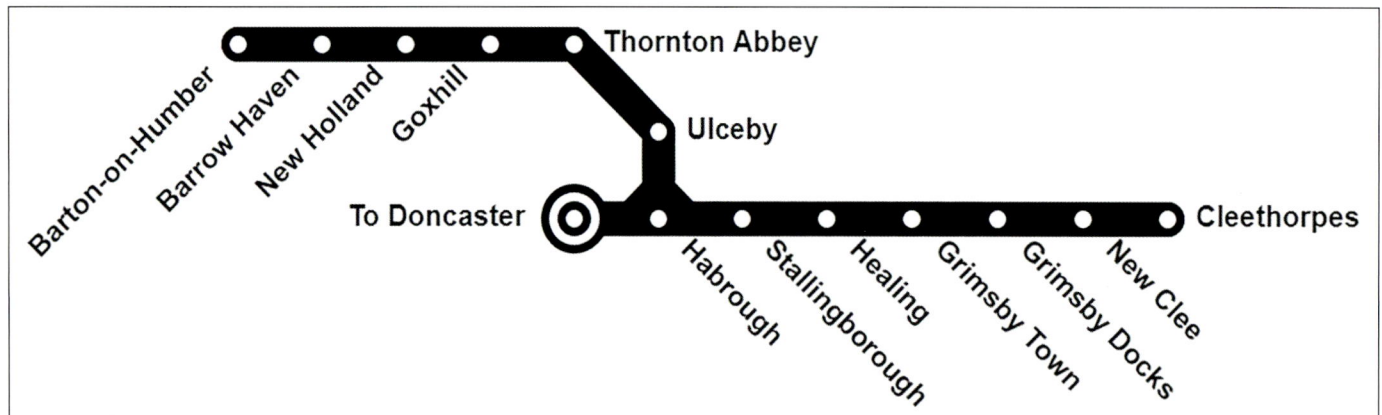

line. The track here was originally double and New Clee had two platforms, with a signal box at the Grimsby end. By the early 1900s the extensive 'Clee Sidings' adjacent to the station were in place. Work in the mid-1980s involved the singling of the line and removal of the signal box, with new colour-light signals replacing the semaphores.

Located on the 'Barton Line', New Clee is close to the docks, something that was clearly evidenced by the strong odour of fish every time the wind blew in from the coast (it was a rather blustery day), but there was no sign of a chippy anywhere, which was a shame as I could have been tempted. Situated in an area of light industrial units I felt the station had very little to offer, other than the fishy odour and the splendid views of a tyre fitting centre and the local Aldi car park. Step-free access, a bus stop-style shelter and a noticeboard about sums it up. There are no other facilities to ease the passenger on his/her way. The redundant second platform is very clearly visible, but I couldn't make out any other tangible signs of what has existed here before.

Bearley looking towards Stratford-upon-Avon on 26 October 2018. The old platform can be seen on the left.

Chiltern Trains 09.40 service from Leamington Spa to Stratford-upon-Avon, formed of a Class 165 Networker Turbo DMU, seen approaching Claverdon on 26 October 2018.

The old station buildings at Claverdon, which are situated above the platform at road level, photographed on 26 October 2018.

On 26 October 2018, the 09.57 Stourbridge Junction to Stratford-upon-Avon service, formed of a Class 172 Turbostar DMU, calls at The Lakes.

Wood End on 26 October 2018, with a Class 172 Turbostar DMU forming the 11.57 Stourbridge Junction to Stratford-upon-Avon service passing through.

WHAT NO CHIPS? • **131**

Danzey, looking north on 26 October 2018.

The 12.57 Stourbridge Junction to Stratford-upon-Avon is made up of a Class 172 Turbostar DMU as it arrives at Danzey on 26 October 2018.

132 • A COMPREHENSIVE GUIDE TO RAILWAY REQUEST STOPS: A PERSONAL ODYSSEY TO VISIT EVERY ONE IN BRITAIN

A Class 172 Turbostar DMU arrives at Wootton Wawen on 26 October 2018, forming the 15.57 Stourbridge Junction to Stratford-upon-Avon service.

Entwistle photographed on 14 November 2018, facing towards Blackburn.

Pleasington on 15 November 2018, and the 09.57 Preston to Colne is about to depart. This service is made up of two Class 142 Pacer DMU units.

Hapton photographed on 15 November 2018, looking towards Blackburn.

Above: The platform at Reddish South looking towards Stalybridge, photographed on 15 February 2019.

Opposite above: The 10.57 Preston to Colne service, comprising of a Class 142 Pacer DMU set, at Burnley Barracks on 15 November 2018.

Opposite below: The garden and shelter at Bures, seen on 5 January 2019.

Left: The once a week 09.45 Stockport to Stalybridge service, formed of a two-coach Class 142 Pacer DMU, is seen arriving at Reddish South on 16 February 2019.

Opposite above: Denton on 16 February 2019, and the Class 142 Pacer DMU forming the 09.45 Preston to Stalybridge is waiting to leave.

Opposite below: A Class 153 Super Sprinter DMU leaving New Clee on 16 February 2019, forming the 12.55 Cleethorpes to Barton-on-Humber service.

The platform at Denton looking towards Stalybridge on 15 February 2019.

WHAT NO CHIPS? • 137

CHAPTER 11

THE HOME OF THE HUMP

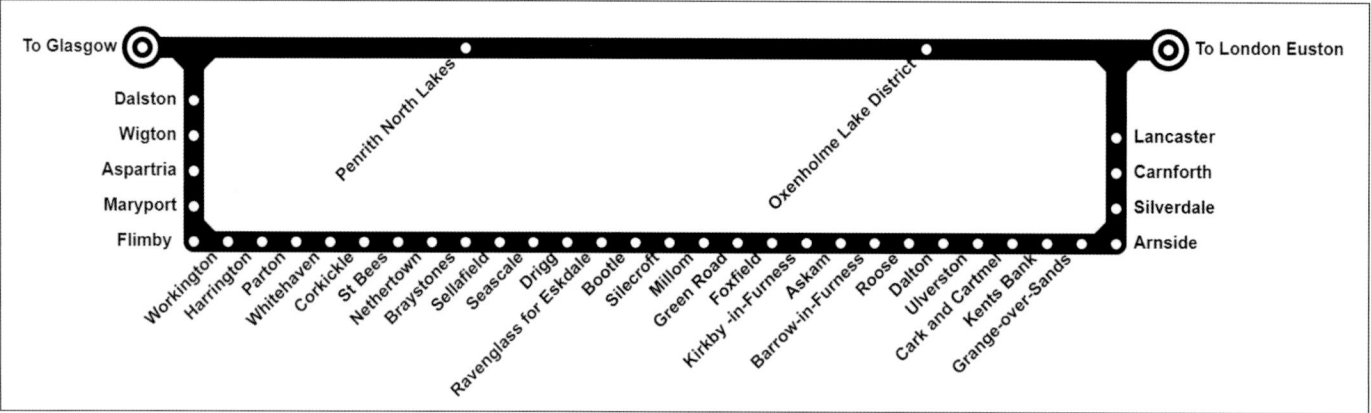

Spring 2019 had finally arrived and my first major outing of the year was planned: a four-night stay in Whitehaven, from where I could explore the 'Cumbrian Coast Line'. The line extends from Barrow-in-Furness in the south to Carlisle in the north, a total distance of 85 miles, with fourteen request stops, although some of these have since become mandatory. This was my first visit to this line, and as such was eagerly anticipated.

Braystones
Annual passenger usage: 992
Least used station rank: 53
Postcode: CA21 2YW
Ordnance Survey national grid reference: NY000060

The Whitehaven & Furness Junction Railway (W&FJnR) opened Braystones in 1849. It is a gorgeous location, literally a few metres from the Irish Sea and, on a stormy day, possibly in it. There are very basic facilities, but there's nothing wrong with that, is there? The platform has a metal shelter, noticeboard and help point, there is also a bench seat, ideal for watching the summer sun set into the sea. A Harrington Hump has been provided because the platform here is very low. The original station building is intact and now a private home. At the end of the platform is a level crossing allowing vehicular access to the beach by means of self-operated gates.

Corkickle
Annual passenger usage: 50,422
Least used station rank: 578
Postcode: CA28 8AP
Ordnance Survey national grid reference: NX977174

First opened by the W&FJnR in 1855 the station has at times been referred to as Whitehaven Corkickle.[1] The Preston Street goods branch, which had its own engine shed and two signal boxes, all of which finally closed in 1997, once existed to the south of the station. Also to the south was the 'Corkickle Brake', a roped incline built to handle traffic from Croft Pit – the last commercial roped incline in Great Britain remaining when it eventually closed in 1986.

During my time at Corkickle it felt quite busy with many passengers both boarding and alighting trains in both directions. This to me is one of the less attractive request stops. The original station building, which backs right onto the platform, is now residential accommodation, the front of which is in good order, while the back (station side) is left looking uncared for and unloved, with its canopy now absent and bricked up doors all adding to a feeling of neglect. The platform has a bus stop-style shelter, a ticket machine and noticeboards, but there is no information screen or help point. It does have one redeeming feature – a semaphore signal with a white sightboard at the tunnel mouth adjacent to the end of the platform. The northern end of this tunnel opens out into Whitehaven station.

Drigg
Annual passenger usage: 9,728
Least used station rank: 239
Postcode: CA19 1XW
Ordnance Survey national grid reference: SD063988

Drigg was opened by the W&FJnR in 1849. To the south of the station there used to be a siding and a goods shed; the siding has since been lifted. Alighting from a Class 156 DMU I found Drigg to be an attractive stop in a quiet location. Most of the facilities that I would expect were missing – there were no shelters nor help points or information screens; concrete bases had been newly laid on both platforms leading me to suspect new shelters were on the way. Metal columns with cables protruding were also evident, presumably awaiting the installation of screens. It is a well-kept and tidy station nonetheless, with lovingly tended gardens. A signal box stands immediately to the southern end of the platforms, used by the level crossing keeper who opens the gates manually. Opposite the signal box is the old goods shed, which is in good condition but now isolated since losing its tracks. The old station buildings are obviously looked after and now contain a café and gift shop. To the north of the station, sidings lead into a low-level nuclear waste repository. Awaiting my train south I made a mental note that when I got back to the hotel and turned the lights out, I should check to see if I glowed in the dark.

Green Road
Annual passenger usage: 6,504
Least used station rank: 186
Postcode: LA18 5HR
Ordnance Survey national grid reference: SD189839

First opened by the Furness Railway (FurnR) in 1853, Green Road once had a goods yard and a signal box close to the level crossing at the end of the platform. Located close to the Duddon Estuary, in what is a delightful rural spot, I was left feeling that I would have liked more time to explore, but I had a plan and plans are not to be deviated from. Green Road has been adopted under the NRT scheme and is an enthusiastically cared-for station. The shelter on the northbound platform is a solid brick construction, while the southbound platform has one of an altogether different type, consisting of concrete columns with a galvanised roof and back; the front and sides are open to the elements. The main station building is brick built and still exists on the platform but it is no longer available for public use. There is however a payphone on the front of the building. Access is step-free from road level. There were no information screens when I visited but it appeared that these were being installed.

Although very overgrown, the old goods yard, which is on the west side of the station, was easy to find. I was able to locate traces of loading bays, and associated ramps, also the base column of a loading crane standing defiant and alone among the brambles; RIP: rust in peace.

Silecroft
Annual passenger usage: 7,030
Least used station rank: 193
Postcode: LA18 5LP
Ordnance Survey national grid reference: SD130819

Opened by the W&FJnR in 1850 Silecroft had sidings and a goods shed. There was also a signal box and a level crossing here at one time. Arriving at Silecroft I immediately noticed the signal box and semaphore signals, a definite plus for me, but the level crossing had been automated, a sign of things to come perhaps, I thought to myself. Neither platform had a shelter or information screens, but there were signs that work already underway would provide both. Access to both platforms is by a ramp from the road, where there is a timetable posterboard. The robust goods shed is still standing but there is little else to indicate the previous existence of the yard; the area is now mostly a car park.

Sitting quietly on the platform I suddenly heard a frightful screeching and two rooks crashed onto the platform almost at my feet. The bigger of the two was on top of the smaller one and stabbing at him with his beak. I have heard the point of view that this is nature and people should not interfere, but because I could see blood being drawn I did intervene and they both flew off. What happened to the smaller one I'll never know, but I do hope he made it.

Foxfield
Annual passenger usage: 22,680
Least used station rank: 367
Postcode: LA20 6BX
Ordnance Survey national grid reference: SD208854

Foxfield was opened in 1848 by the FurnR, then in 1850 when the W&FJnR completed its own line from Whitehaven, it became a junction. The OS 6-inch map of 1850 shows the station name of 'Foxfield Junction'. It also served as the junction for the Coniston branch from 1859 until its closure in 1962. The junction suffix was dropped in 1957.[2] Sidings and a goods shed were all once present here.

I found Foxfield to be quite busy and since my visit it has lost its request stop status with all trains now stopping. There is an island platform with both sides in use, and access is via a barrow crossing and ramp. A wooden signal box is situated at the end of the platform and the waiting shelter forms part of the same structure. In addition, this box is still operating semaphore signals. The water tower still stands and close by is the original and quite large station building. Taking a short walk to the south of the station I found a manned crossing on a lane called Skelly Crag. Seeing my camera the keeper left his hut to see what I was doing. He was a fellow enthusiast it transpired, and he seemed genuinely impressed that I'd travelled from the deep south that is Wiltshire, eventually saying he would have to head south himself one day.

Kirkby-in-Furness
Annual passenger usage: 14,398
Least used station rank: 292
Postcode: LA17 7UB
Ordnance Survey national grid reference: SD226825

Opened as Kirkby in 1846 by the FurnR, the station was renamed Kirkby-in-Furness in 1928 – by which time ownership of the line had passed to the London Midland & Scottish Railway (LMS). The southbound side of the station had a goods yard and shed, while a water tower, signal box and the longest station seat in the country were previously on the northbound platform; sadly all are gone now.[3] To the north of the station a line diverged to a nearby slate quarry.

Kirkby-in-Furness is situated in a superb location on the Duddon Estuary, almost opposite Green Road. Platform 2 still has in use its original stone shelter while Platform 1 has a bus stop-type shelter, the original buildings on this side having been demolished. There is a payphone and timetable boards, but no information screens. Access to the platforms is through a gate, with passage between the two via a barrow crossing or the footbridge.

I found traces of brickwork from the base of the signal box adjacent to the shelter on Platform 2. In the site of the former goods yard I found various derelict and overgrown loading bays and ramps.

Bootle
Annual passenger usage: 10,870
Least used station rank: 251
Postcode: LA19 5TA
Ordnance Survey national grid reference: SD093892

Bootle was opened by the W&FJnR in 1850 and has been in past times a much busier place than it is today. The OS 25-inch map of 1863 shows, at the north end of the station, a goods yard and shed complete with a crane. There was also a coal depot with a weighing machine, and a loading dock.

The main station building, which is on Platform 2, is now privately owned, and for a very rural location a quite expansive structure. Of particular interest is the cast iron guttering in that one of the downpipes bears the mark 'FR 1873', by which date the line was under FurnR ownership. There is no shelter or arrival/departure screen on this platform, but like other stops on this line installation works did appear to be in progress. There is a shelter on Platform 1, which stands apart from the crowd. It is almost certainly part of the original station, built of wood and on a large scale. It has a freshly painted interior and the beams are picked out in a contrasting colour, while the tiled floor adds a fine finishing touch. A signal box stands at the end of the platform, controlling not only semaphore signals but also manually operated level crossing gates. It just kept on getting better, watching the signalman close the gates, and then the signal go to the 'off' position while the motor traffic waited. A sight that has been a part of the rural railway scene for so many years, but increasingly rarely seen today. I wondered how long it would be before Bootle fell prey to modernisation.

The current Carlisle to Barrow journey time is two hours and twenty minutes, with trains that run through some magnificent scenery, often between the sea and the peaks. Automating all the gates on this line would undoubtedly save a few minutes on journey times, but that is a little less time to relish the scenery sliding past the train windows. Are we really in that much of a hurry? A few crossing keepers would be made redundant it is true and the human touch would be lost forever; on the plus side there would be a reduction in the wage bill, with the associated savings possibly passed on to passengers in the form of lower fares.

Dalston

Annual passenger usage: 21,556
Least used station rank: 360
Postcode: CA5 7LT
Ordnance Survey national grid reference: NY366506

The Maryport & Carlisle Railway (M&CR) opened Dalston in 1843, and a busy goods yard was soon established to the south side of the station. This yard contained a saw mill, coal depot, crane and a goods shed.

The original station building on the southbound platform is now in private commercial use. Here a modern brick-built shelter is available for passengers, while the northbound platform has retained its period stone built shelter, which is nicely maintained. A payphone is provided, and information screens were being installed on my visit. Both platforms have step-free access and a footbridge also links them. At the eastern end of the station are sidings leading to a working oil terminal that receives regular traffic.

After an enjoyable Dalston visit the Class 156 DMU that was going to take me the 43 miles south to Nethertown pulled up. Some careful planning had been required for my next stop Nethertown, as few trains are timetabled to call there, even on request, but I had confidence in my planning and sat down and awaited the arrival of the guard.

"Nethertown please," I said,

"I'm sorry, we don't stop there," she replied.

At this point I instantly thought that I had got my timings wrong and was on the wrong train. I must have looked somewhat crestfallen at this point, and taking pity on me the guard said, "Only joking," and went on her way. Cheeky guard I thought, but I rather liked her style.

Nethertown

Annual passenger usage: 536
Least used station rank: 36
Postcode: CA22 2UG
Ordnance Survey national grid reference: NX985079

Opened by the W&FJnR in 1849, Nethertown had a passing loop with two platforms, several sidings and a signal box at the northern end of the station. The line was singled and the passing loop removed in the 1970s.

When I arrived my instant reaction was oh yes, this is why I am doing this. Nethertown is perched between some low cliffs and the sea, there is a house nearby and some beach huts further in the distance. Apart from that I saw no other sign of human life until I climbed to the top of the cliffs and could see inland. Having a full ninety minutes here I decided it was time for tea, and I sat with the warm spring sunshine on my back, the Irish Sea in front of me and a flock of stonechats around me, busily going to and fro, as if oblivious to my presence.

The station has a small aluminium and plexiglass shelter, an assistance phone and a timetable noticeboard. The platform has a Harrington Hump, and access is step-free via a barrow crossing, however, due to the unevenness of some surfaces, it is probably unsuitable for wheelchairs. The whole site is quite open and the unused platform is very evident and easily reached. The former goods yard is also very obvious, and it is possible to make out parts of the base of the former signal box. Nethertown proved to be a most enjoyable visit, and with only 536 passengers annually it is the least used station on the Cumbrian Coast Line.

Parton

Annual passenger usage: 7,426
Least used station rank: 202
Postcode: CA28 6PA
Ordnance Survey national grid reference: NX979206

The Whitehaven Junction Railway (WJnR) opened Parton in 1847. There were various sidings around the station and a signal box at the north end, which was demolished in 2010. The station is located on the edge of the village and close to Parton Beach. It has two platforms with brick-built shelters on both. I found a brick embossed 'ACCRINGTON NORI'. It was a type of iron-hard engineering brick, and it is thought that the name came about because 'iron' was accidently reversed in the brick mould spelling, 'NORI'.[4] A subway links the platforms with stairs going up to platform level. Both platforms have newly installed departure/arrival screens and a noticeboard stands near the main entrance, but there is no help point.

Harrington
Annual passenger usage: 27,776
Least used station rank: 409
Postcode: CA14 5QQ
Ordnance Survey national grid reference: NX990253

Opened in 1846 by the WJnR, this is the last surviving of the five railway stations that once served the Harrington area. A signal box once stood to the north of the station and several sidings also existed with a goods shed to the west.

There are two platforms, both with bus stop-style shelters and information screens. There is no help point but a timetable noticeboard stands by the entry/exit point. Access is step-free to Platform 1, but not to the second platform as it can only be reached by means of a footbridge. The term 'Harrington Hump', which I have used many times so far in this book, is derived from the fact that the first ones ever installed were here at Harrington, in 2008. The humps raise a section(s) of platform to assist passengers with accessibility issues when boarding trains. They can be installed at a low relative cost, and so are a popular option.

Flimby
Annual passenger usage: 9,442
Least used station rank: 235
Postcode: CA15 8QN
Ordnance Survey national grid reference: NY020338

Situated precariously close to the sea, Flimby was opened by the WJnR in 1846. It lost its request stop status between 30 November 2009 and 28 May 2010, following the introduction of an hourly shuttle service between Maryport and Workington, timetabled to call at Flimby. This was done to cope with a large increase in passenger numbers, because flooding had forced the closure of both road bridges across the River Derwent at Workington, the rail bridge remaining as the only river crossing in the area. In January 2014 the line closed for a week because of storm damage to the track just south of the station.

Flimby has two platforms with step-free access to the southbound one, while the northbound platform can only be reached by use of the footbridge or the barrow crossing. Both platforms have shelters, the northbound an aluminium and plexiglass type, the southbound an older metal one. Information screens, a noticeboard and a ticket machine are present, but there are no help points or payphone. No original station buildings remain, with all traces of them having been removed. The exit from the western side of the station leads directly onto the beach, which is only a few metres away.

Aspatria
Annual passenger usage: 22,420
Least used station rank: 365
Postcode: CA7 2AW
Ordnance Survey national grid reference: NY143412

Aspatria was first opened by the M&CR in 1841, and like many others the station today belies its historical importance. Sidings to the north once served a coal and lime depot, and there were cattle pens and two cranes with various sheds and loading docks. A signal box controlled the entrance/exit to the sidings, and to the Mealsgate branch which diverged westward.

Aspatria has two platforms which are connected by a footbridge, with step-free access to both also possible. The old stone station buildings are still extant, but now a private dwelling. Only Platform 1 has a shelter, although it did seem on my visit that preparations for a second were underway along with information screens and a ticket machine.

Platform 2 has a feature that I had not seen before, or since: free range chickens. How or why they were there I can't say, but I did speculate that perhaps NRT was piloting a scheme to attract more passengers: half a dozen eggs free with every day return? Or perhaps restaurant cars were coming to the line, with omelettes on the go a speciality? All I know is they were there, a group of hens watched over by a rooster, and he was very much in charge. Every time I walked past he fixed me with what could only be described as a 'come on then if you think you're hard enough' look; a seriously cocky cockerel one might say.

Aspatria was my last stop on the Cumbrian Coast Line, completing a most enjoyable outing. The next day I headed first to Carlisle, then on to Newcastle using the 'Tyne Valley Line', a route I had not travelled before, and from there south and home.

THE HOME OF THE HUMP • 143

Braystones on the Cumbrian Coast Line, looking south on 26 March 2019.

The 12.06 Barrow-in-Furness to Carlisle service, formed of a Class 156 Super Sprinter DMU, is departing Braystones and heading north on 26 March 2019.

Left: Corkickle on 26 March 2019, with a Class 156 Super Sprinter DMU forming the 14.52 service from Barrow-in-Furness to Carlisle, coming to a halt.

Opposite above: Green Road looking south, photographed on 27 March 2019. The shelter on the right was open for passenger use while the main building was sealed.

Opposite below: Silecroft photographed on 27 March 2019, looking south. Like others on the Cumbrian Coast Line that I visited it appeared to be awaiting the construction of new shelters.

Drigg seen on 27 March 2019, looking towards Carlisle.

THE HOME OF THE HUMP • 145

Left: Foxfield has a working signal box with semaphore signals, this being a fine example of one, photographed on 27 March 2019.

Opposite above: The original shelter on the northbound platform at Kirkby-in-Furness is still in use. The southbound passengers have access to a modern shelter which is just visible under the footbridge. Photographed on 27 March 2019, looking north.

Opposite below: The substantial former station buildings at Bootle seen on 27 March 2019.

Foxfield on 27 March 2019. The waiting room is at the left of the photograph with the signal box rising above it. The old water storage tank is on the right. Just arriving is a Class 156 Super Sprinter DMU forming the 12.08 service from Carlisle to Barrow-in-Furness.

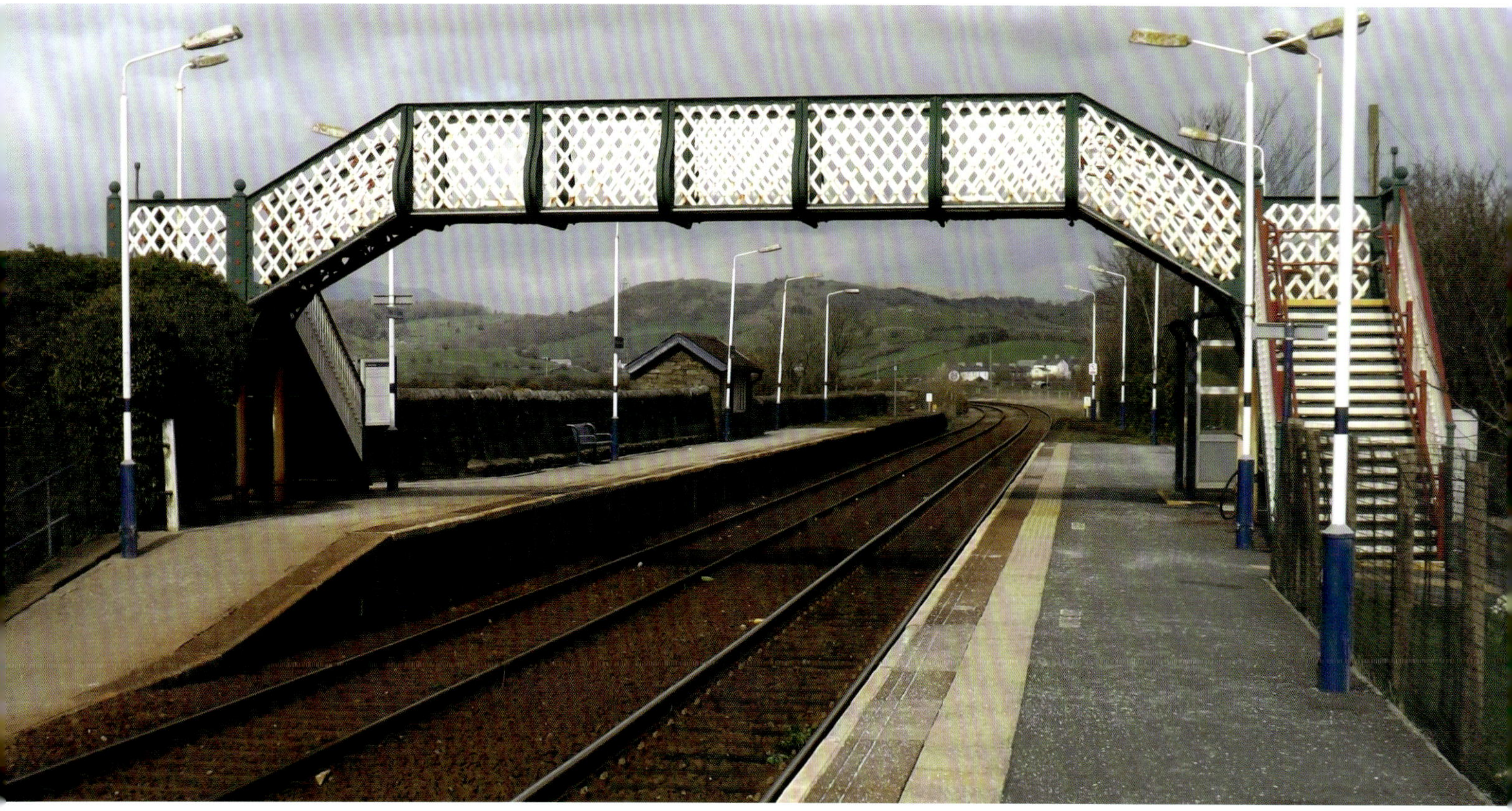

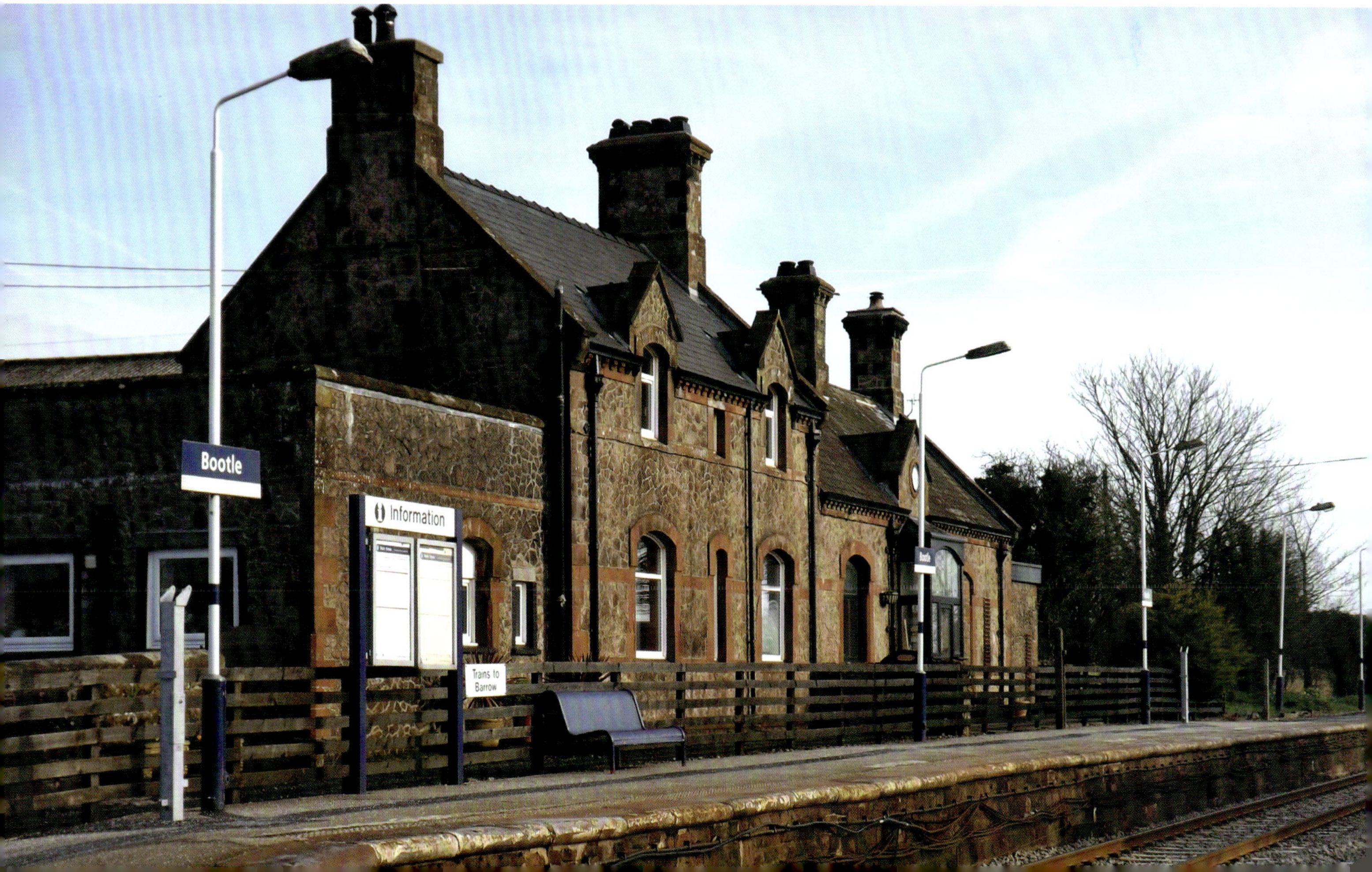
Bootle
Information
Trains to
Barrow

Above: Dalston viewed from the footbridge on 28 March 2019.

Opposite above: The truly wonderful Nethertown seen looking south on 28 March 2019.

Opposite below: Nethertown on 28 March 2019 with the 11.20 Barrow-in-Furness to Carlisle passing. This service was formed of a Class 156 Super Sprinter DMU, and was not scheduled to stop, therefore it is passing at speed.

THE HOME OF THE HUMP • **149**

Above: Parton was, I felt, a little bland. Here looking north on 28 March 2019.

Opposite above: Harrington looking south on 28 March 2019. Not only do both platforms have Harrington Humps, but these particular ones were the first to be installed in Britain.

Opposite below: Flimby on 28 March 2019 with a Network Rail 'yellow' test train travelling south, headed by an English Electric Type 3 Class 37 diesel-electric locomotive 37402.

THE HOME OF THE HUMP • 151

152 • A COMPREHENSIVE GUIDE TO RAILWAY REQUEST STOPS: A PERSONAL ODYSSEY TO VISIT EVERY ONE IN BRITAIN

Aspatria photographed on 29 March 2019 looking towards Barrow-in-Furness.

Keep your eyes off my hens – is that what the rooster at Aspatria on 29 March 2019 is thinking?

CHAPTER 12

THE WILDERNESS

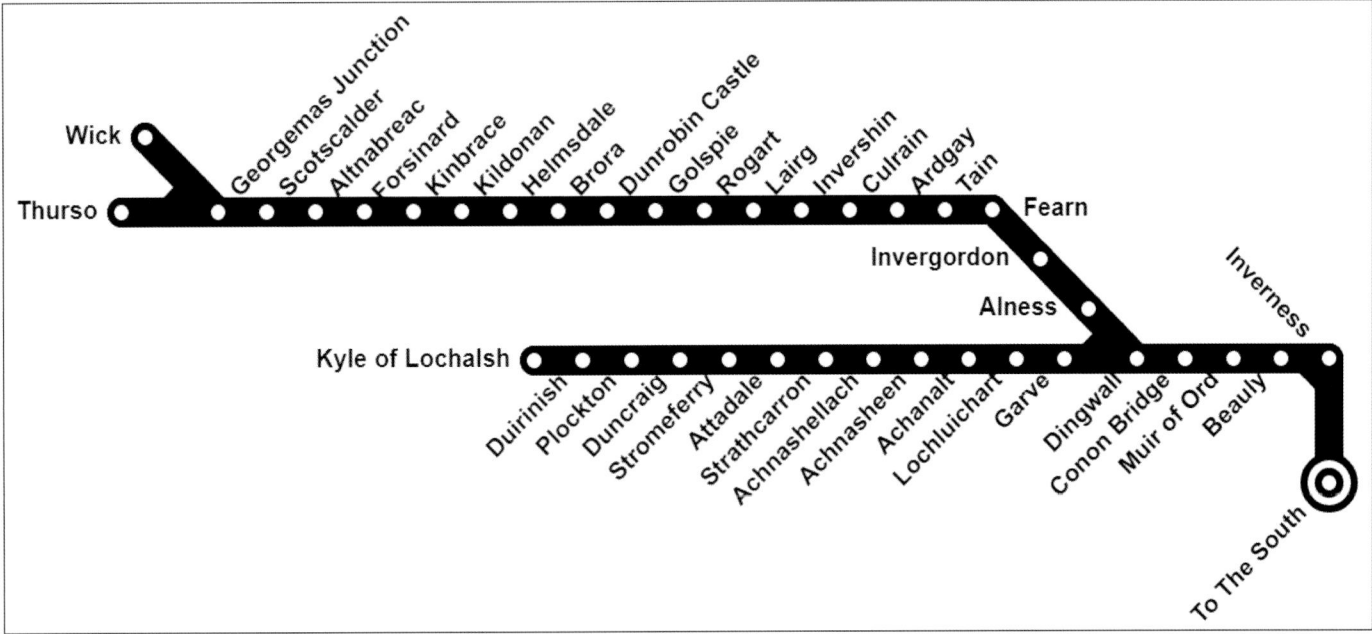

In late April 2019 I headed north, this time to Scotland on the first of two trips north of the border. Staying in Inverness for eight nights allowed me to visit stops on both the 'Kyle of Lochalsh Line' and the 'Far North Line' which included Thurso, the most northerly station in Great Britain.

The Sleeper

Going north I travelled on the overnight sleeper. I have used these services before but I was younger and suppler then, and able to pass the night in seated accommodation. This time I intended doing it in style in a sleeping berth, and I had high expectations. Due to engineering works, the train departed from King's Cross, not the usual Euston. 'Rooms available thirty minutes before departure' the timetable said, but not on this night and it became a case of rooms available an hour after departure. Chaos ruled with no one knowing what platform the train would be on until it actually arrived sixty minutes late, made up of old Mk3 coaches which were overdue for replacement.

Finally underway I checked my cabin out, which looked quite comfortable, but oh dear, it was tired, worn and, worst of all, not very clean. The bedding was thankfully crisp and laundered, but the carpet sadly hadn't seen a hoover in a while, while the washbasin took twenty minutes to empty and smelt of bad drains; luckily keeping the lid down kept the unfortunate odour at bay. Determined to enjoy the experience I left the window blind up and got into bed to watch the lights of stations flash past for a while, eventually pulling the blind down and getting a good night's sleep.

Having washed and shaved the next morning, there was a tap on my door. I opened it and saw the steward.

"Breakfast sir?" he said.

"Thank you," I replied.

He then dropped the bombshell and said, "Sorry there's no porridge this morning, will cornflakes do?"

I answered in the affirmative with a pressing question in my head: we should be in Scotland by now, so how can there be no porridge? Did I get on the wrong train, are we at this moment bearing down on Penzance? If I look out of the window will I see the Cornish coast rushing past? Let's be clear: I do love Cornwall and hope to return soon, but I had a plan and a timetable which needed to be strictly adhered to, and this plan clearly stated porridge for breakfast, then Inverness. I asked the steward where we were.

"We've just passed Blair Atholl and are running on time," he replied.

As I was certain Blair Atholl is in Scotland, clearly I did catch the correct train so why the porridge crisis? Was this a Brexit issue I thought. Has Theresa May created a new Cabinet post, Minister for Scottish Food Supplies, and is the new minister at this very moment diverting all available porridge to a secret warehouse hidden deep in the Highlands where it will be kept secure for future generations of Scots post-Brexit? Or is it more a Scottish independence issue: do we have to listen to Nicola Sturgeon's next speech? Will she promise unlimited porridge if Scotland becomes independent?

When breakfast was over and the porridge trauma had receded we pulled into Inverness on time. Overall my journey had been an enjoyable experience, it was just a shame that a little more care had not been taken with the presentation of the carriages themselves. On a more positive note the crew were all doing an excellent job, but let down by mismanagement, which is so often the case.

Day 1, Kyle of Lochalsh Line

Duncraig
Annual passenger usage: 408
Least used station rank: 29
Postcode: IV52 8TZ
Ordnance Survey national grid reference: NG812332

'Duncraig Platform' was opened in 1897 by the Highland Railway (HighR), then a private station for the use of Sir Alexander Matheson, who had built the nearby Duncraig Castle, after making his fortune in Hong Kong selling opium. Renamed Duncraig by BR in 1962 it then closed in 1964. However, it did remain unofficially open and at one point Ross & Cromarty Council agreed to pay £10 a year for the upkeep of the station as a request stop.[1] It was officially reopened in 1976, and has remained a request stop since that date.

After getting down from the train, and standing alone on the platform, I watched it disappear around the curve of track and through a corridor of brilliant yellow gorse bushes; I then had that marvellous feeling again, that for a short time this place was just for me. A brilliant blue sky and the shores of Loch Carron, with its islands of pine trees and across the water the village of Plockton – a perfect picture. The track at the east end of the platform vanishes through the stone arch of a road bridge and into a mysterious rock cutting. At the other end it follows the curving shore of the loch, on my visit through a blaze of yellow gorse. If the rest of Scotland comes near to this, I shall be very happy, I thought.

Only basic facilities exist: a noticeboard, help point and a seat on the platform. Something I put to good use while watching a heron on the shore and other birds on the water. There is a drop-off point with level access to the platform, although some surfaces are rather rough. Duncraig doesn't have a shelter – it has a waiting room, which may be small in stature, but is grandiose in style. An octagonal vertically-boarded construction with a pyramidal slated roof, and a decorative valance, all the inside timber is varnished and the outside has blue and white paintwork in good order.

Lochluichart
Annual passenger usage: 632
Least used station rank: 39
Postcode: IV23 2PZ
Ordnance Survey national grid reference: NH323625

Lochluichart was opened by the Dingwall and Skye Railway (D&SkyeR) as a private station for Lady Ashburnton in 1871, becoming a public station in 1887.[2] In 1954 flooding caused by the Luichart hydroelectric project necessitated not only track realignment but also the construction of a new station.[3]

Lochluichart is in a wonderful location, standing just above the loch with a real feeling of remoteness. The old station building is still standing but is now in private use, and there is a house nearby. The platform has a small wooden shelter with a help point on the outside wall. There is a drop-off point with step-free, but rather rough, access, and a timetable information board is situated near the entrance/exit gate.

Something that I saw here for the first time in a good many years was a pair of hooded crows, sometimes called the Scotch crow. These black and white birds are strikingly different to the plain black ones we see down south.

Attadale

Annual passenger usage: 1,170
Least used station rank: 62
Postcode: IV54 8YX
Ordnance Survey national grid reference: NG924390

Attadale was opened around 1875 by the D&SKyeR as a private halt for Attadale house. It became available for public use in 1877. A siding and signal box once existed at the eastern end of the station, but the siding closed to traffic in 1966 and was then removed in 1979.

It is a very nicely presented station with a brick-built shelter, containing a help point, and having a door that can be shut, not needed in April perhaps but probably most welcome in January. At road level there are noticeboards, and a short flight of stairs leading up to the platform, which has a bench seat outside the shelter. Part of the buffer stops that would have been at the end of the siding are still visible, pushing up through the undergrowth at the end of the platform.

It is another gorgeous location, with views of Loch Carron and its tidal ponds opposite, and the mountains all around. Even after two and a half hours, when I saw the Class 158 DMU that would take me back to Inverness coming into view, I was still wanting more.

Days 2, 3 and 4, Far North Line

Kinbrace

Annual passenger usage: 376
Least used station rank: 27
Postcode: KW11 6UB
Ordnance Survey national grid reference: NC862316

Kinbrace was first opened by the Sutherland & Caithness Railway (Sld&CnsR) in 1874 and had two platforms connected by a footbridge. There was a passing loop and two signal boxes, which opened in 1894, one at the northern end of the station by the level crossing, and the other at the southern end at the entrance to the goods yard. These boxes and the loop were taken out of service in 1966.

The scenery on the Far North Line is very different to the Scotland of the western side; gone are the lochs and mountains, and in their place a flatter and altogether bleaker landscape, what my landlord at the guesthouse in Inverness described to me as 'the wilderness', and I loved it.

The platform at Kinbrace has a bus stop-style shelter and a nearby help point. There is also an additional bench seat and an information screen. Near the entrance/exit are noticeboards, and access is step-free, although the platform surface is rather uneven. The original station is now a private home, and the disused platform is still clearly visible, as is much of the old goods yard.

Intrigued by a small walled enclosure on the top of a nearby hillock, and having plenty of time, I decided to investigate. I found not only a small cemetery, but a wonderfully atmospheric place enclosed by a low wall, with a single, stunted, wind-blasted tree that was dripping with lichen. The most recent grave was from the 1960s with the majority much older; presumably people had moved to the big towns and cities. I did wonder what life would have been like for these hardy people, living in what can at times be a harsh environment, now finally laid to rest with their low stone wall for protection from the wind and snow.

Scotscalder

Annual passenger usage: 182
Least used station rank: 12
Postcode: KW12 6YH
Ordnance Survey national grid reference: ND096560

Scotscalder was first opened in 1874 by the Sld&CnsR. Two signal boxes, one at each end of the station, came into use about twenty years later. There were two platforms with a passing loop and a single siding with a loading dock which served as a goods yard.

The old station building, which is now someone's home, has changed little since it last welcomed weary passengers, and appears almost ready to do so again. A bus stop-style shelter is provided for today's travellers, and there is also a help point and an arrival/departure screen. A noticeboard stands by the entrance/exit. The now defunct second platform along with the former goods siding and loading dock are both clearly visible.

With just 182 passengers annually, Scotscalder is the least used station on the Far North Line, and at less than 11 miles south of Thurso it is the most northerly request stop in Great Britain.

Altnabreac
Annual passenger usage: 658
Least used station rank: 41
Postcode: KW12 6UR
Ordnance Survey national grid reference: ND003456

Just why Altnabreac was built by the Sld&CnsR in 1874 remains unclear, in view of the fact it is one of the most remote stations in Great Britain. The commonest suggestion is that it served as a passing place and watering point for locomotives, as there was a water tank installed. Two platforms, a passing loop and two signal boxes were all once in place, along with sidings for goods and gravel.

Another favourite for me, Altnabreac is truly remote. The old station building, now a private house, still stands, but there is nothing else, just trees and moor. On the platform is a small wooden shelter containing a help point. Platform lighting is fed by an array of solar panels. There is also a bench seat. Noticeboards are close to the entrance/exit point which is level, but the surface is unmade. Opposite the northern end of the platform the water tank is still standing and the abandoned second platform is obvious, while at the southern end the old goods siding is very evident with some track still in place, albeit overgrown.

After a while two dogs joined me, one young and the other older. Great, I thought, because I do like dogs. The younger decided he liked me to the point where he became a bit of a nuisance – after all, muddy paw prints up clean trousers can eventually become tiresome. The older one, for reasons known only to himself, decided that I had somehow offended him, and proceeded to raise his hackles, bare his teeth and emit what can only be described as a low menacing growl. Luckily the shelter was not only close by, but had a narrow entrance. I backed in, keeping my bag between us, and guarded that doorway like the Roman soldier Horatius guarding the bridge. If you find yourself in a difficult doggy situation, the advice from dog people is *don't show fear*, so I talked to him, continuously, in a very brave voice. Now, bad tempered he may have been, stupid he wasn't, and he quickly worked out just who was the bravest, and that's how we stayed for the next fifteen minutes, at which point he presumably decided he had better things to do and wandered off.

Culrain
Annual passenger usage: 300
Least used station rank: 22
Postcode: IV27 4ET
Ordnance Survey national grid reference: NH576947

Culrain was opened by the Sutherland Railway (SlandR) in 1870 with a single platform, and a small goods yard on the west side of the station. A second platform and passing loop were added in 1902, along with a signal box. The loop, second platform and signal box were all removed in 1962 and the goods yard closed shortly after.

Having just come from Altnabreac I found Culrain to be an altogether different place, but very pleasing in its own way, having that feeling of a green and quiet rural retreat, closed in by surrounding trees. The usual facilities are all here, a wooden shelter painted in ScotRail blue and white, a help point, an information screen – which was not working – a bench seat and noticeboards. The disused platform is heavily overgrown and barely discernible, and the site of the former goods yard is now quite wooded. While exploring this site I found some lengths of rail and associated chairs, also various telegraph insulators, some still attached to pole cross-arms.

Just to the north of Culrain is the rail bridge that crosses the Kyle of Sutherland; as it has a footpath, I decided to walk across to Invershin. Not only is the distance to Invershin less than half a mile, but it afforded me the chance to get a close look at the striking structure that is Oykel Viaduct.

Invershin
Annual passenger usage: 438
Least used station rank: 32
Postcode: IV27 4ET
Ordnance Survey national grid reference: NH579953

The SlandR opened Invershin in 1868 with a single platform and unlike nearby Culrain it was never given a second platform. It did have two sidings and a signal box at the north end of the station.

My instant reaction at Invershin was one of dismay – this is a place that conveys an instant feeling of neglect. There is a small shelter that has the look of having been cobbled together from bits and pieces found in a local scrapyard. It has a small window made of some semi-opaque material, which gives it the appearance of a horrific jail cell, from which, once the door slams shut, there is no escape. An information screen and a bench seat are on the platform. Access from the drop-off point is level but over rough ground, with noticeboards by the entrance/exit. The original station building is still standing, although in a very bad state of repair with most of the roof missing; a pity as it must have been an attractive building in happier times.

Day 5, Kyle of Lochalsh Line

Duirinish
Annual passenger usage: 918
Least used station rank: 49
Postcode: IV40 8BD
Ordnance Survey national grid reference: NG777314

When opened by the HighR in 1897 Duirinish had a single platform with a wooden shelter. During the Second World War a yard was built to the east of the station to enable trains carrying military supplies on the way to the Kyle of Lochalsh to be marshalled. A signal box controlled this yard until the end of the war.

It is a gorgeous stop in another beautiful location, with the station sitting in a patch of green, with Loch Carron to the east and mountains all around. From the drop-off point there is level access through a gate onto the platform where there is an information screen, a bench seat and a small brick-built shelter, which has a help point inside. The station cottages are still standing and well looked after, with one of them let out as holiday accommodation.

Opposite the station is an expanse of common ground where on my visit sheep and Highland cattle were roaming free. The weather was perfect, what better than a walk I thought. Some distance in front of me a couple paused to admire and photograph a Highland bull – after all, he seemed to be a particularly fine specimen, just like the ones on all those Scottish postcards. The sheep paid me no attention at all and carried on doing what sheep do. The bull however fixed me with a most disconcerting stare. I changed course but his eyes still followed me – my imagination surely, as he had paid no attention to the couple who had just passed. I moved again and he was still staring. Now I could never be a matador, I don't have the right legs for those trousers they wear for a start, although I could find a red flag if pressed. I decided to make for the gate in the best nonchalant manner I could possibly manage, occasionally glancing over my shoulder and hoping not to hear the sound of pounding hooves getting ever closer. Once through the gate I began to feel a bit braver and tried to stare him out, but he had clearly done this before and I admitted defeat. At no time did he actually show aggression towards me, but clearly something was going on in his head, and it was obviously to do with me. Needless to say I stayed on my side of the fence until my train arrived.

Settled on the train and thinking to myself, the rooster at Aspatria, the dog at Altnabreac and now the bull at Duirinish, why don't they like me? Silly me, I thought, I'm getting paranoid, it's just one of those things, or should I say three of those things; little did I realise then that worse was yet to come.

Day 6, Far North Line

Rogart
Annual passenger usage: 1,630
Least used station rank: 82
Postcode: IV28 3XL
Ordnance Survey national grid reference: NC724019

Opened by the SlandR in 1868 Rogart had two platforms with a passing loop, plus two signal boxes and a goods yard. The platforms were extended in 1914.[4] The station was closed between June 1960 and March 1961 and was renamed Rogart Halt in June 1961. The suffix was dropped in 1982.

Rogart is in a glen just above the River Fleet with mountains rising up on both sides. It is a beautiful place to pass a couple of hours. The original station building is now a private dwelling, with luggage trolleys and barrows placed outside which give an air of a country station of yesteryear. A small wooden shelter stands on the northbound platform, while the southbound has a bus stop-style shelter. Information screens and noticeboards are both present and access is step-free to both platforms. One of the old Rogart signal boxes has been relocated to the site of the former goods yard for preservation and there are also old railway coaches parked there which form the accommodation for a tourist hostel.

Taking a short walk to the river gave me the opportunity to spend some time watching a dipper. These are marvellous little birds that actually walk underwater to catch their prey. This one also displayed the typical bobbing up and down that they constantly do when perched above the water. There was also a pair of grey wagtails, such eye-catching and always busy little birds. Walking back to the station a rustling in the leaves at the side of the road revealed a quite large common lizard. This was really nice to see because I do like my reptiles. This particular specimen had lost part of its tail, something that is not uncommon.

Dunrobin Castle
Annual passenger usage: 1,030
Least used station rank: 56
Postcode: KW10 6SF
Ordnance Survey national grid reference: NC849012

The Duke of Sutherland's Railway opened Dunrobin in 1870, and it became a private station the following year, although the public were allowed to use it in its later years, before it closed in 1965.[5] The station building was replaced in 1902, and *Railway Magazine* noted that the Duke of Sutherland had determined that Scots pine be used wherever possible in its construction. It also noted that the platform is rather long for a private station, this being necessitated for the duke's special events because his guests, when arriving by rail, could number between 300 and 400.[6] It reopened as Dunrobin Castle in 1985, and although still privately owned by the Sutherland Estates, it is available for the public wanting to use the ScotRail services that call here during the summer months only.

An impressive and rather unusual stop, the 'Hansel and Gretel' timber building is the most obvious feature. This building, which was not open when I visited, is a railway museum, making the only shelter available the awning at the front. Apart from a noticeboard no other facilities are available to passengers. The former bay platform can still easily be seen at the north end.

Kildonan
Annual passenger usage: 206
Least used station rank: 16
Postcode: KW8 6HY
Ordnance Survey national grid reference: NC901217

The Sld&CnsR opened Kildonan in 1874, originally being a two platform station with a passing loop, and two signal boxes which opened in 1894. A siding and loading dock were at the north end of what is today's platform.

This was a fantastic visit, with both the location and weather being absolutely perfect, and a station that really does look like a request stop. There is a new bus stop-style shelter, which is like the rest of the station, clean and functional. On the platform there is an arrival/departure screen, noticeboards and a bench seat. Walking around the site it is easy to find the one-time loading dock. The abandoned second platform is still visible, complete with its wooden waiting shelter, which is still in place. Now having realised it will never again welcome passengers, it is quietly retiring into the undergrowth.

Travelling on the Far North Line I had passed through Brora a total of six times, noticing that when heading back towards Inverness in the evening there was always a group of seals on the beach. The group, which on one occasion numbered about twenty, included both small and large ones. It occurred to me that some could be teenagers just hanging out, while the bigger and probably older ones might have been talking about their youth, the good old days, perhaps even saying, "This beach here is beautiful, and a perfect spot to rest the flippers, but do you remember when we used swim out far across the North Sea without seeing plastic floating in the water? Then the fish – well there were always so many more, was it really like that, or am I just getting old?"[7]

Day 7, Kyle of Lochalsh Line

Achanalt
Annual passenger usage: 434
Least used station rank: 31
Postcode: IV23 2QD
Ordnance Survey national grid reference: NH260614

Opened by the D&SKyeR in 1870, Achanalt had two platforms and a passing loop. Two signal boxes were opened in 1893 and a small goods yard was to the west of the station. The loop and signal boxes were closed in 1966 and the line singled.

It is a lovely location close to the River Bran and Loch Achanalt. The station is clean and functional, if a little unremarkable. The now privately owned stationmaster's cottage backs onto the platform. On the platform is a metal and plexiglass shelter that looked on my visit to be almost new. Noticeboards are present but there is no help point or information screen. Access to the platform is via a kissing gate and, although level, the ground is uneven.

A large garden is separated from the platform by a fence, and walking down the platform I noticed an Irish Setter. I have been fortunate enough to share my life with two of these gorgeous dogs which, apart from stunning film-star good looks, also have a mischievous and yet at the same time loving temperament. I said hello and he bounded straight over. They do love people. His owners followed and told me his name was Riley and we spent some time chatting. When I finally walked away Riley began crying for me to stay, then, when he realised I finally was going he did several laps of the garden at an amazing speed.

Achnashellach
Annual passenger usage: 870
Least used station rank: 47

Postcode: IV54 8YH
Ordnance Survey national grid reference: NH002484

The D&SKyeR opened Achnashellach in 1870. At that time a private halt, it appeared in public timetables from 1871. Prior to 1914 the station name was spelled 'Auchnashellach'.[8] It had two platforms with a passing loop and a signal box from 1893, with a siding at the western end of the platform. The line was singled during the 1960s.

The station is situated in a superb location at the end of a private road in Achnashellach Forest, hiding among the trees and nestled at the foot of the surrounding mountains. Basic facilities only exist here with a tiny brick shelter, noticeboards and a help point. Access is step-free but by way of a rough track and gate.

At Achnashellach, my last stop of this trip, I was shortly to discover I had perhaps saved the best to last. Exploring up a forestry track that led uphill from the station, I eventually found myself above the treeline at the foot of the mountains. After a little while there I heard the unmistakable screech of a bird of prey. When I located the source I saw not one, but a pair of golden eagles. An amazing treat, since I had not seen a golden eagle since the early 1990s when birdwatching with my daughter. I sat and watched these magnificent birds for half an hour before I had to leave them; a tremendous finish to my first Scottish trip.

The platform and the splendid waiting room at Duncraig, photographed on 24 April 2019, looking west.

Above: Duncraig and the shores of Loch Carron seen on 24 April 2019, looking towards Kyle of Lochalsh.

Opposite above: Lochluichart on 24 April 2019 facing west. The wooden hut is for passenger use, all other buildings are now privately owned.

Opposite below: Attadale seen on 24 April 2019. A Class 158 Express Sprinter DMU forming the 17.13 Kyle of Lochalsh to Inverness service is seen arriving.

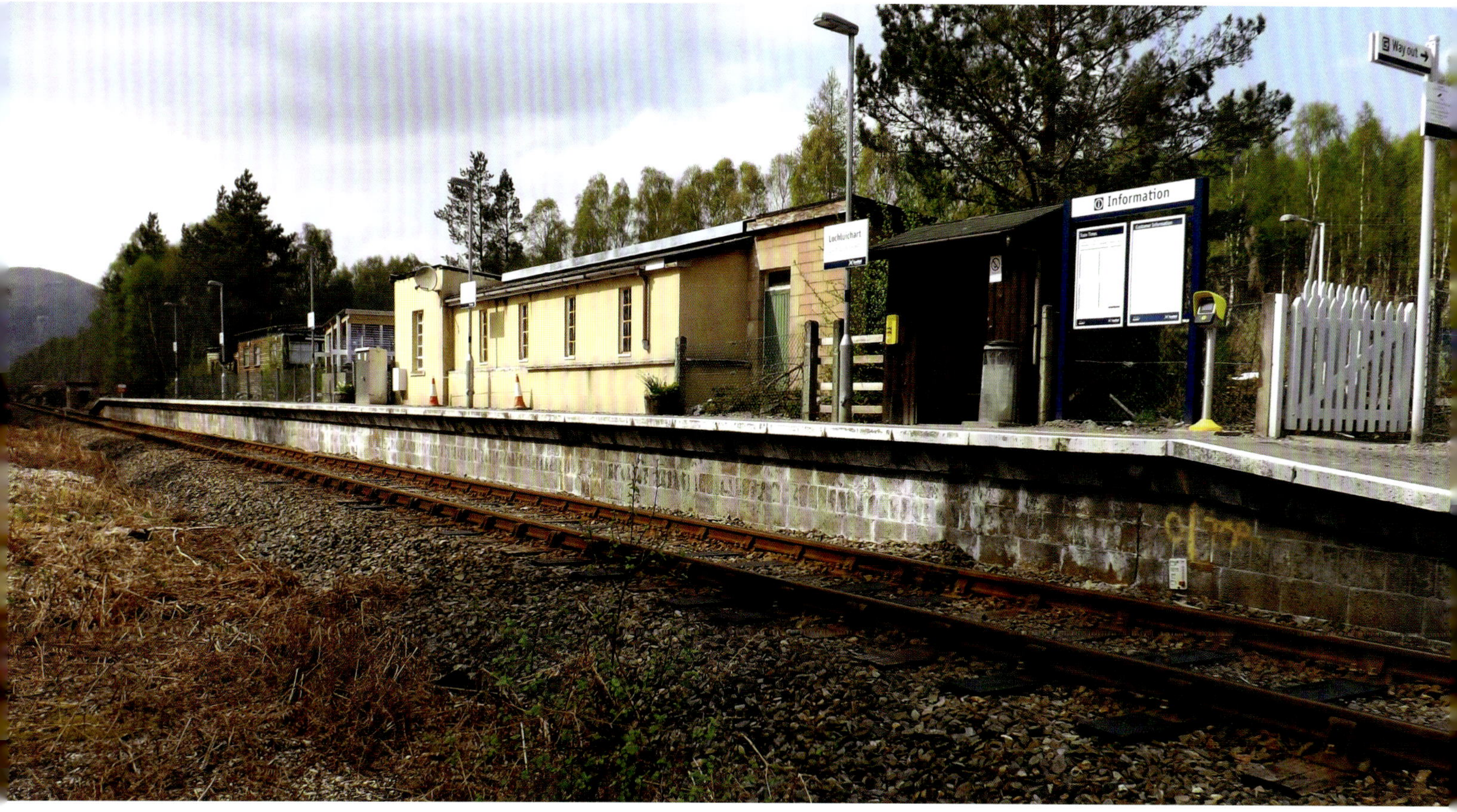
Information
Way out

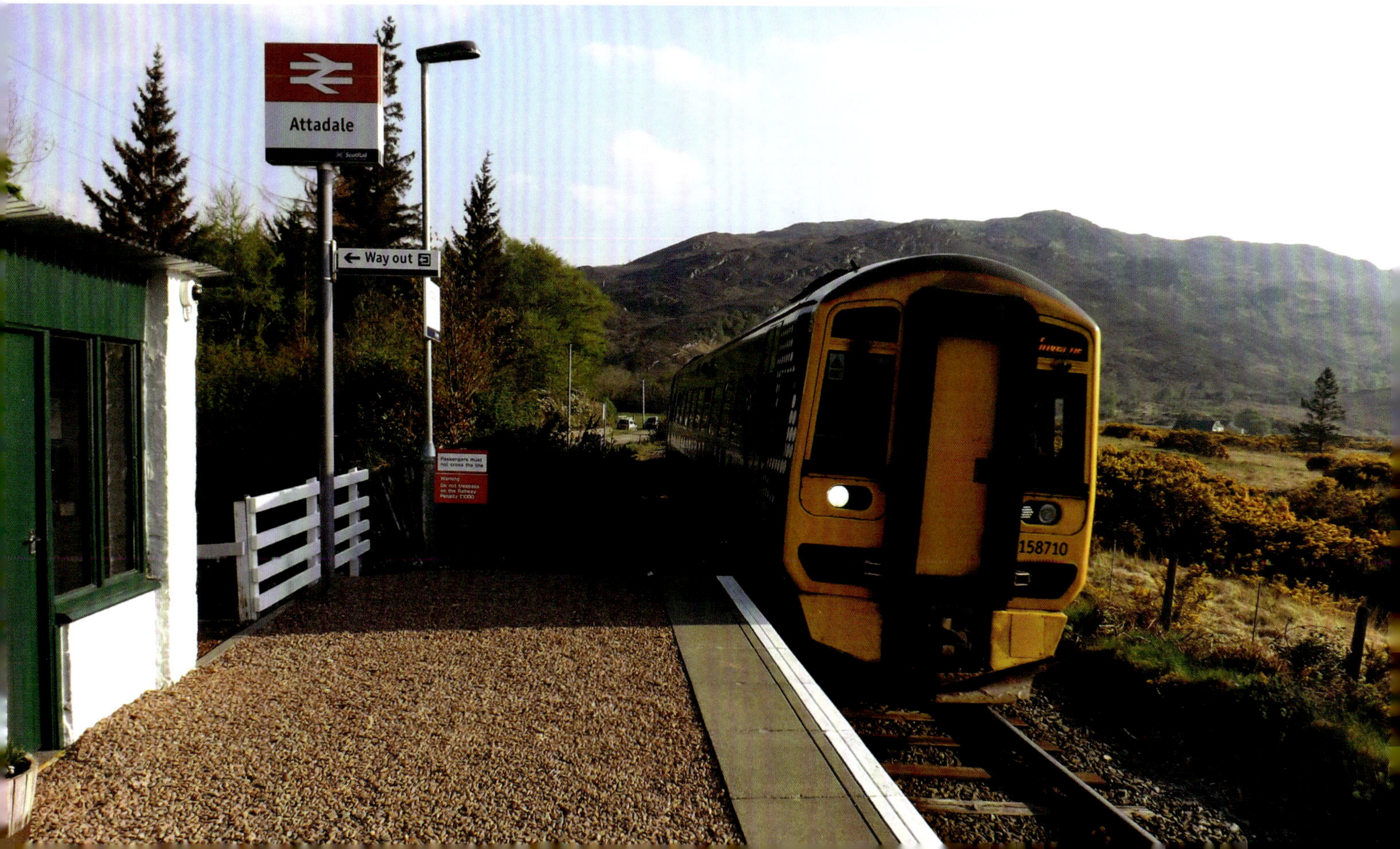
Attadale
Way out
158710

162 • A COMPREHENSIVE GUIDE TO RAILWAY REQUEST STOPS: A PERSONAL ODYSSEY TO VISIT EVERY ONE IN BRITAIN

Kinbrace on the Far North Line, looking towards Thurso on 25 April 2019.

As far north as it is possible to go by rail on the British mainland: Thurso, which is over 900 rail miles from Penzance, the most southerly station. Seen here on 25 April 2019.

A Class 158 Express Sprinter DMU at Thurso forming the 10.41 Inverness to Wick which is about to depart on 25 April 2019.

The very well-kept Scotscalder on 25 April 2019, this view is looking towards Inverness.

Above: The magnificently remote Altnabreac on 27 April 2019. Approaching is a Class 158 Express Sprinter DMU forming the 12.34 Wick to Inverness service. On the left of the photograph can be seen the now redundant water tank and part of the abandoned platform. The shelter is on the right.

Left: The water tank at Altnabreac, still standing but unused for something like fifty years, pictured on 27 April 2019.

Opposite above: Culrain looking north towards Thurso/Wick on 27 April 2019. From here the line crosses the Kyle of Sutherland on a rail bridge, arriving at Invershin which is less than half a mile distant. However, to drive between the two would entail a journey of over 8 miles.

Opposite below: Invershin with its former station buildings in a very poor state of repair. Today's shelter can just be seen at the far end of the platform. Photographed looking south on 27 April 2019.

166 • A COMPREHENSIVE GUIDE TO RAILWAY REQUEST STOPS: A PERSONAL ODYSSEY TO VISIT EVERY ONE IN BRITAIN

Duirinish photographed on 28 April 2019, facing east towards Inverness.

Photographed at Rogart on 29 April 2019, one of the former signal boxes, which has been preserved and relocated to the tourist hostel site adjacent to the station.

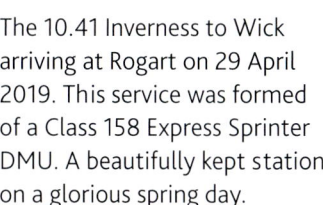

A common lizard seen at Rogart on 29 April 2019. This one has lost part of its tail, which is sometimes done deliberately in order to escape a predator.

The 10.41 Inverness to Wick arriving at Rogart on 29 April 2019. This service was formed of a Class 158 Express Sprinter DMU. A beautifully kept station on a glorious spring day.

Above: Dunrobin Castle looking towards Wick on 29 April 2019.

Opposite above: Kildonan had a superb feeling of isolation, seen here looking north on 29 April 2019.

Opposite below: The wooden shelter on the abandoned platform at Kildonan still survives, photographed here on 29 April 2019.

Above: Achanalt seen here on 30 April 2019, looking towards Inverness.

Opposite above: The delightfully secluded Achnashellach looking towards the Kyle of Lochalsh on 30 April 2019. On the right is the former second platform.

Opposite below: The 13.35 Inverness to Kyle of Lochalsh, comprised of a Class 158 Express Sprinter DMU, is seen arriving at Achnashellach on 30 April 2019.

THE WILDERNESS • 171

CHAPTER 13

GET ON YER BIKE

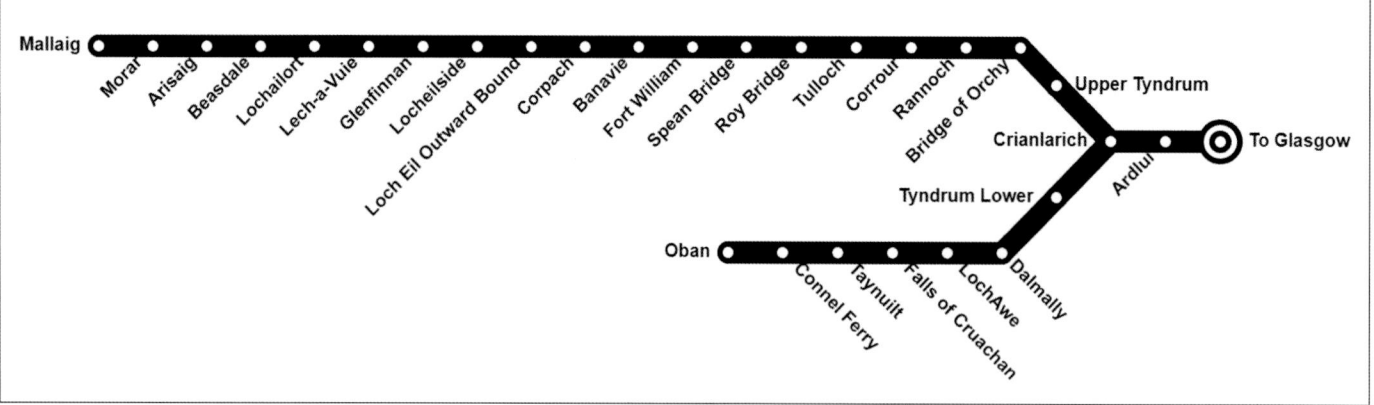

In June I made my second trip to Scotland, with the intention of visiting the nine request stops on the 'West Highland Line', plus Arisaig, which is the most westerly station on mainland Great Britain. Also planned was a steam fix with a trip on the 'Jacobite' from Fort William to Mallaig and back, 82 miles of chuffing; pure joy. I had booked a six-night stay in Fort William and two nights on the Caledonian Sleeper. The overnight train in both directions proved to be a little disappointing as the promise of new coaches still did not materialise. Arriving at Euston, and later at Fort William for the homeward journey, I found the same old, tatty and tired Mk3 coaching stock of my previous trips waiting at the platform, but at least, unlike my first trip, the drains didn't smell.

Ardlui
Annual passenger usage: 5,104
Least used station rank: 161
Postcode: G83 7DT
Ordnance Survey national grid reference: NN316155

Ardlui was opened by the West Highland Railway (WhighR) in 1894, consisting of an island platform with a passing loop and sidings at the northern end of the station. As Ardlui is a request stop but only for the night sleeper services, I duly made my request, and was delighted to find myself the only passenger alighting, just what I had hoped for, making the Caledonian Sleeper stop just for me – a good start to Scottish trip number two. Access to the station is through a subway from road level, then up a flight of stairs onto the island platform. At the top of the stairs there are some rather ornate iron gates and fencing. The old signal box, located on the platform, closed in 1986, and was then converted into a comfortable waiting room. Prior to this a small open-fronted waiting shelter had been attached to the outside, and is still available to those who require a seat and a breath of fresh air.

Arrival/departure screens, a help point and timetables are all in place. The sidings at the north end of the station are still in use for permanent way maintenance purposes. Now privately owned, the stationmaster's house is still visible to the north of the station.

On a lovely sunny summer morning, I was at Ardlui taking in its glorious position on the banks of Loch Lomond. The train taking me on to my next stop appeared to be running on time; things were looking good.

Falls of Cruachan
Annual passenger usage: 726
Least used station rank: 43
Postcode: PA33 1AN
Ordnance Survey national grid reference: NN079267

Opened in 1893 by the Callander and Oban Railway (C&ObanR), Falls of Cruachan has always comprised of one platform, located at the foot of Ben Cruachan in the Pass of Brander, an area notorious for rockfalls. No conventional signalling has ever existed here, but there are 'Pass of Brander Stone Signals' at the western end of the station. These signals consist of wires, alongside the railway, and if these wires are broken by a falling rock, the signals automatically go to danger alerting the driver of the possibility of rocks on the line. This system is sometimes called 'Anderson's Piano' after the name of its inventor and the noise the stretched wires make in the wind. The station is shown on the OS map of 1900 under the name of 'Falls of Cruachan Platform'. It closed in 1965 and then reopened in 1988 as Falls of Cruachan.

Buried between the foot of a mountain and the shores of Loch Awe, this is a very attractive location. It is a well looked after station with a help point, information screen and a timetable posterboard. Access could be problematical with two ramps and three sets of stairs between the road and platform. There is a modern bus stop-style shelter, and planted flower troughs on the platform, some of which take the form of a mini wooden train. Not only is this stop open only during the summer months, trains only call during the daylight hours, due to the fact that there is no lighting.

Loch Eil Outward Bound
Annual passenger usage: 548
Least used station rank: 37
Postcode: PH33 7NN
Ordnance Survey national grid reference: NN054783

This station was opened by BR in 1985 specifically to serve the nearby Loch Eil Outward Bound Centre. It is a neat and tidy stop on the shores of Loch Eil, with views of the mighty Ben Nevis. The platform has a gravelled surface and a wooden shelter, the construction of which is very much in sympathy with its surroundings, due to the use of half-rounded vertical timbers. Both a help point and information screen are in place as is a timetable/noticeboard. The waterfront and the Centre can be reached by use of a barrow crossing at the end of the platform.

Roy Bridge
Annual passenger usage: 3,712
Least used station rank: 136
Postcode: PH31 4AH
Ordnance Survey national grid reference: NN272810

The WHighR opened Roy Bridge in 1894, with two platforms and a passing loop. On the north side of the station was a goods yard, and a signal box once stood on the southbound platform.

Roy Bridge has now been reduced to a single platform with a metal and plexiglass shelter and additional seating outside. An arrival/departure screen, timetable/noticeboards and a help point are here to assist passengers. Access is via a flight of stairs from the road, which leads directly onto the platform, the surface of which is gravelled. The abandoned second platform is still in existence, but there is no sign of the former station buildings or the goods yard, these having all been replaced by modern housing.

Corrour
Annual passenger usage: 13,302
Least used station rank: 283
Postcode: PH30 4AA
Ordnance Survey national grid reference: NN356663

Corrour opened in 1894 as a private station on the shooting estate of Sir John Stirling Maxwell, Tenth Baronet of Pollok, a Tory MP and chairman of the Forestry Commission. It was built with an island platform and a footbridge to take passengers over the adjacent siding. The 1904 OS 6-inch map shows the name 'Corrour Siding', and it first appeared in the public timetable in 1934. A signal box at the southern end of the platform was of the observation tower type.

Corrour is Great Britain's most remote station, having only private road access. The nearest public road is the B846 which is a 10-mile walk away by hill track, and the only vehicular access is along a 15-mile private road to the A86. It is also the highest main line station at 1,340 feet (408 metres) above sea level. The isolation here on the edge of Rannoch Moor is palpable, and it is a truly magnificent and magical place to immerse yourself in. The island platform has a wooden shelter and a picnic bench. A help point, information screen and posterboards are provided. The old signal box is now available for holiday rentals, and the siding is still in place. Something I'd not seen before, at least at a request stop, was a defibrillator. Not sure just why it would be located here, but then I did see several lots of hill walkers striding by.

Lochailort

Annual passenger usage: 1,844
Least used station rank: 92
Postcode: PH38 4LZ
Ordnance Survey national grid reference: NM768826

The Mallaig Extension Railway (MER) opened Lochailort in 1901 with two platforms, a passing loop and a small goods yard. A new signal box was built and the loop extended when the station became much busier during the Second World War. Also at this time Inverailort House, which is nearby, did service as a commando training school, along with much of the surrounding countryside. The loop was lifted and the signal box demolished in 1966, with the original station buildings being torn down in the 1970s.

Lochailort today is a fairly unimposing station in itself, but it is in a magnificent location at the foot of mountains and above the River Ailort where it flows into Loch Ailort. The now defunct second platform is overgrown but still visible, as is some foundation brickwork from the station buildings. The base of the signal box is easy to find at the western end of the platform, and part of a loading dock in the old goods yard can still be found. The platform has an information screen, help point, bench seats and a metal and plexiglass shelter. A timetable noticeboard is by the entrance/exit gate and access is step-free.

Beasdale

Annual passenger usage: 418
Least used station rank: 30
Postcode: PH39 4NR
Ordnance Survey national grid reference: NM709850

The MER opened Beasdale in 1901 as a private station for Mr Nicholson of Arisaig House.[1] A siding and loading dock were at the immediate western end of the platform. The station opened to the public in 1965.

Stepping out of a Class 156 DMU I found myself at an idyllic stop, cocooned among greenery. A buzzard was floating high overhead keeping a watchful eye, adding to the feel of this place and the moment. There is a wooden shelter, so very apposite for its location, on the platform. I decided to check it out and discovered I wasn't alone. Sitting on a windowsill I saw a large black beetle. I don't think he wanted a train, but if he did I suppose he would had to have stood on the platform and raised an antenna, after all this is a request stop. The former station building adjacent to the platform is now privately owned, but still fits in with the general ambience. Access from the car park is level and the platform surface is gravel. A help point, information screen and noticeboards all help to guide the traveller. Parts of the loading dock and siding can still be seen, although the tracks have been lifted.

Locheilside

Annual passenger usage: 300
Least used station rank: 23
Postcode: PH33 7PN
Ordnance Survey national grid reference: NM994786

Built with one platform, Locheilside was opened by the MER in 1901, with a goods siding at the western end of the station. Situated close to the shores of Loch Eil and with mountain views to the east, it is a picturesque location. The actual station however is to my mind the least striking on the Mallaig branch. There is a car park with step-free access to the platform, but this is over a very rough gravel surface. A bus stop-style shelter is provided, as is a help point and information screen, plus noticeboards. I was unable to see any trace of either the former goods sidings, or the old station building.

Lech-a-Vuie

Annual passenger usage: N/A
Least used station rank: N/A
Postcode: PH37 4LT
Ordnance Survey national grid reference: NM860813

Opened by the MER with the line in 1901, Lech-a-Vuie has always consisted of a single platform, built for the use of shooting parties on the Inverailort Estate, which used to be owned by the Cameron-Head family. The agreement to provide a private 'shooting platform' at Lech-a-Vuie was part of a deal to sell land required by the railway company.[2] It is shown on some early OS maps with the legend 'platform'; sheet 61 Arisaig 1908 is one example.[3] It is also shown in the 2001 edition of *Railway Track Diagrams 1: Scotland & the Isle of Man* as being '17 miles and eighteen chains' from the former Banavie junction.[4] This is confirmed at the location with the 17.25 milepost located just past the platform end.

Specific instructions related to this platform existed, and the *LNER Sectional Appendix to the Rules and Regulations* of 1947 states:

LECH-A-VUIE PLATFORM
This platform is situated between Glenfinnan and Lochailort. When passengers are to be set down or taken up, timeous notice must be made to the Station Master at Lochailort, who must give the necessary instructions to the Driver and Guard in the case of up trains and must telephone the Station Master at Glenfinnan, in the case of down trains. Parties using the platform must pay the fares to the station beyond, and the Guard must collect the tickets from those alighting, while those to be taken up must previously possess themselves of tickets. Trains must only call at this platform between sunrise and sunset.[5]

During the Second World War the platform, Inverailort House and much of the surrounding countryside were used by the military for training commandos. When the war ended it reverted to its original use, and according to local signalman Jim Archibald, the platform saw its last passengers in July or August 1973.[6]

Working with the Wikipedia list of request stops, I became very much aware that there were anomalies. Some stations are request stops for one train operating company but not another. Others listed as request stops when I began are now mandatory stops, and only two heritage lines stops are shown, but I know many others do exist. But Lech-a-Vuie is different, in that no passenger has set foot here in almost fifty years. Just how or why it is still listed as a request stop I can't imagine. All I know is that the last time I checked (March 2020), it was still there.

But listed it was, therefore I had to go, and this left me with two problems: firstly how would I locate it, and secondly how would I actually get there? I found a map reference on the internet, and using this in conjunction with satellite map views I found a definite possibility for the location. This just left me wondering how to actually visit – the train doesn't stop and it is not on a bus route. Firstly I considered a taxi, but that would have meant me asking the driver to take me to a place while being unable to tell him exactly where it was. Then it came to me: Lech-a-Vuie is only 3 miles from Glenfinnan; so I would hire a bike, a mountain bike. After all I might have to pedal up a mountain.

On a rather damp Highland morning I alighted from a train at Glenfinnan, with my eye being immediately drawn to the mountain bike locked to the cycle rack on the platform just as I had arranged. This was going to transport me to Lech-a-Vuie, my last stop in Scotland. Donning full wet weather gear I mounted my steed and headed down the slope that leads from the station, although describing an incline of 45 degrees, and in the wet, as a 'slope' is possibly an understatement. In fact I recall picking up speed and thinking, is this safe? But even before I could answer I found myself at the bottom. Pedalling off towards my destination and ignoring the awful crunching sound every time I changed gear, I became focused on what, if anything, I might find when I reached my goal. I am a seventy-something years old and had not ridden a bike for twenty years, so I did find the going a little hard. The constant drizzle also detracted from the enjoyment of the moment, and the road, while not exactly mountainous, did have its ups and downs. I do remember once, or perhaps even twice, feeling the road begin to climb upwards yet again, and thinking, oh no not another bloody hill. Clunking the gears downwards and puffing up the hills, I did at times have doubts about my sanity, but allayed these with a smug personal admiration for my dogged determination. After a few false starts, looking from the roadside down to the railway line and hoping that this would be it, I at last recognised the footpath's stone edging I had seen in those satellite pictures and realised I'd finally arrived. I gave myself a metaphorical pat on the back, and seeing as the drizzle had thankfully at last abated, I sat on a rock and had a cup of tea, postponing my exploration for a few minutes, because this was not only a moment to savour, but also a chance to get my breath back.

From the road it is impossible to see what, if anything, is there. The stone edging marks the line of the footpath that once led from the road down to the platform. I followed it. Several trees have taken root, and on my visit the grass was thick, but the base and shape of the platform is unmistakably still visible. I was just 3 miles from Glenfinnan and a couple of hundred metres from a main road, but down at the platform I could have been in the middle of nowhere. This was a truly wonderful and atmospheric location, the magic of which I instantly felt. Looking eastwards, the line curves quite sharply between rocks on both sides of the track giving the impression that it is coming at you out of nowhere. Towards the west the ground is more open but still enclosed by the surrounding mountains. I spent quite some time in that place, taking in the surroundings and deciding that all the planning and sheer physical effort of getting there meant nothing compared to actually being present. I asked myself what it might have looked like when it was still in use, and wondered why this tiny, abandoned and largely forgotten place had managed to so tightly grip my imagination. I had no answers, but I did know it felt good to be there.

On my return home I set about discovering all I could about Lech-a-Vuie. Disappointingly information is very scant, but the search goes on with the ultimate goal of finding a photograph of it when it was still in use.

Above: On the morning of 10 June 2019 the Caledonian Sleeper, with Class 73 electro-diesel locomotive 73968 at the head, is about to leave Ardlui and continue its journey north to Fort William, after having stopped to allow me to alight.

Opposite above: A glorious early summer morning at Ardlui, looking north on 10 June 2019.

Opposite below: Falls of Cruachan is the only request stop on the Oban branch, and has a train service during the summer months only. Photographed looking towards Oban on 10 June 2019.

GET ON YER BIKE • 177

A Network Rail road/rail tree cutting vehicle passing through Falls of Cruachan on 10 June 2019.

Loch Eil Outward Bound photographed on 10 June 2019. About to stop is the 16.05 Mallaig to Glasgow Queen Street service formed of a Class 156 Super Sprinter DMU.

The truly magnificent Corrour, situated on the edge of Rannoch Moor. It is the highest main line station in Britain, and was photographed on 11 June 2019. To the left the line continues on to Fort William, while to the right it heads for Glasgow.

The platform at Corrour seen on 11 June 2019, facing south towards Glasgow.

180 • A COMPREHENSIVE GUIDE TO RAILWAY REQUEST STOPS: A PERSONAL ODYSSEY TO VISIT EVERY ONE IN BRITAIN

Roy Bridge was, clean and well-presented but rather uninteresting. There was however plenty to read while waiting for my train: a splendid example of corporate signage, all that was needed was a sign reminding passengers to read all the signs. Looking towards Fort William on 11 June 2019.

Beasdale with its wooden shelter, seen facing west on 12 June 2019.

Ex-LMS Black Five 45407 *The Lancashire Fusilier* at the head of a Jacobite service bound for Mallaig, passing the original station buildings at Beasdale on 12 June 2019.

A Class 156 Super Sprinter DMU forming the 08.20 Glasgow Queen Street to Mallaig service passing Lochailort on 12 June 2019.

Locheilside on 13 June 2019, with the 10.10 Mallaig to Glasgow Queen Street service, comprised of a Class 156 Super Sprinter DMU, about to stop. The electronic sign seems a little confused as it shows the next train to be a Mallaig service.

The remains of the platform at Lech-a-Vuie, looking east on 15 June 2019.

The view from platform level at Lech-a-Vuie, facing east, 15 June 2019.

Ex-LMS Black Five 45212 passing the site of Lech-a-Vuie on 15 June 2019. The group of trees alongside the first carriage are growing on the old platform itself, and the low stone wall marks the footpath that leads to the platform.

Arisaig, the most westerly station on the British mainland, looking towards Mallaig on 12 June 2019.

CHAPTER 14

OH BULLOCKS, WHAT DO I DO NOW?

Having completed Scotland, there remained only seven stops, two of which were on heritage lines and five were in East Anglia. I would also be photographing Lowestoft (the most easterly station), completing my journey to the four corners of mainland Great Britain's rail map. I also intended a return visit to Berney Arms, the circle complete, so to speak.

Damems in Yorkshire would be first and involved a two-night stay in Leeds. The second night was not required for the Damems visit, but it did allow me to fit in a journey on the Settle–Carlisle line. My next outing would be Greenway Halt in Devon, which would be easy for me as a simple day trip. East Anglia entailed four nights in Norwich, and required some serious timetable work. The National Rail Enquiries website had four out of the five stops that I would be visiting marked with the warning 'This station is served by a very sparse train service'. So sparse in fact that in three cases out of the five I resorted to arriving by bus, foot and taxi. I did of course leave by train, but in only two instances did I actually arrive and leave by rail. Berney Arms presented its own unique problems, because the station had been closed due to engineering work since October 2018. These works had overrun, meaning the line was still closed for my visit (July 2019). The solution I decided would be pedal power again; how wrong I was.

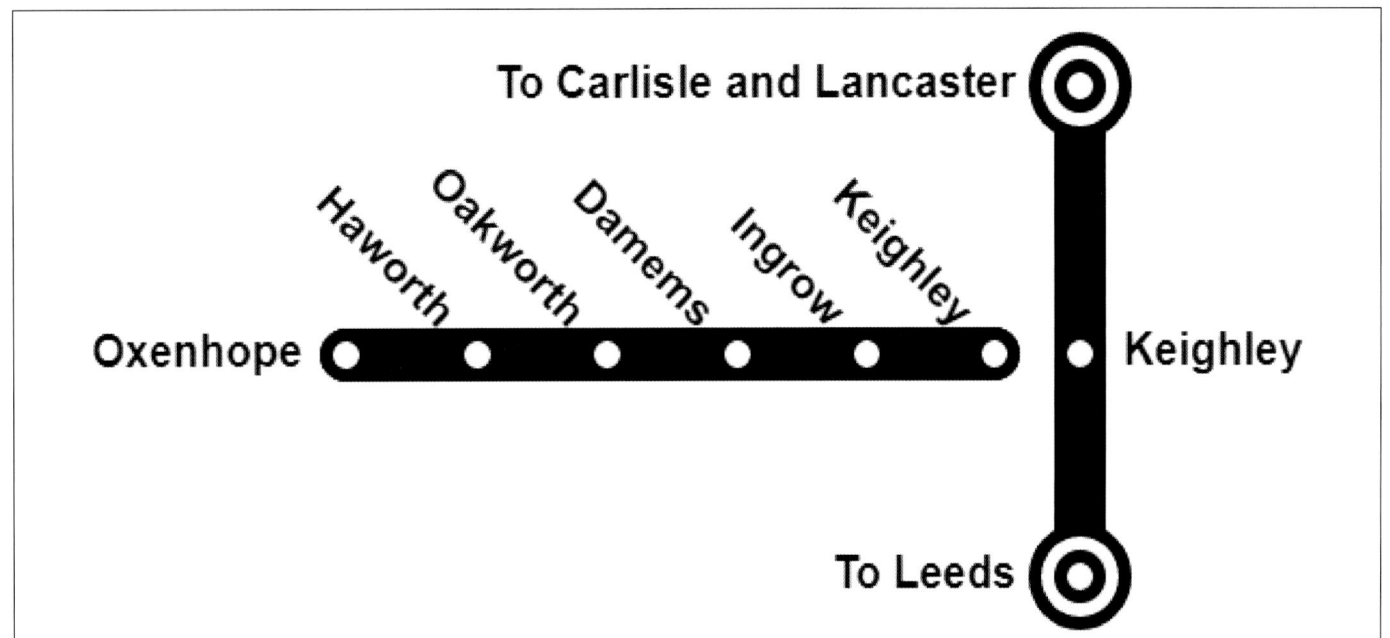

Damems
Annual passenger usage: N/A
Least used station rank: N/A
Postcode: BD22 7AR
Ordnance Survey national grid reference: SE050388

The Keighley and Worth Valley Railway opened Damems station in 1847. Despite the platform being only one coach length, it still had all the usual station facilities: a waiting room, booking office and even a stationmaster. This allowed its claim to be the smallest station in Great Britain, a claim still maintained to the present day. Closed in 1949 by BR it was then reopened in 1968 by the Keighley and Worth Valley Preservation Society. There was a siding which serviced a nearby mill at the northern end of the station and a level crossing at the southern end of the platform which used to be operated from a ground frame in the garden of the stationmaster's house.

I found Damems to be charming, and it was described to me by the signalman there as 'Something of a hidden gem'. A statement I would heartily agree with, as the trains passing through during my stay were busy, but nobody got either on or off – just faces staring out of the windows, not realising what they were missing. A small signal cabin on the end of the platform, which came here from Earby in Lancashire, now houses the ground frame, and the signalman invited me in. I found this signal box to be immaculate; but then they always were. The station buildings, which include a waiting room and toilets, are not original, as they had to be rebuilt, while remaining faithful to the Midland Railway design, and the builders have done an incredible job. Overall, Damems is in a perfect and quiet location, a beautifully preserved and lovingly cared-for station, with manicured gardens, steam trains and semaphore signals: like the man said, a 'real gem'.

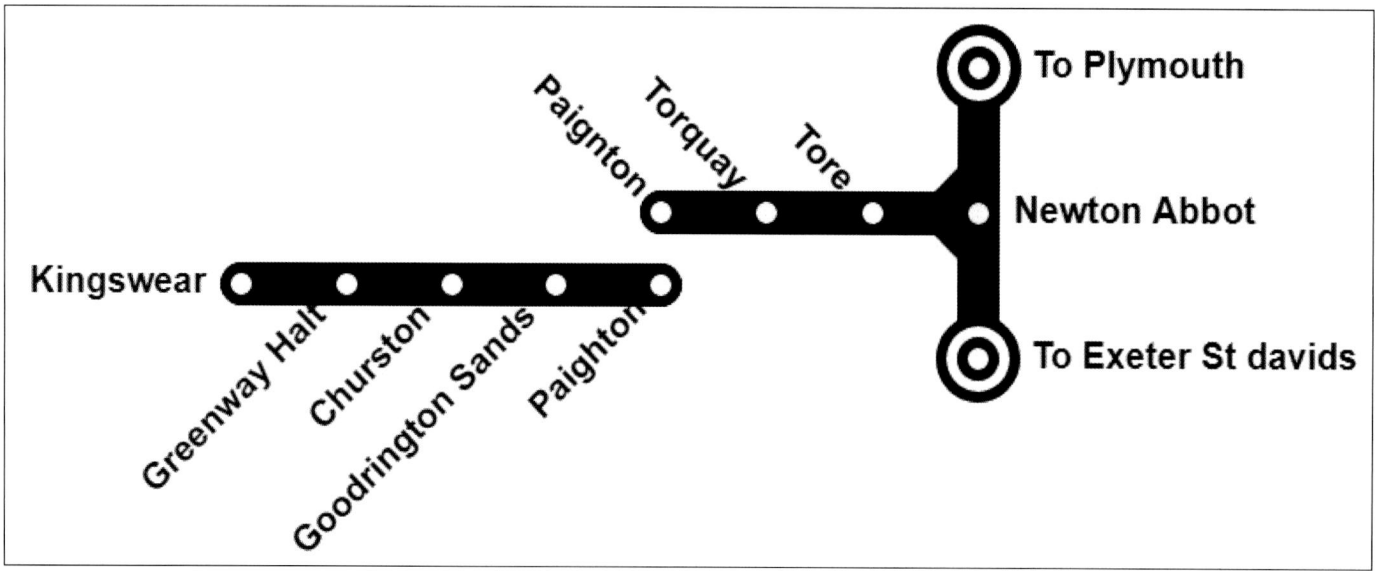

Greenway Halt
Annual passenger usage: N/A
Least used station rank: N/A
Postcode: TQ5 0ER
Ordnance Survey national grid reference system: SX882552

A relatively new stop, Greenway Halt was opened in 2012 by the Dartmouth Steam Railway, a steam operated line, which runs from Paignton to Kingswear. The stop was opened mainly for the benefit of visitors to the nearby Greenway Estate, the former home of author Agatha Christie.

Set among the rural greenery of Devon, and at the northern end of Greenway Tunnel, this is a charming location. It is a basic stop with no facilities other than some bench seats and a parked former railway freight van that serves as a waiting room, which is stocked with local tourist literature. The platform is short and can only accommodate two coaches. A novel feature here is that passengers do not have to signal to the driver of their intention to board – instead a button is provided which when pressed lights a lineside signal that alerts the train crew.

East Anglia, and the Final Five

Brampton
Annual passenger usage: 9,004
Least used station rank: 227
Postcode: NR34 8EF
Ordnance Survey national grid reference: TM411834

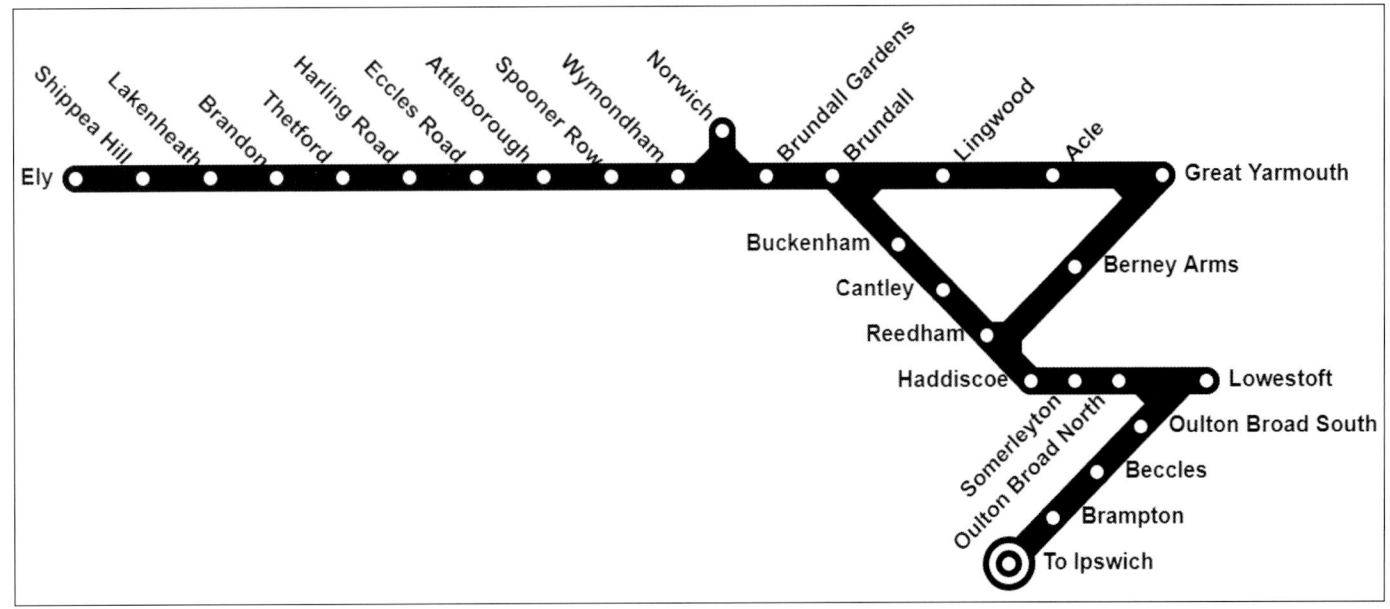

Brampton was opened by the East Suffolk Railway in 1854, and while under LNER ownership in 1928 it became known as 'Brampton (Suffolk)' in order to distinguish it from the station in Cumbria of the same name. It did have, at one point in its history, two platforms, a goods siding and a signal box; no obvious signs remain of any of these today.

This is a rather basic and modern station with limited facilities. There is a small bus stop-style shelter, and at the end of the platform a help point, noticeboard and a red phone box with a payphone. Local volunteers maintain flower tubs, which help to create a cared-for and clean station.

At this point in the day I was still travelling north from London. After stopping a Class 156 DMU, I boarded and headed towards Lowestoft, in order to photograph Great Britain's most easterly station. From there I travelled to Norwich in order to drop my bags at the hotel, and then on to my last stop of the day, Spooner Row, for which, due to its 'sparse service', I resorted to using a local bus service.

Spooner Row
Annual passenger usage: 1,628
Least used station rank: 80
Postcode: NR18 9AH
Ordnance Survey national grid reference: TM094975

Spooner Row was first opened by the Norfolk Railway in 1845, only to be closed in 1847. It was then reopened in 1855, this time by the ECR, closing again in 1860. Finally it reopened in 1882 under the ownership of the Great Eastern Railway (GER). There were two platforms staggered across Station Road, a signal box was adjacent to the level crossing, and there was a small goods siding.

The service at Spooner Row is indeed sparse with a total of three trains on weekdays, two on Saturdays and no service on Sundays. Only half a mile from the bus stop on the very busy A11, I was agreeably surprised to find on my arrival at the station a quiet, rural haven. The southbound platform has a basic bus stop-style shelter, a help point and bench seats. Northbound travellers are not so fortunate as the platform has only a bench seat and a help point, and it also has a Harrington Hump. A posterboard is present and access to both platforms is step-free with a ramp. The signal box is still in situ but boarded up and out of use, and the level crossing now has automatic barriers. No trace of the former station buildings or goods siding remains, and the area seems to have been built over.

Buckenham
Annual passenger usage: 202
Least used station rank: 15
Postcode: NR13 4HW
Ordnance Survey national grid reference: TG350056

The Yarmouth & Norwich Railway opened Buckenham in 1844. It was threatened with closure in 1916. *Railway*

Magazine noted in its May issue of that year that the GER, which now owned the line, intended closure.[1] It then reported in the next (June 1916) issue that there had been an apparent change of mind and Buckenham would remain open.[2] A signal box alongside a level crossing and two platforms staggered on opposite sides of a road, along with a small siding, once made up the facilities at Buckenham.

With no weekday service and only two trains on a Saturday (Sundays are better), I had to get off the train at Brundall and walk the 2.5 miles to Buckenham. Arriving, I found myself in an area which to the north of the station was mostly farmland while to the south lay marshland on the banks of the River Yare. The station is very basic and the amenities on the Yarmouth-bound platform consist of just two seats and several noticeboards. The old station buildings still exist and I believe are now owned by the RSPB. The signal box and siding have both been removed. Using the barrow crossing to go to the Norwich-bound platform, which is a walk of some 200 metres, I found the luxury of a recently installed metal and plexiglass shelter.

What Buckenham lacks in facilities it more than makes up for in its location, which is real Norfolk. What could be better than this quiet backwater away from the hurly burly and noise of Norwich that I had just left? Sitting there the only sounds were birdsong and the reeds blowing gently in the wind. While watching the warblers and linnets going to and fro I was eventually rewarded with a real treat. A pair of marsh harriers were quartering the marsh opposite the platform, something I have not seen in a long time. I felt honoured to be able to watch these magnificent birds for a while. Let us hope human society can find the desire and compassion to ensure these and other beautiful creatures survive, because our world will be a much poorer place if we let them go, and are left with a planet filled with nothing but human greed and ego.

After two hours my time there came to an end and, a Class 156 DMU having been duly flagged down, I boarded. I was now heading back to Norwich but only passing through, on my way to Ely and finally the much anticipated Shippea Hill, the penultimate stop on my around Great Britain odyssey.

Shippea Hill

Annual passenger usage: 276
Least used station rank: 19
Postcode: CB7 4SR
Ordnance Survey national grid reference: TL641841

This station went by the name of Mildenhall Road when first opened by the ECR in 1845. The GER changed it to Burnt Fen in 1885, and a further name change took place in 1905 when it finally became Shippea Hill. Seeing the Shippea Hill of today it is hard to imagine how busy this place would have been in the 1920s. The OS 6-inch map of 1927 shows several tramways coming from the south west that brought produce into the goods yard, and another line coming from a chicory and herb drying factory to the east. Between June and October 1922, 1,259 tons of fruit were loaded onto trains at Shippea Hill.[3]

The only train calling here on weekdays is the 07.27 to Norwich, while on Saturdays the 07.27 is augmented by the 19.27 to Cambridge, so I resorted to a taxi ride from Ely. My driver was a man who one could say saw eye to eye with me on the state of the world, and by the time we got to Shippea Hill we had basically agreed on the best way forward for our world leaders. A most pleasant man who seemed almost apologetic when he told me the fare. I assured him I knew what I was doing, and had earlier made an (fairly accurate) estimate of the fare. He wished me well with the book and went swiftly on his way leaving me alone at Shippea Hill.

I have seen this place described as bleak and desolate. Personally I would describe it as wonderfully bleak and desolate. Surrounded by flat agricultural land, it really did feel like nowhere. That said, the line is fairly busy, with the trains hurtling past, full of people all too busy to stop, which somehow added to the isolation. Did some of these people see me, the strange man in black, alone on the platform? Some, no doubt, were totally focused on hurrying to the next meeting, intent on planning the hoped-for outcome with eyes only for their laptops, lives fixated on climbing up the greasy corporate pole of success in order to claim the perceived prize at the top. They miss so much. Have they ever felt what I had during my eighteen-month trip, do they ever know real calm, quiet and contentment? Hopefully some were hurrying to be with someone they love, now that was a comforting thought and I wished them all possible speed.

Platform 2 is very basic with just two bench seats for anyone waiting for the one train a week to call. Platform 1 has a help point and the luxury of a metal and plexiglass shelter, but then it does have a train almost every day. I noted a newly installed information screen, although it mostly displayed 'There are no trains due to depart from this station', only changing about an hour before the next arrival. Passage between the platforms is by use of a level crossing, with step-free access up a ramp. The signal box is now out of use, but still standing alongside the automatic level crossing, and the area that once comprised the goods yard is easy to make out, but serving no real purpose any more.

The Final One

On Sunday 7 July 2019, I boarded a Class 170 DMU at Norwich and having asked the guard to stop at Lakenheath, I was now only forty minutes from completing a journey that had begun in earnest eighteen months before. Lakenheath was stop number 152, the last one, albeit that the next day I would travel to Berney Arms, but only to revisit.

Lakenheath
Annual passenger usage: 468
Least used station rank: 34
Postcode: IP27 9AD
Ordnance Survey national grid reference: TL723863

Lakenheath was opened by the ECR in 1845 with two platforms. Late nineteenth-century maps show a station with a goods yard and shed, a signal box and a level crossing.

A station with no weekday service, and only two trains on Saturdays, means that on Sundays it becomes almost busy with a total of seven services. Platform 1 has three bench seats, but makes no other provision for passengers aside from the noticeboard by the entrance/exit gate. Platform 2 does have an information screen that gives information for both platforms. It also has a very small aluminium and plexiglass shelter, but there is no seating either in the shelter or on the platform itself. Some of the original station buildings are still standing, but no longer in railway use, while the goods yard, now devoid of its tracks and shed, has become an open-air storage site for what appeared to be enormous rolls of artificial turf. The now no longer needed signal box, with its paint slowly flaking away exposing patches of bare wood that resemble painful sores, is still quietly watching over the level crossing it no longer controls. Gone is the gentle ding of the bells that signalmen used to communicate the passage of trains to each other, usurped by automated barriers, with their warning sirens and flashing lights.

My visit came to an end and it was time to leave. It was a rather strange feeling raising my arm that 'one last time' after the hundred or more that had gone before. I will visit request stops in the future, but never again will I raise my arm that one last time – how can I, for that journey is now finally over.

Berney Arms, the Return

It seemed appropriate to revisit Berney Arms, not only because I was in the area and I wanted to see it again, but to me it would sort of complete the journey, finishing where I started.

There was a problem however, as I have already mentioned Berney Arms had been closed since October 2018 for engineering work, but I did have a solution, hire a bike. At that time there were bikes for hire at Great Yarmouth station and from there, a mere 5 miles following the banks of the River Yare and the Wherryman's Way path to Berney Arms; easy I thought.

I collected a bike and wobbled off through the car park. I soon found the path and the first mile went according to plan, with the ground a little rough but level. True, the ankle-high grass did slow my progress, but I was getting along. Then I came upon a padlocked five-bar gate, with a kissing gate at the side. Fine for walkers but a definite challenge for cyclists, and despite my manoeuvrings the bike would not go through the gate, forcing me to lift it over. This sounds easy but it was one of those city hire bikes and no lightweight. To add to my woes, at about the fifth such gate, my arms had got weaker and the grass steadily longer, to the point of it now being somewhere between waist and chest high; I had to take stock of the situation. The windmill at Berney Arms was now clearly in sight, and probably only a mile distant, but I could see at least two more gates. Also, it had become impossible to ride the bike, I could only walk, forcing it through the grass. I decided I had three choices: give up altogether, after all I had already been there (not an option as I don't give up); take the bike back and see if I could swop it for a combine harvester (but then the bike place probably only hired bikes); go home, regroup, re-plan and come back stronger and better prepared. This last seemed the only viable option – I would return.

On 29 August 2019 I again headed towards Berney Arms, but this time with a brand-new plan. Norwich to Reedham by train, then a bus to Halvergate and finally a 3-mile walk following the Weavers' Way footpath right to the station. Arriving at Reedham I walked over to the bus stop to check the timetable. This was a real country bus route and I knew they didn't run every day. I had got the day right, but what I hadn't realised was that this was a dial-a-ride bus that you have to pre-book. I quickly phoned the booking number and heard that the bus had already been booked and would be with me shortly. The minibus, for that is what it turned out to be, arrived and we were off, calling at various other villages en route.

What followed was without doubt a bus ride like no other I have ever known. We picked up mostly elderly people, who were off to do a bit of shopping, going to the doctors or visiting a friend. What immediately struck me was that this was also a social event, for they all knew each other. Not only that, I wasn't considered an outsider but instantly one of the gang. They were genuinely interested in what I was doing and offered advice on how to get there, tempered with warnings to be careful of the cattle in the fields, as there had been 'incidents'. We got to Halvergate and I disembarked, with goodbyes and hope all goes well messages. The bus pulled away and I began thinking about just how important that bus link is to some people living in isolated villages, not only for doing things that have to be done, but to occasionally escape the four walls and meet other human beings. There are vital bus services all over the country hanging on by a thread, relied on by people who have worked all their lives and contributed to our society. Many rural rail lines were closed, with the promise of better replacement bus services, but if the buses are now abandoned in the drive for bigger profits and people are left isolated, it would indeed be shameful.

Quickly finding the Weavers' Way path I headed off. It was a beautiful day and everywhere I looked there were dragonflies darting across the path. While the cattle standing in the fields were just staring I decided to be brave and carry on. However, with the warnings of my fellow bus passengers still fresh in my mind I decided to be careful. After the Highland bull incident my son-in-law told me that cattle don't like hats. I've no doubt this is true since not only has he worked with cattle, he is also a clever man (so he tells us anyway). I decided therefore that every time cattle were near I would take my cap off. While sightings of me without my cap are rare, I would like to refute any rumours that I wear it in the bath.

Continuing on my way I came to a point where three paths diverged. The one I thought to be mine had a padlocked gate and a sign on it saying 'Private property, beware, bull in field'. Against my better judgement I followed another of the paths (I later learned that illegally closing footpaths is a common practice here) and drifted off course. Realising my mistake and consulting a map I saw a path that would take me to the river. Remembering the further advice from the people on the bus that a good path went all along the river bank to Berney Arms I carried on, although my 3-mile walk had now become 5 miles. Just before reaching the river I passed through a field of young cattle. I removed my cap, but they were not impressed, and with heads down the whole herd decided to charge at me. Calculating that if I ran for the gate I would not get a quarter of the way before I was trampled into the ground, what could I do? I knew they were male cattle because I remember thinking, *Oh Bullocks! What do I do now?* Flapping both arms and shouting as loud as I possibly could caused them to have second thoughts and they stopped, but continued taking a rather disconcerting interest in me until I left 'their' field.

The rest of my walk proved to be mercifully uneventful and I arrived at Berney Arms later than intended and after a longer walk, but I had made it. Subtle changes had been made since my first visit – there was more signage at the end of the platform and some seats had been installed. But the reeds were still rustling in the breeze and the huge Norfolk sky was still overhead. Berney Arms still had the magic I'd felt before. I decided that I would sit there for at least two hours before beginning the long walk back.

Not wishing to have any more bullock or closed path experiences, I followed the advice given on the bus and decided to walk to Reedham along the riverbank. This would mean a 6-mile walk on top of the 5 I had already done, but at least it would, hopefully, be incident free.

Walking along the banks of the River Yare, with my rail odyssey finally over, I considered what I had achieved and asked myself if it had been worth it. The expense, the effort, and for what? True, this journey had proved to be expensive, but then it is sometimes nonsense to put a monetary value on things. The planning, checking timetables, finding hotels and then catching the 05.18 from Swindon more than once were all to me part of the satisfaction. It wouldn't have been the same if it had been easy. As I said in the Introduction, it was worth it: every penny, twice over.

I had said hello to many people, railway staff who were always helpful, locals pleased to guide me and friendly fellow passengers. People who with just one exception had two things in common: they had an interest in what I was doing, and they were genuine and warm human beings, lovely people in fact. I had visited the four cardinal compass points of the British mainland railway system, and discovered the true joy of doing nothing except contemplating the sheer beauty of my surroundings. I had discovered places anew, watched a beetle in Beasdale and golden eagles in Achnashellach. I'd been stranded in Chetnole, threatened by a dog at Altnabreac, charged by bullocks in Norfolk, and eyeballed by a rooster in Aspatria.

Finally, in realising how important this had become to me, I began to think that perhaps I didn't do this just for myself. Is it possible that when those people hurrying through Shippea Hill glimpsed that strange man in black standing alone on the platform, that he wasn't really alone?

Damems on the Keighley & Worth Valley Railway is possibly the prettiest stop of them all, a real overlooked gem which has been beautifully renovated. Photographed looking towards Keighley on 24 June 2019.

The Damems signal box interior seen on 24 June 2019. Note the cloth on the levers and the can of Brasso, so essential for any self-respecting signalman.

Ex-LMS Ivatt Class 2 2-6-2T 41241 passing Damems on 24 June 2019, bound for Oxenhope.

Greenway Halt on the Dartmouth Steam Railway, seen on 28 June 2019, looking towards Kingswear.

This male robin came to sit with me at Greenway Halt on 28 June 2019. He was rather cute and I think he knew it.

Above: Ex-GWR Manor Class 4-6-0 7827 *Lydham Manor* leaving Greenway Halt for Kingswear on 28 June 2019. This locomotive was built in 1950 by BR.

Opposite above: Brampton looking north towards Lowestoft which is about 13 miles distant, seen on 5 July 2019.

Opposite below: Lowestoft, the most easterly station on the British mainland, photographed on 5 July 2019. On the left the 12.07 to Ipswich is made up of a class 156 Super Sprinter DMU and is waiting to depart, while on the right the 10.58 from Norwich, comprised of a class 153 Super Sprinter DMU, has arrived.

OH BULLOCKS, WHAT DO I DO NOW? • 195

Spooner Row photographed looking towards Ely on 5 July 2019 from the westbound platform. The eastbound platform can be seen on the other side of the road.

Buckenham on 6 July 2019 with a Class 153 Super Sprinter DMU forming the 08.55 Norwich to Lowestoft service passing through. This stop is the least used station in Norfolk and has a very sparse service with no weekday trains at all.

OH BULLOCKS, WHAT DO I DO NOW? • 197

The magnificently bleak Shippea Hill with the 16.22 Ely to Norwich service comprised of a Class 158 Express Sprinter DMU rushing through on 6 July 2019.

A Class 170 Turbostar DMU forming the 15.35 Norwich to Ely service passing Shippea Hill and its now defunct signal box on 6 July 2019.

Lakenheath with a Class 158 Express Sprinter DMU making up the 09.47 Norwich to Ely service passing on 7 July 2019. This is another stop that does not have a weekday service.

The signal box at Lakenheath, sadly now unused and unloved like so many others, seen on 7 July 2019. The 10.03 Norwich to Cambridge train, formed of a Class 170 Turbostar, is passing by.

Berney Arms photographed on 29 August 2019, two years and twelve days after my first visit. Little had changed apart from the provision of some seats and a sign at the end of the platform telling passengers to 'Use the subway or footbridge to access other platforms'!

Some of the many tickets I used on my journey.

APPENDIX I

ABBREVIATIONS

A&WCR	Aberystwith (*sic*) & Welsh Coast Railway	LNER	London & North Eastern Railway
BBC&WYorksR	Bolton, Blackburn, Clitheroe & West Yorkshire Railway	LR&DC	Llanelly Railway & Dock Company
		M&CR	Maryport & Carlisle Railway
BR	British Rail	MER	Mallaig Extension Railway
C&HR	Chester & Holyhead Railway	MOD	Ministry of Defence
C&LlR	Conway & Llanrwst Railway	MWidR	Mid-Wales Railway
C&ObanR	Callander and Oban Railway	NDevonR	North Devon Railway
CAMR	Cambrian Railways	NRT	Northern Rail
CWalesExR	Central Wales Extension Railway	NR	Network Rail
CwallMinsR	Cornwall Minerals Railway	ORR	Office of Rail and Road
CwallR	Cornwall Railway	OS	Ordnance Survey
CWR	Central Wales Railway	P&TR	Pembroke & Tenby Railway
D&SKyeR	Dingwall and Skye Railway	RSPB	Royal Society for the Protection of Birds
DMU	diesel multiple unit	S&CreweR	Shrewsbury & Crewe Railway
ECR	Eastern Counties Railway	SlandR	Sutherland Railway
ELancsR	East Lancashire Railway	Sld&CnsR	Sutherland & Caithness Railway
FurnR	Furness Railway	SoAR	Stratford on Avon Railway
GER	Great Eastern Railway	SR	Southern Railway
GWR	Great Western Railway	SWalesR	South Wales Railway
HighR	Highland Railway	VoTR	Vale of Towy Railway
HST	high speed train	W&FJnR	Whitehaven & Furness Junction Railway
KtnR	Knighton Railway		
L&NWR	London & North Western Railway	WHighR	West Highland Railway
L&YR	Lancashire & Yorkshire Railway	WJnR	Whitehaven Junction Railway

APPENDIX II

ALPHABETICAL LIST OF REQUEST STOPS (AS AT DECEMBER 2017) AND DATE VISITED

Station	Date visited
Abererch	2 August 2018
Achanalt	30 April 2019
Achnashellach	30 April 2019
Altnabreac	27 April 2019
Ammanford	4 May 2018
Ardlui	10 June 2019
Aspatria	29 March 2019
Attadale	24 April 2019
Bearley	26 October 2018
Beasdale	12 June 2019
Berney Arms	17 August 2017
Bodorgan	18 September 2018
Bootle	27 March 2019
Brampton (Suffolk)	5 July 2019
Braystones	26 March 2019
Broome	21 June 2018
Buckenham	6 July 2019
Bucknell	21 June 2018
Bugle	10 April 2018
Builth Road	21 June 2018
Bures	5 January 2019
Burnley Barracks	15 November 2018
Bynea	20 June 2018
Causeland	12 April 2018
Chapelton	22 April 2018
Chetnole	13 March 2018
Cilmeri	11 July 2018
Clarbeston Road	2 May 2018
Claverdon	26 October 2018
Clunderwen	2 May 2018
Conwy	18 September 2018
Copplestone	26 March 2018
Corkickle	26 March 2019
Corrour	11 June 2019
Culrain	27 April 2019
Cynghordy	23 June 2018
Dalston	28 March 2019
Damems	24 June 2019
Danzey	26 October 2018
Deganwy	20 September 2018
Denton	16 February 2019
Dilton Marsh	16 February 2018
Dockyard	20 March 2018
Dolau	22 June 2018
Dolgarrog	21 September 2018
Dolwyddelan	19 September 2018
Drigg	27 March 2019
Duirinish	28 April 2019
Duncraig	24 April 2019
Dunrobin Castle	29 April 2019
Dyffryn Ardudwy	2 August 2018
Entwistle	14 November 2018
Exton	22 March 2018
Falls Of Cruachan	10 June 2019
Ferryside	1 May 2018
Ffairfach	10 June 2018
Flimby	28 March 2019
Foxfield	27 March 2019
Garth (Powys)	10 June 2018
Glan Conwy	19 September 2018
Green Road	27 March 2019
Greenway Halt	28 June 2019
Hapton	15 November 2018
Harrington	28 March 2019
Hawarden Bridge	20 September 2018
Hopton Heath	22 June 2018
Invershin	27 April 2019
Johnston	1 May 2018
Kidwelly	1 May 2018
Kildonan	29 April 2019

Station	Date visited	Station	Date visited
Kilgetty	2 May 2018	Penmaenmawr	17 September 2018
Kinbrace	25 April 2019	Pensarn	1 August 2018
Kings Nympton	22 April 2018	Pen-y-Bont	21 June 2018
Kirkby-in-Furness	27 March 2019	Penychain	4 August 2018
Knucklas	10 June 2018	Perranwell	20 April 2018
Lakenheath	7 June 2019	Pleasington	15 November 2018
Lamphey	3 May 2018	Pontarddulais	9 June 2018
Lapford	12 April 2018	Pont-y-Pant	19 September 2018
Lech-a-Vuie	15 June 2019	Portsmouth Arms	15 April 2018
Lelant	10 April 2018	Prees	16 June 2018
Llanaber	1 August 2018	Reddish South	16 February 2019
Llanbedr	1 August 2018	Rhosneigr	18 September 2018
Llanbister Road	11 June 2018	Roche	20 April 2018
Llandanwg	1 August 2018	Rogart	29 April 2019
Llandecwyn	2 May 2018	Roman Bridge	19 September 2018
Llandybie	9 June 2018	Roy Bridge	11 June 2019
Llanfairfechan	17 September 2018	Sandplace	12 April 2018
Llanfairpwll	17 September 2018	Saundersfoot	2 May 2018
Llangadog	4 May 2018	Scotscalder	25 April 2019
Llangammarch	9 June 2018	Shippea Hill	6 June 2019
Llangennech	20 June 2018	Silecroft	27 March 2019
Llangynllo	11 June 2018	Spooner Row	5 June 2019
Llanwrda	10 June 2018	St Columb Road	10 April 2018
Llwyngwril	31 July 2018	St Keyne Wishing Well Halt	12 April 2018
Loch Eil Outward Bound	10 June 2019	Sugar Loaf	4 May 2018
Lochailort	12 June 2019	Talsarnau	1 August 2018
Locheilside	13 June 2019	Talybont	2 August 2018
Lochluichart	24 April 2019	Tal-y-Cafn	19 September 2018
Luxulyan	17 April 2018	The Lakes	26 October 2018
Lympstone Commando	22 March 2018	Thornford	13 March 2018
Menheniot	10 April 2018	Tonfanau	2 August 2018
Morchard Road	26 March 2018	Ty Croes	18 September 2018
Morfa Mawddach	31 July 2018	Tygwyn	1 August 2018
Narberth	2 May 2018	Umberleigh	26 March 2018
Nethertown	28 March 2019	Valley	18 September 2018
New Clee	16 February 2019	Wood End	26 October 2018
Newton St Cyres	22 April 2018	Wootton Wawen	26 October 2018
North Llanrwst	19 September 2018	Wrenbury	16 June 2018
Parton	28 March 2019	Yeoford	26 March 2018
Penally	3 May 2018	Yetminster	13 March 2018
Penhelig	31 July 2018	Yorton	12 June 2018

BIBLIOGRAPHY & SOURCES

Bibliography

Baker, S.K., *Rail Atlas Great Britain & Ireland*, Oxford Publishing Company, 2015.

British Railways, *British Railways Pre-grouping Atlas and Gazetteer*, Ian Allan Ltd, 1980.

Butt, R.V.J., *The Directory of Railway Stations*, Patrick Stephens Limited, 1995.

Cooke, R.A., *Atlas of the GWR 1947*, Wild Swan Publications, 1988.

Frater, Alexander, *Stopping-train Britain*, Book Club Associates, 1984.

Heart of Wales Line, *Heart of Wales Line, Western at Work Series No. 3*, British Rail (Western), 1981.

Ian Allan Ltd, *Sectional Maps of the British Railways as at December 1947*, Ian Allan Ltd, 1987.

Jenkins, Stanley C., *Great Western Railway Journal, Special Cornish Issue*, Wild Swan Publications, 1992.

Jowett, Alan, *Jowett's Railway Atlas of Great Britain and Ireland*, Patrick Stephens Limited, 1989.

McGregor, John, *100 Years of the West Highland Line*, ScotRail, 1994.

McGregor, John, *North British Railway Study Group, Journal 128*, North British Railway Study Group, 2016.

Messenger, Michael, *Caradon & Looe: The Canal, Railways and Mines*, Twelveheads Press, 2001.

Quick, Michael, *Railway Passenger Stations in Great Britain: A Chronology, Fifth Edition* (electronic), Railway & Canal Historical Society, 2019.

Robertson, Kevin, *Great Western Railway Halts Volume One*, Irwell Press, 1990.

Robertson, Kevin, *Great Western Railway Halts Volume Two*, KRB Publications, 2002.

Thomas, John, *The West Highland Railway*, David & Charles, 1992.

Wills, Dixe, *Tiny Stations*, AA Publishing, 2014.

Wilson, J.M., *Imperial Gazetteer of England and Wales*, A. Fullarton & Co., 1870–1872.

Other Sources

Community Rail Cumbria: www.communityrailcumbria.co.uk/

Conwy Valley Railway: www.conwyvalleyrailway.co.uk/

Friends of the West Highland Line: http://westhighlandline.org.uk/

Heart of Wales Line: www.heart-of-wales.co.uk/

Interactive map of request stops in Britain: https://tools.wmflabs.org/osm4wiki/cgi-bin/wiki/wiki-osm.pl?project=en&article=Category%3ARailway_request_stops_in_Great_Britain

Mapmaker: https://metromapmaker.com/

National Rail timetables: https://www.networkrail.co.uk/running-the-railway/the-timetable/electronic-national-rail-timetable/

Old maps: https://maps.nls.uk/

Railway history, particularly Scotland: www.railscot.co.uk/

Rover and Ranger tickets: www.nationalrail.co.uk/times_fares/rangers_and_rovers.aspx

Request stops: https://en.wikipedia.org/wiki/Category:Railway_request_stops_in_Great_Britain

NOTES

Introduction

1. *Beeching Answered*, pamphlet, Communist Party of Great Britain, 1963.

Chapter 1

1. *Railway Magazine*, April 1984, p. 132.
2. Ibid, pp. 132–133.

Chapter 2

1. Robertson, Kevin, *Great Western Railway Halts Vol. Two*, KRB Publications, 2002, p. 81.
2. Robertson, Kevin, *Great Western Railway Halts Vol. One*, Irwell Press, 1990, p. 52.

Chapter 3

1. https://tools.wmflabs.org/osm4wiki/cgi-bin/wiki/wiki-osm.pl?project=en&article=Category%3ARailway_request_stops_in_Great_Britain
2. www.nationalrail.co.uk/times_fares/rangers_and_rovers.aspx
3. www.networkrail.co.uk/running-the-railway/the-timetable/electronic-national-rail-timetable/
4. Ibid.

Chapter 4

1. Jenkins, Stanley, C., *Great Western Railway Journal, Special Cornish Issue*, Wild Swan Publications, 1992, pp. 19–20.
2. Messenger, Michael, *Caradon & Looe: The Canal, Railways and Mines*, Twelveheads Press, 2001, p. 153.

Chapter 5

1. Clark, R.H., *An Historical Survey of Selected Great Western Stations Vol. 1*, Oxford Publishing Co., 1976, pp. 43–45.
2. Clark, R.H., *An Historical Survey of Selected Great Western Stations Vol. 2*, Oxford Publishing Co., 1979, pp. 50–51.
3. Potts, C.R., *An Historical Survey of Selected Great Western Stations Vol. 4*, Oxford Publishing Co., 1985, pp. 117–118.

Chapter 6

1. Quick, Michael, *Railway Passenger Stations in Great Britain: A Chronology, Fifth Edition* (electronic), The Railway & Canal Historical Society, 2019, p. 257.
2. Cooke, R.A., *Atlas of the GWR 1947*, Wild Swan Publications, 1988, map 133.
3. Wilson, J.M., *Imperial Gazetteer of England and Wales, 1870–1872*, A. Fullarton & Co.

Chapter 7

1. *Railway Magazine*, March 1951, p. 195.

Chapter 8

1. Robertson, Kevin, *Great Western Railway Halts Volume Two*, KRB Publications, 2002, p. 34.
2. www.weekendnotes.co.uk/llwyngwril-the-knitted-village/
3. Quick, Michael, *Railway Passenger Stations in Great Britain: A Chronology, Fifth Edition* (electronic), The Railway & Canal Historical Society, 2019, p. 390.
4. Ibid., p. 254.

Chapter 9

1. www.rhosneigr.org.uk/Gallery/ArchiveStation.html
2. Quick, Michael, *Railway Passenger Stations in Great Britain: A Chronology, Fifth Edition* (electronic), The Railway & Canal Historical Society, 2019, p. 340.
3. Ibid., p. 326.
4. Tal-y-Cafn ground frame photo, https://www.geograph.org.uk/photo/4399347
5. *Railway Magazine*, August 1956, p. 564.
6. Quick, Michael, op. cit., p. 147.
7. *North Wales Weekly News*, 19 November 1909.
8. Daniels, Charles and Dench, Les, *Passengers No More*, Ian Allan, 1980, p. 36.

Chapter 10

1. Jenkins, Stanley C. and Carpenter, Roger, *The Alcester Branch*, Wild Swan, 2005 p. 49.
2. Robertson, Kevin, *Great Western Railway Halts Volume Two*, KRB Publications, 2002, p. 80.
3. Ibid., p 101.
4. Quick, Michael, *Railway Passenger Stations in Great Britain: A Chronology, Fifth Edition* (electronic), The Railway & Canal Historical Society, 2019, p. 141.
5. *Railway Magazine*, July 1974, p. 363.
6. Quick, Michael, op. cit., p. 164.
7. *Railway Magazine*, November 1966, p. 653.
8. https://friendsofreddishsouthstation.co.uk/
9. http://dentonstation.co.uk/

Chapter 11

1. Quick, Michael, *Railway Passenger Stations in Great Britain: A Chronology, Fifth Edition* (electronic), The Railway & Canal Historical Society, 2019, p. 427.
2. Ibid., p. 177.
3. https://en.wikipedia.org/wiki/Kirkby-in-Furness_railway_station
4. https://en.wikipedia.org/wiki/Accrington_brick

Chapter 12

1. *Railway Magazine*, November 2016, p. 29.
2. Croughton, G., *Private and Untimetabled Railway Stations*, Oakwood Press, 1982, p. 96.
3. *Railway Magazine*, June 1954, pp. 432–433.
4. *Railway Magazine*, March 1914, p. 262.
5. Quick, Michael, *Railway Passenger Stations in Great Britain: A Chronology, Fifth Edition* (electronic), The Railway & Canal Historical Society, 2019, p. 154.
6. *Railway Magazine*, November 1903, pp. 339–340.
7. See: https://www.theguardian.com/business/2019/aug/18/where-did-all-the-cod-go-fish-chips-north-sea-sustainable-stocks
8. Quick, Michael, op. cit., p. 41.

Chapter 13

1. Quick, Michael, *Railway Passenger Stations in Great Britain: A Chronology, Fifth Edition* (electronic), The Railway & Canal Historical Society, 2019, p. 66.
2. McGregor, John, Lech-a-Vuie Platform – the Landed Interest and the West Highland, *British Railway Study Journal* 128, North British Railway Study Group, July 2016, pp. 37–41.
3. https://maps.nls.uk/view/74490384
4. *Railway Track Diagrams 1: Scotland & the Isle of Man*, TRACKmaps, 2001, p. 22b.
5. *LNER Sectional Appendix to the Rules and Regulations, Scottish Area*, 1 November 1947, LNER, 1947, p. 154.
6. Archibald, J., *Steam Railway* (magazine), 347, March/April 2008, p. 73.

Chapter 14

1. *Railway Magazine*, May 1916, p. 376.
2. Ibid., June 1916, p. 443.
3. Ibid., September 1923, pp. 209–213.

INDEX

Figures in italics refer to illustrations.

Abererch, 93, *102*
Achanalt, 158, *170*
Achnashellach , 159, *171*
Altnabreac, 156, *164*
Ammanford, 57, *64*
Ardlui, 172, *176*, *177*
Arisaig, 172, *184*
Aspatria, 142, *152*
Attadale, 155, *161*

Bearley, 122, *128*
Beasdale, 174, *180*,*181*
Berney Arms, 12, *21*, 189, *199*
Black Five, *181*, *183*
Bodorgan, 105, *112*
Bootle, 140, *147*
Brampton (Suffolk), 186, *195*
Braystones, 138, *143*
Broome, 69, *73*
Buckenham, 187, *196*
Bucknell, 68, *72*
Bugle, 34, *42*
Builth Road, 69, *74*
Bures, 126, *134*
Burnley Barracks, 125, *134*
Bynea, 67, *72*

Castle Class, 10, 12, 38
Causeland, 35, *44*
Chapelton, 39, *50*
Chetnole, 16, *24*
Cilmeri, 80, *86*
Clarbeston Road, 53, *60*
Class 142 DMU, *133*, *136*, *137*
Class 150 DMU, *28*, *43*, *46*, *87*, *112*, *118*, *120*
Class 153 DMU, *44*, *49*, *65*, *73*, *75*, *83*, *86*, *137*, *195*
Class 156 DMU, *21*, *144*, *146*, *149*, *178*, *181*, *182*, *195*
Class 158 DMU, *98-100*, *103*, *111*, *113*, *161*, *163*, *164*, *167*, *171*, *197*, *198*

Class 165 DMU, *129*
Class 166 DMU, *22*
Class 170 DMU, *197*, *198*
Class 175 DMU, *110*, *114*
Class 37 locomotive, *151*
Class 73 locomotive, *176*
Claverdon, 122, *129*
Clunderwen, 54, *60*
Conwy, 105, *112*
Copplestone, 20, *28*
Corkickle, 138, *144*
Corrour, 173, *179*
Culrain, 156, *165*
Cynghordy, 71, *76*

Dalston, 141, *148*
Damems, 185, *191*, *192*
Danzey, 123, *131*
Deganwy, 109, *120*
Denton, 127, *136*, *137*
Dilton Marsh, 15, *22*
Dockyard, 18, *24*, *25*
Dolau, 70, *75*
Dolgarrog, 109, *121*
Dolwyddelan, 108, *119*
Drigg, 139, *144*
Duirinish, 157, *166*
Duncraig, 154, *159*, *160*
Dunrobin Castle, 158, *168*
Dyffryn Ardudwy, 92, *100*

Entwistle, 124, *132*
Exton, 18, *25*

Falls Of Cruachan, 172, *177*, *178*
Ferryside, 52, *58*
Ffairfach, 79, *84*, *85*
Flimby, 142, *151*
Foxfield, 139, *146*

Garth (Powys), 79, *84*
Glan Conwy, 107, *115*
Goring-on-Thames, 9
Green Road, 139, *145*
Greenway Halt, 186, *193, 194*

Hapton, 125, *133*
Harrington, 142, *151*
Hawarden Bridge, 109, *119, 120*
High Speed Train (HST), 12, *25*
Hopton Heath, 70, *74, 75*

Invershin, 156, *165*
Ivatt Class 2, *192*

Johnston, 53, *59*

Kidwelly, 53, *59*
Kildonan, 158, *169*
Kilgetty, 54, *61*
Kinbrace, 155, *162*
King's Nympton, 39, *51*
Kirkby-in-Furness, 140, *147*
Knucklas, 79, *85*

Lakenheath, 189, *198*
Lamphey, 55, *62, 63*
Lapford, 36, *46*
Lech-a-Vuie, 174, *182, 183*
Lelant, 33, *41*
Llanaber, 92, *98, 99*
Llanbedr, 90, *96*
Llanbister Road, 80, *87*
Llandanwg, 91, *97*
Llandecwyn, 93, *101*
Llandybie, 78, *83*
Llanfairfechan, 104, *110*
Llanfairpwll, 105, *111*
Llangadog, 57, *64*
Llangammarch, 77, *82*
Llangennech, 67, *71*
Llangynllo, 80, *86*
Llanwrda, 78, *83*
Llwyngwril, 90, *95*
Loch Eil Outward Bound, 173, *178*
Lochailort, 174, *181*

Locheilside, 174, *182*
Lochluichart, 154, *161*
Lowestoft, *195*
Luxulyan, 37, *47*
Lympstone Commando, 18, *26*

Manor Class, *194*
Menheniot, 34, *43*
Morchard Road, 19, *27*
Morfa Mawddach, 89, *94*

Narberth, 55, *61*
Nethertown, 141, *149*
New Clee, 127, *137*
Newton St Cyres, 39, *51*
North Llanrwst, 108, *118*

Parton, 141, *150*
Penally, 56, *63*
Penhelig, 90, *95*
Penmaenmawr, 104, *110*
Pensarn, 90, *96*
Pen-y-Bont, 68, *73*
Penychain, 94, *103*
Penzance, 10, 33, *40*
Perranwell, 38, *49*
Pleasington, 125, *133*
Pontarddulais, 78, *82*
Pont-y-Pant, 107, *115*
Portsmouth Arms, 37, *47*
Prees, 81, *88*

Reading, 10, 11
Reddish South, 127, *135, 136*
Rhosneigr, 106, *114*
Roche, 38, *48*
Rogart, 157, *166, 167*
Roman Bridge, 108, *117*
Roy Bridge, 173, *180*

Sandplace, 35, *45*
Saundersfoot, 55, *62*
Scotscalder, 155, *163*
Shippea Hill, 188, *197*
Silecroft, 139, *145*
Spooner Row, 187, *196*

St Columb Road, 34, *41*
St Keyne Wishing Well Halt, 36, *45*, *46*
Sugar Loaf, 57, *65*, *66*

Talsarnau, 91, *98*
Talybont, 93, *101*
Tal-y-Cafn, 107, *116*
The Lakes, 123, *130*
Thornford, 16, *23*
Thurso, 153, *162*, *163*
Tonfanau, 92, *99*, *100*
Ty Croes, 106, *114*
Tygwyn, 91, *97*

Umberleigh, 19, *27*

Valley, 106, *113*

Wood End, 123, *130*
Wootton Wawen, 124, *132*
Wrenbury, 81 *88*

Yeoford, 20, *28*
Yetminster, 16, *23*
Yorton, 81, *87*